A
FAMILY'S
TRAGIC
BATTLE
WITH
NAPOLEON
THE LETTERS AND JOURNALS OF THE FRASERS
OF BALLINDOUN and UNETTS OF WOODLANDS

A FAMILY'S TRAGIC BATTLE WITH NAPOLEON

THE LETTERS AND JOURNALS OF THE FRASERS OF BALLINDOUN *and* UNETTS OF WOODLANDS

GARETH GLOVER

Pen & Sword
MILITARY
AN IMPRINT OF PEN & SWORD BOOKS LTD.
YORKSHIRE – PHILADELPHIA

First published in Great Britain in 2025 by
PEN AND SWORD MILITARY
An imprint of
Pen & Sword Books Limited
Yorkshire – Philadelphia

ISBN 978 1 39903 171 4

A CIP catalogue record for this book is available from the British Library.

Typeset in Times New Roman 10/12 by
SJmagic DESIGN SERVICES, India.
Printed and bound in the UK by CPI Group (UK) Ltd.

The Publisher's authorised representative in the EU for product safety is Authorised Rep Compliance Ltd., Ground Floor, 71 Lower Baggot Street, Dublin D02 P593, Ireland. www.arccompliance.com

For a complete list of Pen & Sword titles please contact
PEN & SWORD BOOKS LIMITED
George House, Units 12 & 13, Beevor Street, Off Pontefract Road,
Barnsley, South Yorkshire, S71 1HN, England
E-mail: enquiries@pen-and-sword.co.uk
Website: www.pen-and-sword.co.uk

or

PEN AND SWORD BOOKS
1950 Lawrence Rd, Havertown, PA 19083, USA
E-mail: uspen-and-sword@casematepublishers.com
Website: www.penandswordbooks.com

Contents

List of Plates

Acknowledgements

I must thank the staff at Stafford Archives, who very kindly went to extraordinary lengths to allow me to return to complete photographing the Unett papers during their major refurbishment which has led to an 18-month closure of the archive section.

I must also thank June Black, a genealogist, who was able to pinpoint the weddings of Richard and Ann Unett along with numerous births and deaths which do not appear in any records of the family I was able to access. This really helped to clear up a number of questions regarding the families and how their lives interacted at significant times.

I must also thank my good friend Robert Burnham for helping with the transcription of Alexander Fraser's letters, and someone I regard as a great friend, although we have never met, Ron McGuigan, who has helped enormously in identifying a number of individuals mentioned. I am always certain that if Ron cannot find an answer, then nobody can.

Lastly, I must also thank my wonderful wife Mary, who supports my endeavours in every way she can unceasingly and has the patience of Job. She will, however, be grateful I am sure, to end the interminable discussions we have had regarding various aspects of the relationships of the Unetts and Frasers.

Introduction

> 'You have I suppose by this time received the account of another glorious event, but which like all the others has plunged many families into affliction'[1]

The Napoleonic Wars lasted 23 years from 1793–1815 – or more correctly the Revolutionary Wars lasted from 1793–1802 and after the brief Peace of Amiens, the Napoleonic Wars continued from 1803–15. These wars were global, encompassing not only all of Europe, but also North and South America, North and South Africa, the West Indies and East Indies, indeed few places in the world escaped its ravages completely and there is a very good case for calling it a World War. Indeed, this war was known to most Victorians as 'The Great War', a title it only shed with the ending of the First World War.

The financial cost to Britain was truly enormous, as it not only had to fund its own extensive war effort; but also played banker to most of the other countries of Europe fighting France. This excessive financial burden has been estimated to have reached £1.65 billion by 1815; in today's terms that would equate to approximately £100 billion. More remarkably, only one-quarter of this huge financial cost was met by government loans, the rest being raised by taxation, much of it via the detested Income Tax that was introduced in 1798 for the duration of the war, but somehow has remained with us ever since. These seemingly ruinous levels of taxation were largely successful on the back of the Industrial Revolution, in which Britain was leading the way, with the huge markets opened up for British manufactured goods across the world, only made possible by the Royal Navy's dominance of the seas.

A war on such a scale obviously needed a huge increase in manpower for the armed forces; over the duration of the war, the Royal Navy increased its manpower from its peacetime level by a factor of eight, rising from 16,000 men to 140,000; whilst the Army, including home defence forces, increased six-fold from less than 100,000 to over half a million.

Fighting enemy forces caused a significant number of deaths and mutilations, but of the most recent estimate of just under 320,000 British dead and wounded (of which 210,000 were deaths), far more than half (possibly as much as 75 per cent) of the deaths were caused by disease and infection, contemporary medical knowledge having little answer or understanding of malaria, yellow fever or even how to avoid

1. Letter from Alexander Fraser dated 15 September 1813.

sepsis and gangrene. In a direct comparison to the First World War – although that war was fought over four years, rather than the twenty-three of the Revolutionary and Napoleonic Wars – given that the population of Britain in 1911 (the last Census before the War) was some 2.5 times larger than in 1811, the loss of life (from those purely from the British Isles), standing at 540,000 is remarkably similar to the 210,000 lost in the Revolutionary and Napoleonic Wars. Although the rate of deaths was undoubtedly significantly higher in 1914–18 and far more shocking due to its much shorter duration, the loss to individual families within a whole generation was of a very similar magnitude.[2]

Today, we are only too aware of the terrible losses inflicted on individual families in the First World War. The record for family losses – an accolade no family would ever wish for – is shared by the Badcock-Apps family from Hurst Green who lost five out of six sons; only to be matched by the Shaw family of Rotherhithe who also lost five sons during the war (three of whom had previously emigrated and served in the Australian forces); the Beecheys of Barnard Castle also lost five of eight sons and the Souls of Great Rissington in Gloucestershire tragically lost all five sons. The record number of siblings sent to the war is held by the Giles family who saw ten brothers go, but six luckily came home.

Such macabre records were not created for the Revolutionary/Napoleonic Wars and there has been lamentably little research into the impact on family life in these wars. It was traditional amongst the gentry that sons beyond the first born (who had to be protected as the sole heir to the estate) were divided throughout the three Great Institutions – the Clergy, the Navy and the Army, although the *nouveau riche* of the commercial classes could also accept sons going into the Law, Trade or Medicine, but a significant number of their offspring still found themselves joining one of the armed services.

The Ramsay family of Balmain lost in all four sons, John in 1807 and all three other sons in 1815, Alexander at the Battle of New Orleans, Norman at the Battle of Waterloo and their younger brother David died in Jamaica just after the wars ended in the July. The Fernyhough's of Lichfield (a Staffordshire family) had four sons serving in the wars,[3] Thomas with the Staffordshire Militia and 60th Foot, John and Henry both in the Royal Marines, and Robert in the Royal Navy then the 95th Rifles; John and Henry did not survive the wars. The Duke of Richmond, himself a General, also had four sons serving, Henry had joined the Royal Navy and died in 1812, Charles served with the 52nd Foot, George was an aide de camp to the Duke of Wellington and William was an aide de camp to General Maitland; Lieutenant Charles Fitzroy and General Peregrine Maitland were also sons-in-law; whilst Thomas Bathurst of the Guards was a nephew. Five other officers were related via his aunt. The Hills had four sons in the Army, all fought at Waterloo and survived;

2. This analysis follows the work of Professor Greenwood published as 'British Loss of Life in the Wars of 1794-1815 and in 1914-1918' in the *Journal of the Royal Statistical Society* Vol. 105 No.1 (1942), pp. 1–16.
3. *Military Memoirs of Four Brothers* by Thomas Fernyhough (one of the four) first published in 1829.

three Dawson brothers; three Wildman brothers (who also had the two Hardinge brothers as uncles), three Smith brothers and the two Keppell brothers and their two second cousins all served in the Waterloo campaign.[4] The Bowlbys had no less than six sons in the forces, Edward, Peter and Joseph in the infantry, Thomas in the Royal Artillery, George in the Royal Navy and Anthony in the Royal Marines. The list is endless, but the point is made.

This work follows the fascinating experiences of the Unett family of Woodlands in Staffordshire and the Frasers of Ballindoun who married into the family during the Napoleonic Wars. It provides an intimate family story and their experiences of war.

4. *Then Came a Voice He Knew; An Account of the Extraordinary Number of Related British Officers Engaged in the Waterloo Campaign of June 1815*, by Andrew Prince, published by Ken Trotman Publishing 2007.

The Unett Family

We are fortunate that so much of the correspondence of the Unetts and their daily diaries have been preserved by the family and were eventually deposited at the Staffordshire County Record Office. Together they give a fascinating insight of a family living throughout the Revolutionary and Napoleonic Wars, with all their trials, tribulations and elations.

The Unett family have a fine military heritage running seamlessly from the Napoleonic Wars to India, the Crimea, South Africa, both World Wars and Malaya and Kenya in the 1950s. Initially the family started in the Royal Artillery, but later generations have preferred the infantry or cavalry. All of these family records covering two centuries are deposited together at Stafford Archives and form a fascinating window into the lives of one family in great depth and hopefully will spur further research in this fascinating aspect of the Napoleonic Wars.

The Unett family papers refer to the family of the Reverend Thomas Unett (1731–85), Rector of Coppenhall,[1] in Cheshire, and prebendary of Lichfield Cathedral, who had married Frances Godwin, of Stafford in 1761.[2] The family records online are far from complete and it has taken a great deal of further investigation to identify all of the details produced below.

Their surviving children were as follows:

- Their first child was a daughter, Frances, whose birth year is stated as 1761 but the date is unknown; she was baptised on 28 March 1762 at St Mary's Stafford; she died on 24 November at Chelsea and was buried on 30 November 1839 aged 78, at St Nicholas, Plumstead. She never married.
- The connection with the Frasers (of Ballindoun and Kinneries) comes when their second child, Ann Unett born on 24 July 1764 and baptised the following day at St Mary, Stafford; married Captain John Grant Fraser of the Royal

1. Coppenhall in Cheshire is now part of Crewe. The church is dedicated to St Michael.
2. The Godwins were a Royal Artillery family, including General John Godwin who was heavily involved in the siege of Gibraltar (his journal of the siege is held by Stafford Archives) and his brother Captain William Godwin. It is highly likely that the Godwins helped the Unett brothers enter into the Royal Artillery.

Artillery[3] on 27 March 1792 at St Alfege's in Greenwich.[4] We also have a vivid account of a shipwreck off the Newfoundland coast in 1795 from John's close friend Captain Howard Douglas of the Royal Artillery.[5]

The couple had two daughters and two sons, James Baillie Fraser born 17 January 1793; Mary Anne born April 1794; Alexander John Fraser born 8 September 1795 and Frances Elizabeth born 6 March 1797 and baptised on 26 January 1798. Tragically their mother appears to have died in giving birth to Frances and was buried at St Nicholas, Plumstead on 21 March 1797 aged 32 and their father John also died in late 1797, being buried alongside his wife on 5 November 1797 aged 34.

Both boys followed their father into the army, but they broke with tradition and joined the infantry; James joining the 7th Foot and Alexander the 52nd Foot. We are lucky enough to have the complementary sets of letters from James from 1810–13 and Alexander, 1812–13, on their experiences in the Peninsular War.

The service career of James Baillie Fraser shows that he was commissioned as a Lieutenant in the 7th Foot[6] on 21 June 1810. He served with 1/7th in the Peninsula from September to November 1810; transferring to the 2/7th in December but remaining in Portugal until July 1811; he then returned home but was again sent to the Peninsula with the 1/7th in August 1812. He served at the Battles of Busaco, 1st Siege of Badajoz, Albuera, Vitoria and the Pyrenees.

His brother Alexander John Fraser joined the 52nd Foot as an Ensign on 12 May 1812 and was promoted to Lieutenant on 23 September 1813; serving in the Peninsula from April 1813, serving at Vitoria, the Pyrenees, Bera and the Bidassoa where he was severely wounded.

- The eldest son, Richard Wilkes Unett, was born & baptised on 11 November 1765 at St Mary, Stafford. He joined the Royal Irish Artillery (Kane List No 695); he kept a daily journal from the time he obtained his army commission in 1788, until 1803.[7] These relate mostly to his service in England and Scotland, but there are also letters from Barbados in 1802, in which he describes heavy losses of soldiers through fever and his own hatred of the

3. John Grant Fraser was the second son of Alexander Fraser of Ballindoun, he inherited the estate when his elder brother James Fraser, ex-Paymaster in the Royal Artillery died unmarried at New York in 1791. There was a third younger brother Hugh Fraser, who became a Lieutenant Colonel. He eventually became the heir after his elder brothers and their offspring all died, he sold all of the family lands off in 1818. Lord Lovat paid £2,500 for Kinneries and Alexander Fraser paid £3,750 for Ballindoun.
4. Records show that Elizabeth and George Unett were present at the wedding and also Hugh Grant the brother of John.
5. Stafford Archives reference D3610/6/1.
6. The 7th Foot (Fusileers) did not have the rank of Ensign, officers joining as Lieutenants.
7. Stafford Archives reference D3610/12/1-5. It is presumed that he continued to write up his diaries, but the later ones do not now exist.

Caribbean climate. Richard was never completely comfortable as a soldier, but he rose to the rank of Lieutenant Colonel and retired on Full Pay on 17 November 1809 and was appointed to the Invalid Battalion of the Artillery on 23 January 1813. Records show that Richard married Ann Steele who was then residing at Perth. They were married at Perth on Monday 16 April 1792, but they do not appear to have ever had any children. Ann died in 1814 aged 50 and she was buried at St Nicholas, Plumstead on 23 May 1814, Richard died at Woolwich on 21 October 1815 aged 49 and was buried alongside Ann on 28 October 1815.

- A third sister, Elizabeth, was born on 13 May 1767 and baptised on 15 May at St Mary, Stafford, she died unmarried in 1835 aged 67 and was buried at St Nicholas, Plumstead on 30 January.
- A second son, Thomas Wilkes Unett, was born on 16 April 1769 and baptised on the 17th, he does not appear to have married and little can be discovered of his life. He died on 6 January 1829 at Margate aged 59, without a wife or any children and was buried on 13 January 1829 at St John the Baptist in Thanet.
- John Wilkes Unett, a third son, was born at The Woodlands, Harborne, Staffordshire, England, date unknown. He was christened on 11 June 1770 at Saint Mary's in Stafford. He did not follow the family tradition into the forces and became a solicitor, living at No 6 The Square[8] and the offices of Barker & Unett were next door in No 5. He was a founder member of the Birmingham Law Society and a property developer in the Smethwick and Filey Company, Yorkshire. His papers quoted in this work comprise his journal of a visit to occupied Paris in 1815 to see his brother George Wilkes Unett.[9] He died on 12 November 1856 in Leamington. John married Elizabeth Unett daughter of Thomas Unett (of Stone)[10] on 6 April 1795, Elizabeth was christened on 18 November 1770 at Stone, Staffordshire, she died on 19 May 1860. They had the following ten children:

    1. Mary Unett was stillborn on 18 January 1796.
    2. William Unett was born on 17 November 1797, but he died on 25 May 1798.
    3. John Unett was born on 2 April 1799, he married Caroline Pidcock in 1835 and had issue.
    4. Thomas Unett was born on 12 November 1800, he became a Lieutenant Colonel in the 19th Foot. He married Mary Ann Ditmas and had issue.

---

8. Later known as the Old Square, Birmingham. Reference *Memorials of the Old Square: being some notices of the Priory of St Thomas in Birmingham and the lands pertaining thereto; also the Square built upon the Priory Close, known in later times as the Old Square; with notes concerning the dwellers in the sixteen houses thereof, and of some notable persons associated therewith*, by J. Hill and R. Dent, Birmingham 1897.
9. Stafford Archives reference D3610/13.
10. These Unetts were from a different branch of the family based on Tittensor, Staffordshire.

He died on 8 September 1855 at the Siege of Sebastopol, Crimea. He is buried at St Oswald's Church, Filey, North Yorkshire

5. Richard Unett was born on 30 January 1803, he died unmarried.
6. Elizabeth Unett was born on 9 April 1805. She died about June 1805.
7. James Robinson Unett was born on 23 April 1806, he died unmarried.
8. George Unett Esq. was born on 21 June 1809. He married Elizabeth Unett (Freen Court branch) in 1843.
9. Walter Unett was born in 1811, he became a Lieutenant Colonel in 3rd Light Dragoons.
10. Letitia Unett was born in 1813. Letitia married Lodge Morres Murray Prior Esq of the 12th Lancers in 1836 and died in 1853–4.

- The last child, George Wilkes Unett who was born on 2 May 1772 and baptised the following day at St Mary, Stafford; as the fourth son George followed the example of his elder brother Richard, by entering the Royal Artillery (Kane 913), and rose to the rank of Major. He was present at a number of engagements in the West Indies and at the taking of Copenhagen in 1807 and the capture of Martinique in 1809[11] and we have a number of his letters from these campaigns. He was also at the Battle of Waterloo in 1815 and afterwards participated in the advance on Paris including the siege of Cambrai. On 22 July 1822, when he was about 50 years old, he married Eliza Jones, the sister of Sir John Thomas Jones, Royal Engineers at Bathwick St Mary, Somerset and they had a daughter Frances-Eliza (1824–44). George was buried on 21 December 1825 aged 53 at Holy Trinity, Cheltenham.

11. Stafford Archives reference D3610/14/1.

THE UNETT STORY

Before the War

The story of the Unetts actually starts 11 years before the wars began, when a 17-year-old Richard Wilkes Unett joined the Royal Military Academy as a Cadet in 1782, almost certainly under the influence of his great uncle Major General John Godwin Royal Artillery[1] and uncle (on his mother's side) Captain William Godwin.[2]

Immediately on being commissioned in the Royal Irish Artillery[3] in 1788, Richard began writing up his daily journal and continued religiously jotting down something every day until 1802, contained in four journal books; it is highly likely that he continued to write a daily journal beyond this, but all searches have failed to discover their whereabouts today and it is feared that they have been lost forever. Richard wrote a great deal about the weather and his journal has been used to help record the weather in the 1790s for modern comparison; he also records the numerous afternoon teas or dinner parties he attends, which are sometimes interesting for the identity of their fellow guests (as a veritable who's-who of the late eighteenth-century artillery) and was also a keen gardener, religiously recording new plantings and plant health. The reader will be pleased, I am sure, that I have chosen to omit much from these mundane entries, particularly previous to the beginning of the War in 1793 but the occasional military notes are of interest and have all been preserved.

Richard initially entered the Royal Military Academy (affectionately known as 'The Shop') which had been established in 1741 at Woolwich 'Warren', which later became better known as Woolwich Arsenal. The Gentlemen Cadets who attended (both for the Artillery and the Engineers), ranged initially in age from 10 to 30 years and were formed into a Company of forty-eight Cadets, overseen by a Captain-Lieutenant. Their Barracks, built along the southern boundary of the 'Warren', was demolished in 1980. The young Cadets joined the Lower Academy, where they were taught reading, writing, arithmetic, Latin, French and drawing.

1. Kane 66.
2. Kane 288, he removed to the Invalid Battalion in 1787 and died at Abbots Bromley Staffs on 24 July 1800.
3. The Irish Artillery had been formed in 1755 as The Artillery Company of Ireland; in 1760 its name changed to The Royal Regiment of Irish Artillery and it remained independent (even though its officers were trained together at Woolwich) until it was absorbed into the Royal Artillery in 1801, following the Act of Union, their units largely forming the 7th Battalion of the Royal Artillery.

Having passed their examinations, they progressed to the Upper Academy, where they learnt advanced mathematics, the scientific principles of gunnery and fortification and further French (for an additional fee). The Cadets of both colleges also undertook practical training, including gunnery, bridge building, surveying, riding and fencing. It could take up to four years to achieve the required level to advance beyond the Academy.

1788 Journal with observations &c since getting my Commission

> Richard Wilkes Unett, born 11 November 1765 about 4 in [the] morning, came to Woolwich 11 February 1782. Was made an Extra-Cadet in May 1782 by [George] Lord Townshend (Master General). Admitted into the Upper Academy in July 1782. Made a Cadet 7 October by His Grace the Duke of Richmond[4] (Master General). Made a Corporal of the Company of Gentlemen Cadets on the 15 of June 1784 (in the room of G Cooke who got a commission in the Foot Guards[5]). Examined for my Commission on 2 June 1787 but owing to the manoeuvres of Colonel St[eheli]n,[6] did not obtain it. Was examined again on the 9 July 1788 and got my Commission the 14 July, it being dated the 1st of the same month.[7] [The] Examination lasted 13 hours. Obtained a fortnight's leave from General Pattison[8] and joined again at Woolwich 28 July 1788. Have been reviewed twice by His Majesty[9] with a firelock [musket] on my shoulder, once on the 7 June 1785 and the other 9 July 1788, both of them at Woolwich.

4. He would appear to have written this introduction later and got his Master Generals confused. Kane records that George Viscount Townshend was appointed Master General of the Ordnance on 17 October 1772 until 31 December 1781 when he was superseded by Charles Lennox 3rd Duke of Richmond; but resumed the position on 1 April 1783 until again superseded by Charles Duke of Richmond on 1 January 1784. Therefore, the Duke of Richmond was in post when he became an Extra Cadet in May 1782 and was still in post when he was appointed Cadet on 7 October 1782.
5. It is difficult to reconcile this statement with the official records. Kane does not record George Cooke as a Cadet, although this would not be surprising if he then went to the Guards. No history of General Sir George Cooke mentions him being a Cadet in the Royal Artillery before joining the Foot Guards as an Ensign in 1781.
6. He can be identified with certainty as Colonel Benjamin Stehelin Royal Artillery (Kane 161) who was Lieutenant Governor of the Gentleman Cadets at Woolwich 1781–94. It is not clear why Stehelin would have connived to stop Richard being commissioned as although Stehelin had three sons in the artillery, all three had successfully gained their commissions previous to his examination.
7. He was appointed 2nd Lieutenant in the Royal Irish Artillery on 1 July 1788.
8. Major General James Pattison Royal Artillery was Colonel Commandant (Kane 55).
9. King George III.

1788

His first entry of interest records the dangers of observing artillery fire.

> 19 August Mortar practise as usual. This morning, I went to the range with Lieutenant Pattison[10] to observe the ranges of the shells upon Woolwich Common; when the 5½ inch shell took quite a different direction from the range, owing to the unskilfulness of one of the recruits who laid it. We guessed it was out of the line of direction by the unusual and different whizzing which it made in the air, however the atmosphere being very thick and hazy, we could hardly distinguish it before it fell amongst about 20 soldiers and Pattison and myself. I may safely say, I was never in such *real danger* before; fortunately, no lives were lost, although it struck a soldier over the hat, broke the loop of it and knocked him down. It fell within about 7 yards of myself.
>
> 21 August. Gun and mortar practise as usual. Breakfasted with Captain Dixon[11] (Captain of Practise).
>
> 22 August. Attended gun practise in the Warren. Breakfasted with Lieutenant Lewis.[12]
>
> 23 August. Rode on horseback to London and called upon the Duke of Richmond, Honourable Edward Monckton[13] and Colonel Morse of the Engineers,[14] the two first of which were in the country, and the last was not at home.
>
> 24 August. The regiment had Divine Service in the foundery[15] [*sic*] this day.
>
> 25 August. We had a field day this morning from 9 till 11 o'clock. Was at long gun practise[16] in the Warren[17] from 2 till 4 o'clock. Colonel

10. 1st Lieutenant Mark Pattison Royal Artillery (Kane 607) died at St Lucia on 24 October 1796.
11. Captain Francis Dixon Royal Artillery (Kane 399); he died at Woolwich on 20 August 1797.
12. 2nd Lieutenant George Lewis Royal Artillery (Kane 703); he was killed at San Sebastian on 30 August 1813.
13. Edward Monckton was then MP for Stafford, the family then owning Somerford House.
14. Colonel Robert Morse Royal Engineers.
15. The Royal Arsenal Brass Foundry had been built in 1716 for the production of cannon.
16. Cannon of each weight were produced in long and short barrel versions; long barrels gave greater accuracy and power, but short barrels reduced weight, making the piece more manoeuvrable.
17. The Warren at Woolwich had been used for proving cannon, to which a range was added in 1787 for gunnery practice.

MacBean[18] ordered all the Second Lieutenants of the regiment to the Cadets Green, where we manned a light 6 pounder and went through all the exercise &c for 2 hours, viz from 5 till 7 o'clock. Supped at the Mess Club.

26 August. Mortar practice this morning from 8 till 10 o'clock, it rained nearly all the time. This day an order was given out for all the 2nd Lieutenants of the regiment to attend 6 pounder exercise three times a week till further orders. Long gun practice in the Warren from 2 till 4 o'clock.

27 August. Practice twice today as usual.

28 August. Practice as usual, both morning and evening.

29 August. Practice in the morning; the weather so bad we had no practice in the evening.

Richard was required to observe his first Punishment Parade and he did not like it.

16 September. The whole regiment were ordered under arms at 6 o'clock this evening in the front of the barracks, when 9 prisoners were brought out of the Guard Room to be punished for different crimes; six of them were pardoned and two of the others received 200 lashes each and the other 300. This is the first flogging I have ever seen since I came to Woolwich, although it is nearly 7 years; it is by far the most disagreeable part of an officer's duty and I hope it may be the last [I see].

1789

Richard records another potentially lethal accident in the ice.

5 January. On guard at the New Barracks.[19] In marching the guard from the Warren, one of them, it being very slippery fell down; he gave a terrible groan just as he reached the ground, it was very lucky however, he did not hurt himself or at least any of his comrades, for his firelock flew out of his hand a great distance and it had the bayonet fixed to it at the time.

18. Colonel Forbes Macbean Royal Artillery (Kane 129) died at Woolwich on 11 November 1800.
19. The New Artillery Barracks overlooking Woolwich Common were completed in 1776.

10 January. Today the regiment fired a Royal Salute with three vollies [*sic*] on account of His Majesty['s] happy recovery.[20] I had the command of one of the six pounders (there were only two) that fired the Royal Salute, which was an exceeding bad one owing to the cartridges being so large they would hardly go into the muzzle of the gun. In the evening there were 280 rockets let off in the front of the barracks and afterwards a ball and supper given by the officers in the Mess Room. All the soldiers had a pot of porter [beer] given them by the Commanding Officer.

23 January. All the regiment was under arms at half after 9 o'clock when three men tried last week by a Garrison Courts Martial for deserting, were flogged. Within the last ten days there have been 8 men flogged, it is now very frequent.

16 February. The whole regiment were under arms at a ¼ after one o'clock, marched past and performed the manual exercise before General Pattison.

17 April Today, Captain Ross's Company,[21] [to] which I belong to, received orders to march to Scotland on this day week viz 24th.

The 8th Company of the 4th Battalion of Royal Artillery, commanded by Captain Thomas Ross was ordered to march to Scotland, his future brother-in-law amongst the officers.

Journal of my march from Woolwich to Perth commencing the 24 April and ending 27 June [May] 1789

24 April
Marched from Woolwich, a little after 5 o'clock with the company of artillery, with Captain Ross and Lieutenants, Scott,[22] Fraser[23] & myself. The two former only marched the first day with us. Arrived in London about 8 o'clock [a.m.], where we halted an hour and breakfasted at a Captain Macdowall's[24] a friend of Captain Ross and got into Highgate about 12 o'clock. Walked about in the evening

20. The recovery of the King's health in 1789 was celebrated widely.
21. Captain Thomas Ross Royal Artillery (Kane 433) commanded the 8th Company of the 4th Battalion; he died in the East Indies on 10 July 1794.
22. 1st Lieutenant George Scott (Kane 558); he died at Woolwich on 26 March 1806 as Inspector of the Royal Carriage Department.
23. 1st Lieutenant John Grant Fraser (Kane 613); he died at Woolwich on 1 November 1797. He later married Richard's sister Ann, bringing the families together.
24. Captain Lieutenant Henry Thomson (Kane 505); he was mortally wounded on 9 May 1801 and died on 8 June in Egypt.

Forth Leith.

> and saw the illuminations in London on account of the king's recovery. The city was to appearance all in a blaze. The wind was very high during the day, which was disagreeable marching. There are some very good houses in the town.

The rest of the journal of the march to Perth is a mere travelogue, simply listing the places they passed through and where they stopped each night and therefore is not reproduced here. Arriving at Perth, they were ordered to proceed to Fort Leith, just outside Edinburgh.

> [Early] May. Arrived at Leith Fort,[25] being 8 miles by half after 10 o'clock. We dined with Captain Thompson of the Royal Artillery,[26] who was Captain Lieutenant[27] of Captain Shand's company,[28] which we were sent down to relieve, it being under orders for Jamaica. Captain Thompson was an old acquaintance of mine.

25. Leith Fort was originally an enclosed battery constructed in 1780, this was expanded into a barracks in 1804. The principal battery comprised of eight 24-pounders, one 18-pounder, one 13in mortar and one 68-pounder carronade.
26. This must refer to Captain Lieutenant Henry Thomson (Kane 505); he was killed in Egypt in 1801.
27. Captain Lieutenant was a rank in the Artillery at this time and was usually the rank of the second in command of a company.
28. Captain Alexander Shand (Kane 355) died at Aberdeen on 7 April 1803. He commanded the 3rd Company of the 2nd Battalion.

They returned to Fife by ferry, disembarking at Kinghorn and marching to Crieff.

> 27 May. After a march of 32 miles from Kinghorn,[29] I being the only officer with the company, I marched them that far to get it over and done with. [To] Perth, Gowrie Castle.[30]

Gowrie Castle.

He makes no mention of it, but they had returned to Perth by July.

> 25 July. This day Lord Adam Gordon the Commander in Chief[31] came to Perth; I was ordered immediately with two non-commissioned & 20 men to mount guard over him. I marched to the inn, but as he would not accept of it, and begged not to have the same compliment paid to him again. He only staid [for] dinner and set off again for the north.

Richard again moved to Leith for nearly two weeks.

> 27 July. Went to Leith Fort and stayed till 8 August.

The company was to remain based at Perth for a considerable number of years, with occasional periods at Leith Fort and it is hardly surprising that there were fewer and fewer diary entries of any military importance, much of his time being taken up with hunting and fishing, but in May 1791 Richard could record some very good personal news.

---

29. Kinghorn is a small coastal town in Fife.
30. Gowrie Castle or House in Crieff was used by the government as a military barracks.
31. Major General Lord Adam Gordon was appointed Commander-in-Chief, Scotland in 1789.

1791

Richard does not record it in his diary, but Captain Ross was ordered to the East Indies and Captain Samuel Rimington Royal Artillery (Kane 477) took command of the company on 24 March 1791.

> 2 April. Received an official letter informing me that I was made a First Lieutenant, my commission being dated the 24th of last month.

1792

> 25 November. Went to church in the morning. Called in the evening with Captain Rimington upon some officers of the 4th Regiment of Dragoons who arrived here today on their march to Dundee.

Revolutionary ideals were spreading from France and they reached Perth in late 1792, the Perth Society for Parliamentary Reform being established that August. The riots of November were triggered by the news that the French army of General Dumourier had entered Brussels; the demonstrators even demanded the end of monarchy and the aristocracy and opposed war with France. Things slowly calmed down in Perth after the arrest and deportation of a number of radicals who were implicated in planning an armed uprising including the ordering of 4,000 pikes.

> 26 November. This evening a mob assembled and made all the inhabitants illuminate their houses &c on account of the success of the French in taking Brussels &c. They made a large bonfire at the cross, round the Tree of Liberty[32] they set up. They were very riotous, breaking a vast many windows and burning a number of carts, barrels & boxes &c. They also broke into the Bellfry [*sic*] and rung the fire-bell and which they continued till 6 o'clock next morning.
>
> 27 November. It was given out by the mob that they were to break open the prison, custom house &c. The Provost[33] called out the Burgesses,[34] who paraded the streets till 12 o'clock, but all was peace and quietness. We were prepared for them at the barracks.

32. The French Revolutionaries began in 1790 to plant a 'Tree Of Liberty' in the main square of towns and villages, which was used as a powerful symbol of the revolutionary idea. By 1792 it was attracting attention across Europe.
33. The Provosts were Mr Fechney and Mr Alison.
34. Burgesses were originally any inhabitant who owned land in the vicinity, later it generally denoted the merchants and craftsmen of the town.

Although things calmed down, there was a continual undercurrent of unrest.

> 11 December. This day there was a fair and it was given out there was to be a serious riot; we were all in readiness at the barracks, but there was no appearance of any.
>
> 13 December. Went in the morning to a meeting, which was called by the Magistrates in order to draw up an address to be published in the newspapers, showing their loyalty to the King & Constitution at the present crisis of affairs, it was a very confused meeting, as there was a strong party for reform in parliament &c so that very little was done.

The French Revolutionary War – Home Service

1793

With the obvious build-up to war, followed by the declaration of war by France on 1 February 1793, Richard's diary immediately fills with more military issues. However, as the threat of an invasion loomed large, particularly in Ireland, some two-thirds of the Army, including Militia and Fencibles, remained at home on defence duties and it was many years before Richard would serve abroad.

> 10 January. Had to dinner and drink tea with us, Ensign Wishart of the 19th Regiment[1] who is here Recruiting.
>
> 13 February. The newspapers today mention the French having declared war against Great Britain & Holland.[2]
>
> 21 February. Captain R[imington] sent off this morning 23 recruits to Woolwich.
>
> 11 March. Three companies of the 53rd [Shropshire] Regiment came here today from Dundee, on their way to Leith where they are to embark for Holland;[3] was asked by Ensign Robertson[4] of the same regiment to dine with him to meet them, but excused myself.
>
> 13 March. Today's Gazette mentioned great successes of the Austrians & Prussians over the French in Holland; and which was taken notice of here by a general illumination of all ranks, except a few people who call themselves the *Friends of the People.*
>
> 18 March. Wrote to [John Grant] Fraser by some recruits which Captain R[imington] sent off to Woolwich this evening.

1. Ensign William Wishart 19th Foot.
2. The news took 13 days to get to Perth from Paris.
3. The 53rd served with the Duke of York in the Flanders campaign of 1793–5.
4. Ensign Daniel Robertson 53rd Foot.

The government sought to increase the number of troops in Britain for home defence while the line regiments were serving in Holland. A large number of Fencible regiments were raised for Home Service for the duration of the war only. Officers of Fencible Regiments held temporary commissions while the regiments remained in existence and were listed in the Army Lists alongside regular officers but were specifically junior to regular officers of the same rank.

> 28 March. Captain Rimington and myself waited upon the Earl of Bredalbine [Breadalbane][5] who arrived here last night in order to raise a Regiment of Fencibles, of which His Lordship is to be Colonel.[6] We were asked to dinner which we accepted, and at night we went round the town with drums beating &c; His Lordship ordering some hogsheads of porter to be given away to the populace.

Richard suffered with a bad headache the next day, but it is dubious whether it was due to excessive shouting!

> 29 March. Had a bad headache today, having *shouted* too much in going round last night with the drums &c wishing success to the *Bredalbine* [Breadalbane] *Fencibles.*
>
> 17 April. Dined with Colonel Morrison[7] of the Bredalbine [Breadalbane] Fencibles.
>
> 30 April. Lord Bredalbine [Breadalbane] this morning marched into town at the head of 300 of his Fencibles which he has raised upon his estate in about a fortnight.
>
> 8 May. We expect to march from this place in a very short time for Leith.

Everyday emergencies occurred alongside the warlike preparations.

> 9 May. Between 12 & 1 o'clock this morning, the town was alarmed by the ringing of the fire bell. I got up and staid there for more than an hour. There was only one house burnt as fortunately there was no wind, but six people lost their lives, viz a mother and two daughters,

---

5. John Campbell 4th Earl of Breadalbane.
6. The Earl of Breadalbane actually raised three battalions of the Breadalbane Fencibles between 1793–4, 1,600 of the 2,300 recruits being raised from the Breadalbane Estates alone and he became a Lieutenant Colonel. He eventually rose to the rank of Lieutenant General.
7. Lieutenant Colonel William Maxwell Morrison commanded the 1st Battalion Breadalbane Fencibles.

> two other women and an old man; another child is much burnt and a man much bruised.
>
> 13 May. Wrote to sister Elizabeth, to [brother] George and to [John] Fraser by Sergeant Brewer who sails tomorrow morning with some recruits for Woolwich.
>
> 14 May. This morning 30 recruits went off for Woolwich.
>
> 22 May. Dined at the Mess with the Bredalbine [Breadalbane] Fencibles (asked by Lieutenant Drummond[8]).
>
> 27 May. General Leslie[9] and [his] Aide du Camp arrived from Edinburgh to inspect the Bredalbine [Breadalbane] Fencibles. Captain R[imington] and myself waited upon him, when he asked us to dinner to meet the officers of the Fencibles; about 50 sat down to dinner; there were only five or six [men] rejected out of the two battalions of 1,200 men.
>
> 28 May. We went this evening to a ball & supper given by the officers of the Fencibles; very full and crowded, returned about 3 o'clock in the morning.

Richard records a public hanging, but it is unclear whether he witnessed it. James Dormand was hung at Perth on this day for four crimes of highway robbery.

> 31 May. At 3 o'clock this evening a man was hanged, he having been condemned about 3 weeks ago for robbing on the highway. The first division[10] of the 2nd Battalion of Fencibles marched from here for Dumfries.
>
> 3 June. Wrote to sister Fanny. Waited upon Lord Bredalbine [Breadalbane] by order of Captain R[imington] to ask His Lordship if he had any commands about the guns tomorrow, being the King's birthday.
>
> 4 June. Fired a Royal Salute with the two six-pounders in honor [*sic*] of the king's birthday. Asked by the Provost and Magistrates to drink the king's health, came home before 9 o'clock.
>
> 11 June. Had company to tea & supper viz Captain & Mrs Rimington, Lieutenant Baillie of 72nd Regiment[11] who is here Recruiting . . .

8. Lieutenant Gavin Drummond 1st Battalion Breadalbane Fencibles.
9. Major General John Leslie.
10. Battalions of ten companies were split into two divisions of five companies.
11. Lieutenant Isaac Bayley 72nd Foot.

> 15 June. Had company to dinner & supper viz Captain & Mrs Rimington & Mr & Mrs Davy from Fort George the Commissary of Artillery.
>
> 5 July. Had a letter from [John] Fraser & his wife.[12]

In late July the company were ordered to move to Leith Fort permanently.

> 30 July. A Route came this morning to Captain Rimington for the company to march to Leith Fort and for that place in future to be [our] headquarters.
>
> 3 August. Employed as yesterday and in putting the things on board a ship which is taken for the purpose in order to carry the artillery stores &c to Leith, by which means it saves me the expense of paying for my baggage &c.
>
> 5 August. Was up this morning by half past 3 o'clock and marched at half past 4 o'clock. Intended setting off before, but the men in taking leave of their acquaintances had drank too much which prevented me from marching sooner. Did not halt till I got to Falkland[13] which was 15 miles, where I breakfasted and after dressing myself and leaving the men to stay all night, I set off and walked forwards for some miles when a gent of my acquaintance overtook me and gave me a lift as far as Kinghorn,[14] where I staid all night.
>
> 6 August. About 9 o'clock the company arrived and halted for some time to clean and refresh themselves, when I crossed the ferry and arrived at Leith Fort before 2 o'clock to relieve Captain Smith,[15] who immediately after set off for Perth to relieve Captain Rimington. Walked up to Edinburgh and left my card at Lord Adam Gordon's who was at his country seat.
>
> 7 August. The baggage arrived, when I ordered all the men to parade in their working dresses and begin to unload the ship.
>
> 8 August. At 9 o'clock Captain R[imington] arrived from Perth and brought me a letter from my wife.[16]

---

12. His sister Ann had married his friend John Grant Fraser on 27 March 1792. Richard was not present.
13. Falkland is just north of Glenrothes.
14. A port on the Fife coast, opposite Leith.
15. Captain William Smith (Kane 462); he died at Leith on 23 July 1806.
16. Strangely this is the first time he mentions his wife in the journal. Records show that Richard married Ann Steele who was then residing at Perth. They were married by Mr Adam Peebles, Minister of the Episcopal Congregation at Perth, on Monday 16 April 1792

9 August. Employed all morning in seeing the stores properly disposed &c.

10 August. Seeing the stores as yesterday &c.

12 August. Had a letter from my wife informing me she was to set off this morning [from Perth] and desiring I would give her the meeting in Edinburgh.

13 August. We were very busy all day in arranging our new quarters.

18 August. Wrote to sister Elizabeth. Went in a chaise with Captain Rimington's to dine with Lord Adam Gordon at his country seat (according to invitation) had a very sumptuous dinner, came home by 9 o'clock.

20 August. Went with Captain R[imington] to Leith Pier at 12 o'clock to see the 57th Regiment[17] embark for Foreign Service, but the wind was so very high, that it was not thought safe. Lord Adam Gordon came and examined the barracks.

21 August. Walked to the pier and saw the 57th embark.

25 August. Wrote to Mr Adair, Paymaster of Artillery.[18]

In September Richard learned that he was the beneficiary of a small property in Warwickshire from a cousin and he arranged to travel to see it with his brother John and to sign the relevant legal papers.

2 September. Had a letter from brother John at Birmingham, giving me an account of the death of Cousin Unett at Warwick,[19] to whom I am heir at law and come in for a small estate in Warwickshire. She had been dead since the 28 June and the executors had lost my direction and did not know where to write to me. Wrote a letter to John telling him I would set off in a few days for Warwick.

5 September. Walked to Edinburgh and took a place in the diligence[20] for Carlisle, which sets off at 4 o'clock tomorrow morning, intend going to sleep in Edinburgh this evening. Walked to the Black Bull Inn[21] to sleep.

6 September. Up at 3 o'clock and arrived at Carlisle (91 miles) between 11 & 12 o'clock at night where I slept.

17. The 57th (West Middlesex) sailed for Flanders to join the Duke of York's army.
18. Mr Adair was Paymaster to the Company of Cadets.
19. I have been unable to discover a Unett who died at Warwick in 1793.
20. The diligence was a four-wheeled enclosed coach, usually associated with France, but was used in Britain as well.
21. The Black Bull on Leith Street, Edinburgh.

7 September. Up again this morning before 3 o'clock and went in the mail to Manchester (118 miles) where I arrived before 12 o'clock. Had some supper, which made it nearly 2 o'clock before I went to bed.

8 September. Sunday. Sent by 8 o'clock to enquire for brother Tom,[22] when I learnt he was at Oldham, about 8 miles off. Took a chaise and brought him with me back to Manchester.

9 September. At 9 o'clock set off for Stafford on the top of the coach, the inside being quite full.

10 September. Rained all night and till 8 o'clock this morning, when it became a fine day. Found riding upon the coach much easier than I imagined; arrived at Stafford a little after 9 o'clock, where I breakfasted and after dressing walked and met sister Fanny, who staid and dined at the Swan Inn[23] with me and after dinner we set off for Acton Hill, where I met brother George from London, who was come down for a month's shooting. We rode to Warwick.

14 September. Set off at 10 o'clock for Birmingham, where I met brother John.

16 September. Went to the lawyer's by appointment at 9 o'clock this morning and received all the writing &c belonging to my estate at Snitterfield called Heath Farm,[24] and which lies about 4 miles from Warwick. Rode over to Snitterfield and walked over the estate. Set off for Birmingham where we arrived about 10 o'clock.

29 September. Rode to Stafford and got from the Post Office two letters from my wife and one from John.

1 October. Wrote to John. Had two letters from my wife which had been laying some time in the Post Office at Warwick.

Having completed the legalities, Richard returned to Leith Fort.

2 October. Up this morning at 4 o'clock and rode on top of the coach to Manchester, there being no room in the inside. Arrived at Manchester about 4 o'clock. Mail [for Scotland] that I had taken my place in set off at 2 o'clock, did not go to bed.

3 October. Arrived at Carlisle between 11 & 12 o'clock at night, went to bed for two hours and . . .

22. Tom was at school
23. The Swan Hotel still exists on Stafford High Street.
24. Now Heath End Farm. Snitterfield lies about 8km south-west of Warwick on the A46.

4 October. Set off at 4 o'clock this morning for Edinburgh where I arrived at the Black Bull and staid all night.

5 October. Up at 7 o'clock and was down at the fort to breakfast, Captain & Mrs Rimington & Major & Mrs Hosmer.[25]

25 October. This being the King's Accession I went to the castle to see the guns fired.

Richard had toothache and was seen by a surgeon.

4 November. Sent for Mr Cheyne[26] and had a tooth pulled out, which plagued me a good deal. Pain still very bad, had but an indifferent night.

5 November. Was no better with the pain last night.

6 November. This day I was so much worse, that Mr Cheyne was sent for and I have been confined to the house and some days to my bed for nearly this fortnight. Mr Cheyne says it is the gout. I have had my left hand much swelled and very painfull [*sic*], which by keeping warm with flannel is now gone away. I have still at times some pain in my stomach particularly in an evening. Had a letter about a week ago from sister Fanny and another from [John] Fraser.

18 November. Had a letter from sister Elizabeth, as also received a present of tea and sugar from sister Anne Fraser.

3 December. Walked with Mrs [Ann] Unett, Major Imrie Brigade Major,[27] and Colonel Mackay Adjutant General[28] called upon me.

1794

19 January. Was up in Edinburgh Castle with 20 of the men in order to put the heavy field train into store &c, it having been surveyed.

20 January. Received two parcels by sea from Staffordshire; the one containing 6 bottles of Catchup[29] and the other two large hams and three cheeses. Wrote to brother George.

25. Major Thomas Hosmer Royal Artillery (Kane 300) died at Greenwich 8 April 1805.
26. Surgeon John Cheyne of Leith.
27. Major Ninian Imrie 1st Foot.
28. Lieutenant Colonel Alexander Mackay 69th Foot, Deputy Adjutant General in North Britain.
29. In the eighteenth century, English Catchup (later changing to Ketchup) was made with anchovies, shallots, white wine, vinegar and spices.

> 1 March. Lieutenant Rey[30] of this company from Tynemouth was at Captain R[imington's] and came and slept at our quarters.
>
> 3 April. The Duke of Gordon's Regiment of Fencibles[31] embarked on board of transports for England, they had for some time refused to go, being under the idea that as soon as Government had them on board, they would send them to the continent, but at last they consented, upon their colonel assuring them they were not to leave England.[32]

From this point onwards he regularly records abdominal pain and less often joint/muscular pain. Consulting with my good friend Michael Crumplin he believes there is some small chance that he suffered with migraines and either a peptic ulcer or lead poisoning, but more likely that the symptoms may well be psychosomatic.

> 15 April. Return of the pain in my stomach and today I still have it.
>
> 16 April. My pain in my stomach troubled me a good deal and prevented me sleeping last night.
>
> 18 April. Took some castor oil today.
>
> 19 April. Had a good night and much better today.

Richard was able to record a litany of good news.

> 23 April. We had a letter from Mrs Godwin[33] giving us an account that sister [Ann] Fraser was brought to bed of a daughter.[34]
>
> 24 April. The guns at Edinburgh Castle fired one and twenty rounds at 1 o'clock on account of the taking of the Island of Martinique in the West Indies by Sir Charles Grey KB.[35]
>
> 6 May. The guns at the Castle of Edinburgh fired a Royal Salute for the taking of Landrecies.[36]

30. 1st Lieutenant Francis Rey (Kane 717).
31. The Gordon Fencibles had been raised by Alexander, Duke of Gordon.
32. They were garrisoned in Kent and were reviewed by the king in London. They returned to Scotland in 1798.
33. The Godwin's were their mother's family.
34. Named Mary Anne.
35. Martinique surrendered on 24 March 1794.
36. The fortress of Landrecies surrendered to the forces commanded by the Prince of Orange on 30 April 1794, but was recaptured by the French on 17 July 1794.

11 May. Wrote to [John] Fraser and another letter to General Stehelin to recommend me to be a Cadet Officer.[37]

15 May. Major Hosmer left this place this morning, being ordered to Woolwich.

19 May. The castle guns were fired today on the news of St Lucia[38] being taken in the West Indies without the loss of a man.

22 May. The guns at the castle fired a Royal Salute for the taking of the Island of Guadeloupe.[39]

29 May. The guns at the castle fired on account of its being King Charles 2nd Restoration,[40] as did also the ships in the roads.

4 June. At 12 o'clock we fired a Royal Salute, it being the king's birthday. The ships in the roads also fired at 1 o'clock. It was expected there would have been some disturbance in Edinburgh, but everything passed very quietly.

7 June. Had a letter from Mrs Wood inclosing one from Colonel Graham of Balgowan[41] offering me a company in the 2nd Battalion of his regiment, which he is just now raising.

13 June. Lieutenant Douglas[42] called to take leave, he being promoted to a First Lieutenant and ordered to Tynemouth to relieve Lieutenant Rey who is to join at Woolwich.

14 June. Had a letter from [John] Fraser and another from Mrs Godwin in answer to mine respecting the company in Colonel Graham's regiment. She does not approve of my leaving the artillery, so that plan is done with. We had a Gazette today giving an account that Earl Howe had on the 2nd of this month given the French fleet in the Channel, a complete drubbing; 2 eighty-gun ships being taken and 4 [5] seventy-fours, one of which sunk before she was taken possession of. The action was exceedingly desperate and both fleets

37. Teaching cadets at Woolwich.
38. St Lucia was captured on 1 April 1794.
39. Guadeloupe was captured by the British on 24 April 1794 but was lost again on 4 June 1794.
40. The Restoration of the monarchy on 29 May 1660 was a public holiday known as 'Oak Apple Day'.
41. He was to become General Sir Thomas Graham of Lynedoch. He raised the 90th Foot (Perthshire Volunteers). The raising of a second battalion caused him serious financial concerns. It was unusual but not impossible for artillerymen to transfer into the infantry but it did not happen because Mrs Godwin did not approve.
42. 1st Lieutenant Sir Howard Douglas (Kane 783) eventually exchanged into the infantry (Royal York Rangers) in 1804, serving in the Corunna campaign, Walcheren and in the Peninsula. He rose to full general and died in 1861.

have lost an immense number of men.[43] In consequence of this signal success, the guns at the castle were fired between 11 and 12 o'clock and at 1 o'clock the ships in the roads saluted; in the evening the whole town, Leith &c was illuminated, the fort amongst the rest. There was also a Gazette for the taking of Bastia.[44]

17 June. At 3 o'clock pm, Colonel D[uncan] Campbell of Lochnell's Regiment[45] embarked for England. Wrote to sister Elizabeth.

24 June. Did not sleep last night with my old complaint of a pain in my stomach, had a piece of flannel put to my breast.

25 June. Was very restless and did not sleep last night with the pain in my stomach.

26 June. Went to Edinburgh with Captain Rimington and called upon Sir Alexander Campbell, Lieutenant Colonel Argyle Fencibles.[46]

30 June. Was in great pain last night &c.

1 July. Still in great pain with my stomach all last night. Sent this morning to Mr Cheyne who let me blood, which did not relieve the pain.

2 July. Was in violent pain last night, so that I took about 50 drops of laudanum which made me sleep though the pain is still very bad this morning.

3 July. Today I had a large blister put upon my stomach, the pain last night was very violent, which prevented my getting any sleep. Captain & Mrs Rimington dined and supped with us, and to dinner, we had also Major Ramsay.[47]

4 July. Slept better last night than I have done for some time past. Wrote to sister Fanny. Was in violent pain all the evening.

7 July. Had a very bad night.

8 July. Slept very well last night.

43. This refers to the Battle of the Glorious First of June when Lord Richard Howe's fleet engaged a virtually equal fleet under Admiral Villaret-Joyeuse, which was protecting a vital grain convoy en route to France. Two 80-gun ships were captured, *Sans-Pareil* and *Juste*, the 74s captured were *America*, *Impetueux*, *Achille* and *Northumberland.* The 74-gun *Vengeur du Peuple* sank.

44. The fortress of Bastia on Corsica capitulated on 19 May 1794.

45. Duncan Campbell of Lochnell raised a regiment in February 1794 which was initially numbered as the 98th Foot. In October 1798, it was renumbered as the 91st Foot.

46. George, Marquis of Lorne raised the Argyle Fencibles in 1793. Lieutenant Colonel Alexander Campbell, Argyle Fencibles later joined the Argyll Volunteers in 1803.

47. Major John Ramsey Royal Artillery (Kane 449), he was Commandant of the troops at Woolwich from 1806. He died on 9 February 1827.

9 July. Had a good night, put a flannel shirt on this morning next my skin. Captain & Mrs Rimington and ourselves went in the Passage Boat to Kinghorn where we staid [*sic*] the day and returned the next tide, which made it 12 o'clock pm.

11 July. Had a good night but feel a good deal of pain during the day.

12 July. My stomach pains me a good deal today but I slept well last night.

13 July. Had a restless night and was in a good deal of pain in the evening.

14 July. Slept very little last night as I was in a good deal of pain.

16 July. Very good diversion at the races.[48] Was in great pain yesterday but am much better today having slept well last night.

19 July. Am still in great pain during the day though I have slept better lately than usual.

21 July. Have slept better for some nights past than usual, though I have been at times during the days in violent pain.

22 July. Some recruits went to Woolwich.

24 July. Was in violent pain all the day.

25 July. Have got a little of a sore throat, but I think the pain is not so bad as usual.

26 July. Find myself better.

27 July. Pain much as usual. Bathed my feet in hot water and took a glass of warm rum and water when I went to bed to make me perspire.

28 July. Had a most unpleasant night, as I was in great pain and had a very great perspiration upon me, which prevented me from moving about, being afraid of catching cold; I never closed my eyes all night, but about 8 o'clock in the morning I fell asleep and did not get up till 11 o'clock, think I am a little better.

29 July. Walked to the coffee room[49] and read the newspapers; did not do myself any good by going out, as I was not so well in the evening as I had been in the morning.

---

48. Edinburgh held an Annual Race Meeting at Leith Sands which was the highlight of the Scottish racing season. It moved to Musselburgh in 1816.

49. Although coffee houses were now very popular, records show only one at Leith, called Gibb's Coffee House.

> 30 July. Pain not so bad, had a fire in the evening.
>
> 2 August. Much better today.
>
> 8 August. Breakfasted with Captain R[imington] when we walked to Bruntsfield Links[50] and saw the Argyleshire Fencibles[51] reviewed by Lord Adam Gordon. Called upon General Martin of the artillery.[52]
>
> 11 August. Had a bad night with the pain in my stomach.
>
> 12 August. Did not sleep very well last night.
>
> 17 August. Had a packet from Woolwich, containing a letter from sister [Ann] Fraser, from John [Fraser] and another from Elizabeth [Unett].

The arrival of a Russian fleet at Leith was a novelty.

> 26 August. At 3 o'clock this day a fleet consisting of six sail of the line and four frigates belonging to the Empress of Russia[53] anchored in the roads, the admiral of which saluted us with seven guns and we by order of Lord Adam Gordon returned him the same number. The admiral had previously to coming to an anchor sent his lieutenant on shore to know if his salute would be returned.
>
> 5 September. Had company to dinner viz General & Miss Martin, Captain Boag of the artillery,[54] Mr Simpson and Captain & Mrs Rimington.

Richard had a run-in with a local hackney driver.

> 11 September. Went to the council chamber and lodged a complaint against a hackney coachman for charging me above his fare and for insulting me on the evening when I returned from Lord Adam Gordon's, when I got him fined five shillings.[55]
>
> 12 September. This morning between 5 & 6 o'clock the wind coming fair (w[est]) the Russian fleet weighed anchor and saluted us, when

50. Brunstfield Links Golf Course is the fourth oldest in the world and only three miles from Edinburgh.
51. The Argyllshire Fencibles consisted of two battalions, their Colonel being George Marquis of Lorne.
52. Major General William Martin Royal Artillery (Kane 109) died in London on 12 July 1799.
53. Catherine the Great was Empress until her death in 1796, when she was succeeded by Paul I.
54. Captain James Boag; he retired on 1 September 1803.
55. About £25 today.

> we returned eleven guns, which was two more than their number, owing to a mistake of our having miscounted and given them two less when they arrived here first.
>
> 22 September. This being the King's Coronation, the guns at the castle fired at 12 o'clock and at 1 o'clock the ships in the roads saluted.
>
> 27 September. Had a letter from [John] Fraser which I answered by return of post. Wrote also to the Duke of Richmond about my being appointed Cadet Officer.
>
> 2 October. Was employed all the morning in marking linen with the permanent ink &c.
>
> 3 October. Had company to dinner viz Mrs & Miss Drummond and Lieutenant Mackenzie of the artillery[56] who staid [*sic*] to supper.

Finally Richard's canvassing had succeeded in obtaining a position commanding a company of Cadets at Woolwich.

> 12 October. This morning I had orders to proceed to Woolwich immediately being appointed by the Duke of Richmond to do duty in the Company of Gentleman Cadets of which His Grace is Captain.
>
> 14 October. My head aches this morning having drank rather too much yesterday.
>
> 15 October. At 12 o'clock a man of the name of Robert Watt was hanged in the High Street, Edinburgh, and beheaded for high treason.[57]
>
> 16 October. Called upon Lord Adam Gordon to take leave, who was very civil.

Richard and Ann set out for Woolwich together.

> 18 October. We were up this morning by 4 o'clock and at 5 o'clock Lieutenant Mackenzie arrived with a chaise and we set off for

---

56. 1st Lieutenant Robert Mackenzie Royal Artillery (Kane 811); he died at St Domingo on 12 September 1795.

57. David Downie, a goldsmith of Parliament Square, and Robert Watt, a wine merchant, planned an uprising armed with pikes, setting fire to buildings and then overpowering the troops as they emerged from the castle to fight the fires. They got as far as distributing seditious pamphlets and ordering 4,000 pikes from two local blacksmiths. They were arrested after forty-seven pikes were discovered at Watt's house. Both were found guilty, but the jury recommended mercy for Downie, who had persuaded them that he was not the main instigator. Watt was executed at Old Tolbooth, being hanged then beheaded as mentioned. Downie was sentenced to a year in gaol and then moved to America, where he died aged 80.

London. We staid a night at Doncaster at Mr Cave's (Monday night 20th) and arrived at Mrs Godwin's on Thursday evening at 4 o'clock.

24 October. Saw [John] Fraser and sister Ann.

27 October. Walked to Woolwich and dined at the Mess.

29 October. Dined at [John] Fraser's at Shooters Hill, came home to tea. Called upon Colonel Farrington.[58]

He took up his new role at Woolwich.

3 November. Came on duty as Cadet Officer. Had a letter from John [Unett] inclosing my half year's rent. Dined at the Crown and Anchor;[59] supped at the Mess.

4 November. Duke of Richmond came down. Wrote to Fanny. Breakfasted yesterday with Captain Godfrey[60] and today with Lieutenant Vivion.[61]

5 November. Breakfasted with Lieutenant Douglas of the Navy.[62]

9 November. Called upon General Macbean.[63] Came back to the parade at 6 o'clock.

10 November. Came off duty and went to Shooters Hill to stay till my own apartments are vacant and my baggage arrives from Scotland.

27 November. We have been staying at the Fraser's till today, when I came on duty again and slept last night in my new quarters for the first time.

28 November. Received all my baggage from the Tower[64] &c.

30 November. Called upon Captain [George] Scott.

---

58. Colonel Sir Anthony Farrington Royal Artillery (Kane 214) died at Blackheath on 3 November 1823.
59. The Crown & Anchor at 33 High Street, Woolwich, was demolished in 1974 to make way for the Waterfront Leisure Centre.
60. Captain Lieutenant Charles Godfrey Royal Artillery (Kane 716); he retired on half pay on 7 May 1811.
61. 1st Lieutenant John Vivion Royal Artillery (Kane 799); he died in October 1832.
62. There were no less than five named Lieutenant Douglas in the Royal Navy in 1794, none closely related to Howard Douglas. It is has therefore been found impossible to identify this officer with any certainty.
63. Major General Forbes Macbean Royal Artillery (Kane 129); he died at Woolwich on 11 November 1800.
64. Tower of London.

> 6 December. To supper we had Mr Macdonald Gentleman Cadet.[65]

The Christmas holidays did not have an auspicious start.

> 7 December. Yesterday the vacation commenced for a month, when an unfortunate accident happened, for as one of the stages was going to London, it being too much loaded with cadets, trunks &c overset in Woolwich and Sir David Murray[66] (one of them) had his arm broke and a soldier who was upon the top, had his thigh with both his legs broke, he was just returned from the West Indies, where he had had his arm shot off. There were several of the other cadets much bruised.

1795

> 8 January. Called upon Colonel Huddlestone.[67]
>
> 10 January. Wrote to Captain [William] Smith at Perth.
>
> 12 January. Came on duty this morning and was up at 7 o'clock.

He had to part with his regimental servant.

> 13 January. My servant Hugh Ross left me this morning, he having some business that required his presence in Scotland, whither he set off today; he was to leave me in May, so that I have taken another servant as it was not worthwhile for me to wait his return. He has lived with me about 5 years, and the reason of his going away was that he wanted to be promoted, which I shall endeavour to obtain for him in the summer.
>
> 14 January Called upon General Phipps.[68]
>
> 18 January. We had a new man servant came to us today. To supper we had also Lieutenant Adye.[69]

---

65. Gentleman Cadet Robert Macdonald Royal Artillery (Kane 858) died at Inchkenneth on 10 November 1856.
66. Sir David Murray does not appear in Kane and it is presumed that he never went beyond cadet.
67. Lieutenant Colonel William Orcher Huddlestone Royal Artillery (Kane 277); he died at Woolwich on 13 February 1814.
68. Major General John Phipps Royal Engineers, he commanded the Invalid Engineers.
69. 1st Lieutenant Ralph Willett Adye Royal Artillery (Kane 645); he died at Gibraltar on 22 October 1804. He was the author of *The Bombardier and Pocket Gunner*, in 1802.

9 February. Came on duty again this morning for the week, for Lieutenant Adye.

11 February. Had company to dinner viz Captain Maclean[70] & Lieutenants Colebrook[71] and Vivion and to supper we had Lieutenant Macdonald & Mr Deacon Cadet.[72]

17 February. Marquis Cornwallis the new Master General[73] came down this morning and all the officers &c were introduced to him. Lieutenant Vivion and Mr Pearson Cadet[74] drank tea and supped with us.

While stocking up on wines before a new tax was imposed, Richard notes some serious effects of the very cold winter.

23 February. The pain in my stomach is very bad and I am afraid of increasing it by going out this disagreeable weather. Received a hamper containing 6 dozen of port and 2 dozen of sherry from Mr Lee, Wine Merchant, London.[75] I also commissioned 12 dozen of port and 6 dozen of sherry and 1½ dozen of rum from Provost Alison at Perth,[76] which I got safe a few days ago. There is an additional duty going to take place upon wine immediately. The oldest person in the country scarce ever remembering so long and so intense a winter, the poor have suffered greatly though there have been subscriptions in almost every parish.

25 February. I have been keeping [to] the house with my old complaint, a violent pain in my stomach. Newspapers make mention of dreadful inundating in different counties owing to the thaw and rains which took place, particularly on the banks of the Trent; it is supposed that half the bridges in England are carried away and the loss to individuals in cattle, horses, sheep, hay and the winter wheat has been prodigious and will entirely ruin some of them and perhaps occasion a shortage in the country.

70. Captain Lieutenant Sir Joseph Maclean Royal Artillery (Kane 659); he died at Woolwich on 19 September 1839.
71. 1st Lieutenant Paulet Colebrooke Royal Artillery (Kane 678); he died at Shooters Hill on 29 September 1816.
72. Gentleman Cadet Henry Deacon Royal Artillery (Kane 873), he resigned on 15 October 1807.
73. Charles Marquis Cornwallis became Master General of the Ordnance on 15 February 1795.
74. Kane does not record a Cadet Pearson.
75. The 1794 London Directory does not list a Mr Lee as a wine merchant, but there were a few general merchants of this name.
76. William Alison was a Provost at Perth.

A trip to London had an eventful finale.

> 2 March. We went with a party, viz Captain & Mrs Scott, Captain [John] & Mrs [Ann] Fraser in a coach and four to Drury Lane to see (the second time of acting) *The Wheel of Fortune* written by Cumberland[77] and the pantomime of *Alexander the Great*,[78] we were all very much entertained, but unlucky in returning home, one of our wheels broke down and after waiting some considerable time we fortunately got two return post-chaises and arrived safe about 3 o'clock in the morning. The roads were exceedingly heavy and bad.
>
> 4 March. Wrote to General Pattison to ask him for the [position of] Quarter Master of his battalion.
>
> 12 March. We had company to dinner and supper viz, Captain & Mrs Scott, Captain & Mrs [John] Fraser and my brother George who is just come from the country in the hopes of obtaining a commission in the artillery.[79]
>
> 28 March. A General Court Martial sat this morning in the Repository upon Captain Lieutenant Robert Wright[80] on charges preferred against him by Captain Robison.[81]

Richard took leave to oversee improvements to his property in Warwickshire.

> 29 March. Took an early dinner and set off in the stage for London. Walked from Westminster to the city where I found a coach just setting off for Birmingham, but which was quite full in the inside, so I got upon the top. It was a fine moonlight night from 7 till 9 o'clock when a very thick mizzling mist came on for the rest of the night.
>
> 30 March. Arrived in Birmingham at 1 o'clock [pm] and called upon my brother John.
>
> 4 April. My horse was so lame this morning that I set off as soon as I had appointed a carpenter to meet me to examine what repairs were wanting to the tenant's house &c [at Heath Farm]. The house is

---

77. A comedy written by Richard Cumberland and first presented on 28 February 1795. As there would not be a show on Sunday 1 March, they saw it on its second night.
78. D'Egville's *Alexander the Great*, or, *The Conquest of Persia*, had its first night on 12 February 1795 at the Drury Lane Theatre.
79. George was never a Gentleman Cadet, but was successful in becoming a 2nd Lieutenant on 14 April 1795.
80. Captain Lieutenant Robert Wright Royal Artillery (Kane 657) died at Edinburgh on 2 October 1833.
81. Captain Charles Robison Royal Artillery (Kane 515); he died in Ireland on 4 July 1811.

> old and what is called half-timbered; the front is to be new built up from the foundation with bricks; the end and other side is to be new bricked in the squares; the whole is to be new tiled and some of the rooms and passages are to be new floored and the stairs to be new &c. The estimate £40,[82] beside the timber being cut upon the estate.

He then went on to attend the marriage of his brother John Wilkes to his cousin Elizabeth Unett.

> 6 April. Left Warwick as soon as dinner was over and on to Stratford upon Avon where I met with my brother and his bride, they were married this morning at Stone[83] and set off post immediately with her sister to Greenwich to stay some little time. She is a relation and namesake, being [Aunt] Elizabeth's oldest daughter and one of the co-heiresses of Thomas Unett of Stone. Staid supper with them and at 11 o'clock [pm] got into the coach . . .
>
> 7 April. . . . and arrived at Greenwich to dinner.

Shooters Hill at night was a dangerous place, but thankfully nobody was hurt.

> 19 April. Mrs Godwin &c in going home last night from us, was unfortunately stopped at the bottom of Shooters Hill by three footpads and robbed, Mrs Godwin lost about three guineas; sister Elizabeth 5 guineas; brother John one and a half; his wife twenty-three and a half and her sister Miss Unett about 4 guineas. They did not take their watches, nor did they use them ill.

His brother George Wilkes received a commission for the Royal Artillery as a Second Lieutenant just as he was turning 23.

> 7 May. My brother George was in orders yesterday as a 2nd Lieutenant; his commission is dated the 22nd of last month.
>
> 23 May. Signed a lease a few days ago for a house near the New Barracks from Mr Sanders for a term of three years from Xmas next and for which I am to pay £19 19s[84] besides all taxes except the Land Tax.[85]
>
> 4 June. Walked to the New Barracks at 1 o'clock when a Royal Salute was fired for the king's birthday.

82. About £4,000 in modern terms.
83. Stone lies about 6km south of Stoke-on-Trent.
84. Equivalent to about £1,800 today.
85. Land Tax was fixed from 1776 at 4 shillings for every pound.

21 June Sunday. Went to church and heard our new Chaplain, who gave us a very good discourse; he reads and preaches too fast (Mr Sandby[86]).

His wife now became quite unwell.

22 June. Mrs [Ann] Unett has complained all day, with a violent pain in her face, which is much inflamed and swelled.

23 June. Mrs [Ann] Unett's face is exceedingly swelled and she is so unwell that she did not get up till 1 o'clock [pm].

24 June. Mrs [Ann] Unett still very unwell. Dr Rollo[87] visited her and says it proceeds from her teeth, which are bad ones and has ordered her not to do anything to her face.

26 June. Dr Rollo called and lanced a large gum boil, which had formed in Mrs [Ann] Unett's mouth; her face was exceedingly swelled and she had suffered a great deal from it. This evening the swelling is in some measure gone down.

27 June. Mrs [Ann] Unett better today.

30 June. Dr John Cheyne from Leith, who is just appointed Surgeon's Mate to the Artillery[88] and my brother George dined with us.

1 July. Walked to Blackheath and saw the City Cavalry[89] reviewed.

3 July. Walked to Shooters Hill to see the 42nd Regiment[90] pass, marched with them to Greenwich. Was pressed to dine with them but declined.

5 July. Lieutenant Campbell of the 42nd Regiment[91] called upon us.

6 July. Mrs [Ann] Unett is today much worse than she has been for some days, she imagines she caught cold again last night.

7 July. Mrs [Ann] Unett was so indifferent that she declined.

10 July. Mrs [Ann] Unett much the same.

86. Charles Sandby was appointed Chaplain to the Royal Artillery on 1 May 1795.
87. Surgeon General of the Artillery John Rollo. (Kane Medical Staff 22); he died at Woolwich on 24 December 1809.
88. John Cheyne became a Surgeons Mate in the artillery on 26 February 1795 and became an Assistant Surgeon in June 1797, but resigned his commission immediately (Kane Medical Staff 36).
89. The Review of the London Yeomanry Cavalry.
90. The 42nd (Highland) Regiment of Foot.
91. Lieutenant Archibald Campbell 42nd Foot.

> 21 July. Mrs [Ann] Unett went to Shooters Hill to stay a few days to try a change of air, her face is still much swelled. Bread is now 1s a Quartern loaf[92] & wheat from 90s to 100s per quarter,[93] which is astonishingly high.
>
> 24 July. Found Mrs [Ann] Unett much better.
>
> 26 July. Lieutenants English and Phillot[94] supped with me.
>
> 27 July. Supped at the Mess with Lieutenant Heaven.[95]
>
> 3 August. Mrs [Ann] Unett has found very great benefit from the change of air and taking the bark.
>
> 9 August Sunday. Came on duty for Lieutenant Vivion today.
>
> 24 August. Had a letter from John [Unett] with a parcel containing a mortgage for £1,000, which he has got for me upon my estate in Warwickshire, which he sent for me to sign &c, which I did and returned it again to him to finally settle. We had company to tea and supper viz Colonel and Mrs & Miss Douglas with their son Robert D[ouglas][96] who is a cadet; Captain & Mrs Godfrey, Lieutenant & Mrs Adye.
>
> 3 September. For these three or four days I have felt a touch of my old complaint in my stomach; this evening in particular.

The news of the harvest was very good. Richard believed that the country had been extremely charitable during the last bad winter.

> 4 September. Had but an indifferent night owing to the pain in my stomach. This day the quartern loaf was reduced in price from 13d to 1s. The newspapers speak of an abundant harvest in almost every county. God send that it may be so, for the poor have suffered most severely for nearly this twelvemonth past, owing to every necessary of life being more than double the price it was prior to that period. No nation in the world possesses more charity and humanity than the English, the Poor Rates are calculated to produce per annum 3 millions of money, and yet notwithstanding this immense sum, it is supposed that within this twelvemonth there has been 2 millions

92. Worth about £4.50 today, the Quartern loaf weighed 4lb 5oz.
93. A quarter was eight bushels or approximately ¼ ton of grain.
94. 1st Lieutenant William English (Kane 872) and 1st Lieutenant Henry Phillott (Kane 755) Royal Artillery.
95. 1st Lieutenant Joseph Heaven Royal Artillery (Kane 700). He died at Battle in Sussex on 30 October 1802.
96. Gentleman Cadet Robert Douglas Royal Artillery (Kane 958); he died at Claygate near Esher on 10 February 1871.

more collected for the relief of the poor during the last severe winter and the present scarcity, which I hope is now pretty well over.

6 September. Took some physick last night which Dr Rollo sent me, which prevented me going to church.

7 September. Continued on duty for Lieutenant Adye, it being his week, which he is to make up to me when I am in the country.

8 September. Had a letter from brother John inclosing me a draft for £1,000, [payable] seven days after date.

9 September. We dined and spent the day at Colonel Twiss's Lieutenant Governor of the Academy,[97] this is the first house we have ever been in since we have lived in the Warren, except the Cadet officer's, which is nearly a twelvemonth and in all probability we should not have visited here had not Miss Twiss and Mrs [Ann] Unett been old school acquaintances; so much for the hospitality of the field officers of artillery in the Warren!!!

They were off to Birmingham and Warwick again.

14 September. Very busy in packing up as we set off tomorrow for Birmingham.

15 September. Set off at 9 o'clock with Mrs [Ann] Unett on our way to Birmingham; at ½ past 4 o'clock got into the coach, travelled all night and arrived at Warwick about 12 o'clock the next day.

17 September. As soon as breakfast was over, we set off in a chaise to Heath Farm; the repairs are not near finished.

There was nearly a terrible accident.

1 October. We all set off this morning for Stone, where Mrs [Ann] Unett and self are to stay some time at Mrs Unett's. Mr & Mrs Ward and sister Fanny went back to Stafford in the evening, when it rained very hard and the two latter, who were in Mr W[ard]'s carriage were near being killed, for the night was so dark that the post boy drove them into a marle-pit[98] and they fortunately got out when the chaise tumbled over and was much shattered.

4 October Sunday. My brother George arrived to dinner, having obtained a month's absence from Woolwich.

97. Lieutenant Colonel William Twiss, Royal Engineers, was appointed Lieutenant Governor of the Royal Military Academy at Woolwich on 1 January 1795, replacing Colonel Stehelin.

98. Marl is a mixture of clay and carbonate of lime which was used as a fertiliser.

> 6 October. In the evening we saw the bull baited,[99] as it is Stone Wakes.[100]
>
> 11 October Sunday. Rode with Mr [John] Unett to Hill Top and to Groundslow Fields, two places where the Unett's have been seated some centuries; the latter is still in the family, but the former by marriage is in the possession of Mr John Rutter (as well as a large farm at Tittensor) whose mother was a Miss Sarah Unett of Stafford and carried between £3 & £400 out of the family.

The repairs were now complete, but the good life was having a toll on Richard.

> 27 October. Rode to Heath Farm with brother John; the repairs of my house nearly finished.
>
> 30 October. I weighed myself again and found I was 12 stone 6 lbs, so that since 19 September when I weighed before and was only 11 stone 7lbs, I have increased 13 lbs.

Finally they could return to Woolwich.

> 31 October. At 7 o'clock this evening we set off for Greenwich, travelled all night and arrived there 7 o'clock of this (Sunday 1 November) evening.
>
> 2 November. We staid [*sic*] at Mrs Godwin's last night and at 10 o'clock this morning Mrs Godwin brought us in a coach to Shooters Hill, where we stopped for ten minutes and then came home to dinner, after being absent two months tomorrow. Came on duty for the week.
>
> 6 November. Last night was one of the most tempestuous ones ever remembered and this morning a number of houses &c are down.

He received promotion on his birthday and was now awaiting orders to join his new company.

> 11 November. This day is my birthday. Employed all morning in taking my wine to Mr Thomson's, where it is to remain for some time at least, as I am this day in orders as a Captain Lieutenant, my commission being dated 3 October.

---

99. A blood sport entailing dogs being set on a tethered bull. It was finally outlawed in 1835.

100. Wakes week was virtually the only public holiday week in the entire year for the pottery workers of Staffordshire, but it was probably in October in Stone as it was an agricultural area, so after the harvest.

> 18 November. Slept at our [new] house for the first time. Have obtained two or three weeks leave from General Drummond[101] before I go to Plymouth to join my company.

The newspaper reports were not good.

> 22 November. The newspapers mention dreadful accidents at sea with our West India fleet, which is dispersed and obliged to run into different ports; a number of vessels are shipwrecked with the loss of a great many souls; it had sailed but a day or two and consisted of above 200 transports with more than twenty thousand soldiers onboard and a large fleet of men of war.[102]

Richard was a godfather to the third child of Ann and John Fraser. The christening took place at St Nicholas, Plumstead.

> 24 November. Spent the day at Shooters Hill, it being the christening of [John] Fraser's third child, to whom I stood as one of the godfathers. He his [*sic*] called Alexander John.
>
> 25 November. Today we had a Gazette for the taking of the Cape of Good Hope.[103]

---

101. Major General Duncan Drummond Royal Artillery (Kane 162), Commander of the Field Train Department 1793–5, died at Woolwich on 27 June 1805.
102. This was the outbound West India fleet under Rear Admiral Christian, part of which was driven onshore by a gale around Portland Bill with hundreds of lives lost.
103. The Dutch colony at the Cape of Good Hope was forced to surrender on 16 September 1795.

A Canadian Drama

Contained within the papers is a letter from Lieutenant Douglas to his friend Captain John Fraser, regarding the shipwreck of the *Phillis* Transport on Newfoundland, Mr Lisle Passmore, Master, carrying six officers and seven men of the Royal Artillery and an officer of the 5th Foot as a passenger. Besides this letter sent to his friend, there is a journal written soon after this incident held by the Memorial University of St John's. Newfoundland. This contains further details and I have therefore incorporated this additional information within the letter to Fraser, but highlighting this in italics.[1] It is clear that the journal was written in 1796 by 1st Lieutenant John Caddy, clearly utilising a copy of Douglas' letter and expanding from there, as there are many similarities of language used. The journal is a contemporary copy[2] of the original written by Caddy.

Lieutenant Douglas's letter to Captain [John] Fraser, being a narrative of the Shipwreck of a detachment of the Royal Artillery[3]

Great Jervis[4] [*sic*] in the Island of Newfoundland 2 December 1795

Dear Sir,
A small vessel which sails by the first fair wind for England gives me the opportunity of sending you, for the information of General Pattison, the following melancholy account of the detachment of Royal Artillery which embarked for Quebec onboard the ship *Phillis* in August last.[5]

1. The Journal is held by the Memorial University in St John's, Newfoundland, reference MF 338.
2. The copy was made by Sophia Brownrigg (née Bissett) in October 1811, wife of Lieutenant General Robert Brownrigg and there are some errors in the spelling of names in this copy.
3. Staffordshire Archives D3610/8/1-16.
4. Great Jervais on Newfoundland.
5. The *Phyllis* or *Phillis* transport sailed from Gravesend and then Cowes on the Isle of Wight in August 1795, bound for Quebec but ran aground and broke up on 12 October 1795.

Tuesday 7 October. Wind West-South-West, at one pm unsteady and squally, handed top-gallant sails and single reefed the topsails. At 2 pm hard squalls . . . at 11 pm blowing a hard gale with a very heavy sea . . . lay to under a close-reefed main topsail.

Wednesday 8 October. Blowing a very heavy gale of wind and the ship labouring much when she fell off into the trough of the sea. At 4 am, in rolling to windward we shipped a sea, which broke over the waist and weather bow with great violence and cleared the deck fore and aft. We found the boats nearly half over the lee-side, but still held by two of the lashings, got tackles hooked and hove them onboard with great difficulty. They were considerably injured . . . sounded the well and finding 2 feet water in the hold, rigged the pump. Having secured the boats for the present and finding the water gain on us, we rigged the other pump and set all hands to work at regular turns. The ship having lain a considerable time previous to our voyage in ballast, her upper works were very leaky and in rough weather we had always found it necessary to pump every two hours, this regular leak was now increased by the seas which the vessel shipped in rolling, getting down between the timber, where the plank-sheer was torn open. At 6 am made sail and wore ship to repair the injured gunwhale on which (now become the weather side) a piece of tarred canvas was nailed, the water in the hold was soon afterwards got under. At 1 pm the wind began to moderate, at 2 South-South-East with rain, set double reefed topsails, the people were employed in securing the boats, which from the chocks having been carried overboard, we were obliged to lash with their bottoms upwards, to the deck. We fixed the cooking place (which had likewise been upset) on the quarter deck and repaired to the best of our power the other damage we had sustained. Amongst our other losses we found that a pig which had been killed the night before the gale, and which was hanging on the gallows near the mizzen-mast had been washed away and [as] this was the last of our fresh provisions, we were now reduced to the ship's stores. At about 3 pm wind East, light breezes with rain, made more sail, at 4 spoke a Banker from whom we learnt the bearings and distance of Cape Race and obtained a cask of water.

Saturday 10 October. At 4 pm looking out for the Island of St Peter's [Saint-Pierre] which we made at 7 am, North by West, distant 4 leagues, calm, clear weather. At ½ past 4 pm, we had a fine breeze from South-East which soon began to increase.

On Sunday the 11th of October, which made exactly the ninth week of our voyage, we had only got as far as the island of St Peters [Saint-Pierre], about 40 leagues to the Eastward of the southern entrance of the Gulph [*sic*] of St Lawrence, during which 10 weeks, we suffered every hardship which could arise from bad weather and a scarcity of fresh provisions; it is necessary to mention that on the

Thursday which preceded, in a very severe gale of wind, a heavy sea broke both our boats from their lashings upon deck, a circumstance which greatly contributed to our future misfortunes, as in securing them again we were obliged to lash them with their bottoms upwards, the chocks having been lost.

On the night of Sunday the 11th, a gale of wind sprung up from the Eastward, which continued till 1 o'clock in the afternoon of Monday the 12th, *as we were running down a lee shore, [I] should have pointed out to the captain the necessity of hawling [sic] up a point or two, to the South-West, the propriety of which measure was suggested by the Mate without effect. The Captain persevered in shaping a direct course to Cape Reay[Ray], urging that if the wind continued in the same direction and strength, we should make the entrance of the Gulph [Sic] of St Lawrence before dark and having once seen the Cape and the Island of St Pauls, be enabled to run all night without risk* when in an instant it fell quite calm; between 6 & 7 in the evening, the Chief Mate of the ship came into the cabin and called out the captain in a very mysterious manner *convincing us that all was not well. We observed him take down the chart from the Mate's berth at the cabin door, which having examined for some time, he said something to the Mate in a low voice, who immediately replied loud enough to be heard by us 'But it is so Sir, and if you will go upon deck you'll hear them yourself'* and soon after, some of us going upon deck, heard very plainly the noise of breakers . . . that noise increasing every instant, we were soon convinced we had got into a strong current which set us towards the shore and that we were inevitably lost unless a breeze sprang up from that quarter. *Lieutenant Douglas pressed the captain in the strongest manner, the captain however obstinately depended on his own reckoning and appeared confident of our safety and that the noise we heard was not that of the surf, but merely the sea to leeward. The noise continuing however to increase, the threatening cause could no longer be doubted. The captain at last alarmed gave orders for* our cables being unbent, all hands were turned up to bend them, which being done, we *sounded* let go our best bower anchor[6] in about 26 fathoms of water, the land beginning to appear on all sides of us. We soon

6. The underlined section is not in the journal. There it states after sounding, *the ship drifted fast in the direction whence the noise proceeded, and the sparkling foam of the breakers began to appear through the darkness of the night still concealed the land. Finding the bottom hard and rocky we were unwilling to let go the anchor, at least until we could better ascertain our situation and in hopes that we may drift to a better anchorage. In this interval of inaction, we ate some cold meat, and drank a glass or two of wine, without which refreshments we must have sunk under the distresses and hardships of the two following nights. At about 10 pm we saw the land close to leeward and immediately let go the best bower anchor in 20 fathoms.*

perceived our anchor did not hold, and as the last resource, set to work to get out the boats, which on account of their being turned upside down, was a very difficult piece of work; *having got the long boat ready for hoisting out, we put into her the carpenter's tool chest and some provisions, all our firearms, powder and shot, a quadrant, and compass and set to work to get her over the side, the weight of the boat and the motion of the ship labouring in a heavy swell* this however we might easily have accomplished, had the ship's company behaved like men, but as soon as they knew their danger, *despite a breeze appearing driving us off the coast, we sought to set the top sails, the English seamen were employed trimming the sails, but the foreigners* they left the sails and stood like cowards *praying and crossing themselves on the quarterdeck*, waiting the fate they had not courage enough to endeavour to avoid. *The Mate made an appeal to them in such extraordinary terms 'Damn your Eyes you [Bastards?] do you think God Almighty is to come from heaven and take our ship by the top mast head and pop her into deep water? Go to work ye [dogs?] and perhaps God Almighty may help you.' One of the seamen, a Canadian now went aloft and loosed the main top gallant sail and Lieutenant Douglas with one of the English seamen let the reefs out of the mizen-top sail. The Captain ordered the cable to be cut, which was done without observing a splice in it between the windlass and the hause-hole [sic] which as the ship was now ahead of the anchor, jammed it and threw her round, head to wind with all aback, we now attempted to hold fast the cable, but loosened by the next plunge the ship made, the splice passed through and left us almost without hope. Having no other cable bent, we paid the ship's head round once more off the land. We saw the breakers a little to the leeward of our course, and hauled up to weather them, but as the wind was not steady we had not much prospect of effecting it and therefore made another effort to get the longboat out, we soon got her hoisted off the deck, but all our strength was not sufficient to stand against her, as she vibrated in the tackles; when the ship rolled in the opposite direction. In our struggle to effect this, a sea struck the boat, dashed her to pieces and carried overboard every article we had placed in her. It was most miraculous that many of us did not share the same fate, some were bruised by the pieces of the boat and others were thrown against the rigging and side rails with great violence, by which they caught hold. When we were nearly abreast of the breakers, the breeze suddenly failed, our fate now seemed certain and a mournful silence was preserved as we marked the rapidity which each succeeding wave drove us towards the rock; when close to it the sea broke over us.* In short, at about ½ past 11 that night, we struck with astonishing violence on a rock about a quarter of a mile from the mainland. That horrible scene baffles all description, nor I'm sure can even the most lively imagination conceive half its horrors; after shaking very violently two or three times, the ship drifted again towards the shore *about a quarter of a mile away, but the water rushing in she soon became water-logged*, where she settled upon a rock, just as she was sinking.

In this situation we turned our thoughts once more towards the boats but could get nobody to work at them except the Captain, 2 Mates, Carpenter, Caddy[7] & myself. With great difficulty we got the small *jolly-boat* over the side, when Caddy, Forbes[8] and myself *with one or two of the men* got into her to prevent her from staving against the ship's side, but in spite of all our efforts she was soon nearly half full of water, so that we were obliged to leave her again. In getting back to the ship, I missed my hold and fell down between the ship and the boat. I swam a few strokes to the boat and was taken in by Forbes, who with Caddy and myself soon after got safe onboard again. The boat we left was soon in pieces, and the longboat which was still hanging in the sails was also soon demolished [see previous for a different timing for this]. *It was now nearly high water and every sea striking the ship on the starboard quarter rolled over her whole length and the greatest exertions were required to afford aid to the women and children and at the same time to afford to our own safety. The ship struck with great violence as the sea passed over and she strained very much abaft from having a quantity of shot and shells in the after hold (on the run as it is called) and which in the hollow of each wave, not being water-borne threatened to destroy the wreck. So it happened, for after the strain of a heavy sea, the stern frame and the stern port gave way and a great number of casks of pork and butter floated out from the hold.* Being now in momentary expectation of the ship's parting; those who could swim stript [*sic*] themselves, to be in readiness to make that last struggle for their lives. *We were now standing in the fore rigging and on the bowsprit, rendering all the aid we could to the poor women and children, who senseless from fear and benumbed by the cold, were so incapable of any exertion, that though we held them from being washed overboard, they all perished on the deck, excepting the wife of Lieutenant Douglas' servant and when death had terminated their sufferings their bodies were let go.*

Thus, we stood during the remainder of that long, long night, wet through with the continual dashings of the breakers, eagerly wishing for day, in hopes that as soon as it dawned, the inhabitants would see us and come to our assistance. At length it came, but only served to augment our distress by presenting to our view, a rough uncultivated,

7. 1st Lieutenant John Thomas Caddy Royal Artillery (Kane 815); he died in 1827.
8. 1st Lieutenant Thomas John Forbes Royal Artillery (Kane 869); he died near Colchester in 1868.

mountainous country, without the least vestige of human beings. We discovered that the rock on which the ship was now settled, was about 15 yards *[35 yards]* from a point of the mainland, which we have since heard is named Little Bay Head, about 3 leagues to the Eastward of Cape Bay in this island, which point of land terminated towards us in an almost perpendicular rock, and we feared the heavy sea occasioned by the preceding day's wind would render our landing in any manner impossible, by the violence with which it broke against the rocks. *The ship being now nearly on her beam end and quite a wreck, we cut all the masts away, and in doing this kept the fore topsail standing, that the mast might fall towards the land; but unfortunately the topmast head broke off with the shock and carried away the jibboom as it fell. The hope which had supported us through the night having now vanished and no other prospect of safety remaining than the chance of drifting to the shore on the pieces of the wreck, the fortitude of several of our fellow sufferers began to fail.* This we were soon convinced of by the dismal fate of poor Barclay[9] and one of the seamen *who went first*, who although they were very expert swimmers, were unable to struggle long with the breakers, they left the ship to try to swim ashore about 9 o'clock. *A Newfoundland dog belonging to Lieutenant Douglas was pushed overboard by Lieutenant Barclay; the dog reached the shore with great difficulty and clambering up the rocks, her success determined Barclay to follow.* The seaman (*Heasy*[10] by name) had just reached the shore, when a breaker with great violence dashed him against the rocks and we saw him no more. Poor Barclay (from what cause I know not) had only swam a few yards when he stopt [*sic*] and after struggling a few moments in the agonies of death and waving his hands to us upon deck, he sunk for ever. The composure with which he bade us all farewell before he committed himself to the waves, was affecting and admirable. In his efforts to gain the shore, he was stimulated as much from an idea of saving our lives as his own, but what renders his behaviour still more wonderful is that he did not leave the ship till he had seen the seaman dashed against the rocks. Poor Barnes[11] soon followed him, for as he was standing on the forechains, a wave swept him from thence into the deep and as he could not swim, his sufferings were soon at an end, *this similarly happened to one of the men.*

9. 1st Lieutenant Francis Barclay Royal Artillery (Kane 843); drowned.
10. The journal says Casey but Douglas says Heasy. The journal is a copy of the original made by Sophia Brownrigg (née Bissett), wife of Lieutenant General Robert Brownrigg, in October 1811 and there are some other errors in spelling names in the transcription, such as Imscott instead of Truscott; the latter in Douglas' letter being proven to be correct in the records.
11. 2nd Lieutenant John Barnes Royal Artillery (Kane 889); drowned.

To relate separately the many awful scenes of death, which we now beheld, would augment my distress in recalling so exactly to my memory that fatal day, suffice it to say that during that day, Mrs D'Estemauville was swept by the waves from the arms of her husband Chevalier D'Estemauville,[12] a French emigrant passenger in the ship *whose brother was established at Quebec*, John Grant, Lieutenant Barclay's servant was washed overboard and drowned and the soldier's wife, who with her two children embarked with us, shared the same fate, one of the boys of the ship was also drowned. *Two gunners, three seamen, two women and two children had by now perished as well as the officers mentioned.*

Towards evening, one of the seamen unfortunately got a cask of wine, with which many of them got intoxicated, a very common thing among sailors in like cases; it proved fatal to the Cook of the ship and Thomas Coutts, Lieutenant Caddy's servant. I am happy in being able to say the rest of our men were perfectly sober. We remained the whole of this day, being Tuesday the 13th and that night, on the wreck without anything to eat, except a piece of pork and a cheese which we found floating on the deck.

On the morning of Wednesday the 14th, the weather was so moderate and the sea so smooth, that it appeared practicable to make a raft capable of taking two or three men on shore *by which means we might get a rope from the wreck to the rock [shore]*, who as soon as they landed, might come to our assistance. We accordingly set to work and made one *from the side and quarter rails and planks from the deck which was now breaking up in the waist,* on which two seamen *(A Canadian and a Genoese) each furnished with a stave of a cask as a paddle, the raft drifted to leeward past the headland, into smooth water in the opening of the bay, where using their paddles it went ahead and we then lost sight of it behind the point [presumably]* got in safety to shore; but after waiting two hours, finding they neglected us *we concluded that the people had perished in the surf,* we made another larger one *by 2 pm* with which *eight of the people got upon it, overloaded with the weight it overset, but disengaging itself of the greater number, it righted with four men and like the former drifted towards the mouth of the bay, all the people who had been thrown off the raft again reached the wreck; those remaining on it were* the Second Mate, Carpenter & two seamen *their course was that of the former and in the same manner were soon hidden from our view; [but they]* landed in safety and who immediately *in about half an hour [we] were relieved from our suspense by seeing them advancing upon a cliff opposite to the wreck [&]* came to assist us in

12. Chevallier Jean-Baptiste-Philippe d'Estemauville who was married to Charlotte Dailleboust of Louisbourg, Canada.

endeavouring to get on shore. *We had in the meanwhile prepared a small rope by throwing which to those on the cliff, we were to send a larger one and thereby establish a communication. The First Mate made several attempts to throw it from the bowsprit end to the rocks where the people stood, but without success; on which the Second Mate with one end of a web of linen (which had been washed on shore from the wreck) fastened [it] round his waist, and [with] the other [end] held by those on the cliff, leapt into the water at the moment the line was thrown and caught the end of it in his hand [&]* by their means we got a rope from the end of the bowsprit to the shore, on which one by one we all landed about 4 o'clock that afternoon. *We were shocked to hear that the two [original] fellows into whose hands we had in a great measure committed our fate, [had] formed the diabolical determination to leave us to our fate; they were found by the second party, nearly intoxicated with wine from a cask which had drifted from the wreck and dressed out in Lieutenant Barnes' clothes whose trunk had also floated onshore, in this state we joined them, they met us with the most hardened indifference and freely expressing in the most insolent terms their opinion that all distinctions were then levelled.* To our infinite joy we found great quantities of cloaths [*sic*] of all kinds had come on shore from the wreck, part of the ship's cargo, from which we each of us took a large cloak and *good water, also some pieces of pork floating amongst the rocks, of which having ate a morsel (raw for we could not get a fire)* there took up our lodgings for the night in a small thicket of a spruce tree, *lying down on the wet ground, overcome by our three day's fatigue [we were] soon lost in sleep.* Soon after dark it rained very fast *till about 2 am, and a sudden change of wind bringing a sharp frost,* which soon pierced the slender shelter they afforded us, and made us completely uncomfortable *we were awakened half frozen.*

About 12 o'clock my servant's wife *(the only surviving woman)* – (who had been very ill ever since we landed) went delirious and raved during the whole of the night in the most shocking manner, which prevented our enjoying that rest, of which we now stood so much in need.

Towards the morning, Thursday the 15th, it cleared up and soon after day, the sun shone with great power, certainly the greatest blessing the Almighty could have sent us; as by its influence we were enabled to dry our tinder (which in spite of all our endeavours had got wet in bringing on shore) and kindle a fire, but we did not get it in time enough to be of service to those who most wanted it, for my servant's wife died about 10 o'clock that morning, her death was certainly occasioned by the cold. Not having implements of any kind wherewith to dig a grave, we *tied some stones in the cloth that contained the body and* committed her body to the deep.

This morning we found Lieutenant Truscott[13] and Ensign Bennett of the 5th Regiment[14] (passenger) who were taken ill the preceding night, so very ill that we had no hopes of their recovery.

The ship having been laden chiefly with pork and butter for the King's stores in Quebec, great quantities of each of these articles were driven on shore *considerable quantities of pork washed from the wreck were by this time found floating amongst the rocks and seen floating near the shore, whence they were brought to land by the dog, who was of the greatest service ever after*; as also 3 casks of wine, which I know not whether to call a fortunate circumstance or not, as some of our men were often intoxicated, which generally ended with argument. Having pressed a few pieces of pork, we all sat down and made a hearty meal, as you may suppose after having passed three nights and somewhat more than two days [without]. After dinner we all met to consult upon the most eligible plan we could adopt for our future safety, when in consideration of our not having tools of any kind to build a house wherewith to shelter ourselves from the inclemency of the weather in so rigorous a climate, nor provisions to last us long, it was unanimously determined that after remaining where we were a few days to see if Messieurs Truscott and Bennett recovered so far as to be able to accompany us, we should each of us furnish ourselves with as much provisions as we could conveniently travel with and set out and endeavour to find an inhabited place.

On *Friday the 16th the weather clearing up after sunrise, we set about drying our tinder which the Mate had fortunately had the foresight to put in his pocket before leaving the wreck, which being accomplished after many ineffectual attempts, a fire was kindled, and having dried our clothes and regaled ourselves with a slice of pork broiled on a kind of gridiron made of an iron hoop, we lifted up our hearts with feelings of the warmest gratitude to the great disposer of all things. The two greatest invalids appeared to suffer much from the cold; to cover them from it and the rain that fell in the afternoon, we brought from the beach two empty wine pipes (the ends of which had been stove in) and applied them to the purpose of cover, putting one in each and placing them close to the fire. They were still in in a state of utter insensibility and so unconscious of pain, that on the return of some of the people to the fire they were found with their feet literally in the flame, having slipped out of their casks towards the fire; to this circumstance their future preservation may be perhaps in some measure owing, as the effect of the fire certainly checked*

13. 1st Lieutenant Robert Truscott Royal Artillery (Kane 836) died at Breda on 16 February 1814.
14. Ensign Robert Bennett of the 5th Foot.

the progress of the mortification. The evening of Friday the 16th we found Messieurs Truscott and Bennet instead of recovering, had got so much worse, that far from there being any possibility of their accompanying us in our intended journey; there was scarcely any [hope] of their living many days and as our staying in that place would be only sacrificing ourselves without being of the smallest service to them, the frost having already seized on both their feet, we determined (distressing as it was thus to be obliged to leave two of our companions behind in such a situation) to set off the next morning in search of inhabitants or die in the attempt.

Accordingly, we assembled early on the morning of Saturday the 17th, each of us with a cloak & provisions and began our march about sunrise this morning. Messieurs Truscott and Bennett were in a state of insensibility and in this state, in anguish of mind indescribable, we left them with a good fire and provisions within their reach, fervently recommending them to the care of an Almighty power.

In solemn silence we continued our day's journey *to the Eastward to attempt to reach the coast some 20 miles away where from the hill we were on, we could see a deep bay* over almost inaccessible mountains and through almost impenetrable woods, till about two o'clock *night closed in*, when we took up our quarters for the night in a wood on the rise of a hill, well covered with wood and plenty of water near us. After making a fire we eat [*sic*] a small piece of pork (which only served to sharpen our appetite) and then endeavoured to get some rest; and for a few hours to smother our distress in sleep. *Before night closed, it was our constant practise to send all hands to gather a supply of wood for the night and to keep up a good fire, a kind of guard was mounted, who took it [in] turns every hour to add fuel, the time being marked by a watch which was not so far injured (though all the rest were) by the salt water. This night on relief of one of the foreign seamen, the watch could not be found, he pretended to have dropped it in putting wood on the fire; the fact was evident that it was stolen, but it was not proved; and willing in our unhappy situation to avoid dispute, for the present the matter was waved.*

On Sunday the 18th we proceeded on our journey, but soon found it impossible to penetrate any further into the country, we found ourselves in a valley covered with impenetrable woods, skirted by inaccessible mountains & frequently interspersed with impassible rivers, from which it was impossible to get out except by the way which we came. This soon convinced us of the impossibility of pursuing our journey and determined us to return to the unfortunate spot of our shipwreck, there to build some kind of a hut, to secure all the provisions we could and there await our fate. This plan being universally agreed to, we measured back our steps to the place where we had stopt [*sic*] at the night before and where we also remained. Then three of our party went on to the place where Messieurs Truscott and Bennett were, to save their lives if they still existed; *they had crawled out of their casks from the fire and endeavoured to fly from the pursuit of their friends in a state of delirium, but in the course of the day they became quiet,* and on Monday the 19th we returned also and immediately set to work in securing our provisions. We were inexpressibly happy to find Truscott and Bennett alive, although their feet were severely frostbit.

On Tuesday 20 October a party of four men were sent out to pick up what provisions might be seen floating about, whilst the rest were employed in planning and beginning a hut *with the planks and other means which the wreck furnished and keeping a signal flying in the day time rest[ing] our hopes of relief on its being observed by vessels passing Cape Reay [Ray], which forms with the Island of Cape Breton, the southern entrance of the gulph [sic] of St Lawrence. We knew the Quebec fleet homeward bound had not yet passed and as with a northerly wind they would keep near to the Newfoundland shore, we watched in anxious suspense whenever the wind was in that direction.* We chose a situation for it [the hut] in a small thicket of spruce where we cleared a space sufficient for our purpose, leaving such trees *[stumps]* as were in a right line *for the corner posts of the building* and would serve for the direction of its sides and ends. *The trees we removed were actually dug out by the roots and the branches of the other four, we cut off with great difficulty with a broken sword, which had been found in Lieutenant Barnes' trunk by the two fellows who rifled it before we landed.* After which we got four strong planks from the wreck (the ship went to pieces the day after we landed) which we lashed to the trees we had left, at about 3½ feet from the ground, securing them well where the trees were not strong enough with stakes driven well into the ground. This done, we built a wall of [dry] stone on that end which was most exposed to the sea *in which a opening for the door was left*, on the outside of which we put a thick coat of sods, which to supply the want of spades, we dug with the staves of a cask, *hardened in the fire* & sharpened at one end *and carried home on a sort of handbarrow.* For the other end and sides leant short planks from the ground against the top of the beams which were first placed on the outside of which all around we built a thick wall of sods. The formation of its top *[roof]* was exactly after the form of an English cottage, although a very humble imitation. After the rafts were placed *which rested on the ground to support such a weight*, we laid planks over them, above which we put a covering of sods; leaving a small hole in the center [*sic*] of the top for the smoke. According to this plan we all worked very hard till it was nearly finished . . . *and the form of a journal has been discontinued.*

I forgot to mention that on our return from our journey, our first employment was to erect a flagstaff on the highest ground *on the headland we afterwards learnt was called Little Bay Head about 3 leagues to the eastward of Cape Reay [Ray]* we could find, upon which we hoisted a black and white flag, *the only stuffs we had to make a flag of, were two pieces of white linen and one of black bombazine;*[15] *a housewife*[16] *well filled with needles and thread was found in Lieutenant Barnes' trunk and this furnished the means of making a flag. The black was placed horizontally between the two white pieces and the main yard of the vessel erected on the top of the hill* in hopes it might be perceived by some small boat going along shore.

The conduct of the foreign seamen (six in number) and who kept continually together, was now such as to increase the distrust and suspicion which it will be allowed we had already much cause to feel towards two of their party, from the first day of landing, they would not work at the hut though they were glad to take shelter under its roof, and as they passed the whole day by themselves and did not appear even at meals, there could be no doubt of their having broken our law against individual appropriation and we had good reason to believe had besides secreted all they found. It was not only on these occasions that they acted thus, but on every opportunity purloined whatever could be of any use; the only vessel we had to drink out of was a tin pot we had found on the beach and which was always left by the side of the spring where we got water; one of these fellows had just drank when Lieutenant Douglas went to the spring and found the cup missing. It was looked for in vain and on returning to the hut (it was night and all the party was present) he did not hesitate to accuse the person, to whom suspicion attached the theft. It was denied and much violent[ly] and very serious discord threatened in the contention it brought on, which however ended for the time in the cup being given up. Our people were with difficulty restrained from coming to blows and their violence intimidated the rascal to surrender his prize and so far the object was gained; but with such wretches as these, it hushed the present only to kindle greater animosities later. They were all armed with knives and did not conceal the revenge they meant to take; and one of them openly threatened Lieutenant Douglas' life. In short, from this day the most violent contentions continually arose and to those who did feel, this circumstance added largely to their other troubles. Our small parties continued to range the coast; a considerable quantity of pork was recovered from the sea by means of the dog, and after every gale of wind, some dead fish of a glutinous substance were found dead amongst the rocks which provided a good meal; they were called squids by the Newfoundland men to whom we

15. A twilled dress fabric used regularly to produce mourning dresses.
16. A sewing kit.

afterwards described them. Besides the wreck of our ship, the coast was strewed in several places with that of some former misfortunes; we found laying on the beach, two topmasts, a great quantity of planks, timber and staves, and the stern frame of a vessel all bleached by the water and in one of our excursions to a neighbouring swamp to gather cranberries, we found the skeleton of the arm and shoulder of a man which must have been dragged there by the wolves; and this was the only vestige we ever saw of the people who had belonged to the unfortunate vessel and who had met the fate it was probable awaited us. A day or two after our return to the coast, one of our people picked up on the beach a large bottle covered with basket work, containing bark, a great quantity of which most likely had been onboard our vessel either as government stores or private trade to a country where this medicine is so necessary, however it was this most providential supply of an antidote to check the mortification, which had yet disappeared on the feet of our companions. About this time the oven of the ship's cooking place was found on a part of the wreck and although it was cracked we repaired it sufficiently to use it as a boiler, but it was large and so difficult to heat that it was a very inconvenient utensil. In the evenings we employed ourselves if fashioning to a convenient shape, the cloth we had found and in making substitutes for shoes etc. In the crowded manner in which we lived and most of the party without even a second shirt, there were reasons why it was necessary to keep the hair of the head as short as possible, a knife was the implement used and the want of hair supplied by a cap of cloth. It is mentioned in a former part that several pieces of a coarse kind of cloth were found, about one yard and a half of this, formed the principal garment, which was made by cutting a hole in the middle for the head, and binding the part which hung down round the body, the arm being partly covered though not confined by the sides of the piece hanging loose over the shoulders. A large box of ribbons addressed to a Miss Brandon, a milliner in Quebec, was driven onshore and amply furnished the means of lacing or tying our inconvenient covering, though it added very much to our grotesque appearance, for the lower part of our dress, many had a kind of Indian legging, made of cloth laced (it could not be called sewed) with ribbon, or rope yarn and a sort of sandal cut to the shape of the foot out of the most curved part of the stave of a cask, was our substitute for shoes; besides these expedients, most of the people had preserved several articles of their former dress, which added to the non-descript costume in which we were now equipped, Our two invalids began sensibly to recover a very short time after the bark was administered to them; it was applied externally as well as internally in the wine driven on shore, which in this case only proved a blessing and alone prevented our destroying it, as from the intemperate use of it many little differences were inflamed to a degree that often threatened bloodshed. Besides our two brother officers, many of the people were severely injured by the hardships we had undergone, the Captain and the Carpenter were scarcely able to walk from the effect of the wet and cold, the 1st Mate was not much better and one of our soldier, one seaman and Mr d'Estemauville added to the list of invalids. We continued in this state daily labouring at the completion of our hut, according to the plan described until it was so far finished as to enable us to spare some people to examine the further side of the bay (from which we were separated by a river not fordable anywhere near us) on which we hoped to find some provisions and other articles driven from the wreck and which we had postponed till now to complete our shelter against the fast approaching winter. When the measure was now proposed our opposite party immediately offered to go, but having stronger grounds than ever to believe they were taking daily means to preserve themselves at our expense, by secreting all they found. We did not choose to trust to their report, and as they were not willing to be entirely left out, there was no other way of accommodating the difficulty than by sending two of each party; which was accordingly formed of Lieutenants Douglas and Caddy together with the two fellows who had so inhumanely neglected us on the landing.

At daylight on the 25th we four left the hut[17] *and having crossed the river some miles above, proceeded to the part of the coast where from the direction of the wind it was expected a considerable part of the wreck had drifted. It turned out according to that expectation and on our arrival we found the beach covered, in some parts with the fragments of the vessel, the quarterdeck was found almost entire and in the companion lockers two bags of nails, a gimblet*[18] *and a chisel, these were articles of the greatest use and value to us, as we had in contemplation, if we could find any means to accomplish it, to make a small boat in which two people might be sent along the coast in calm weather, as the best chance of finding inhabitants. A little beyond this spot, we discovered a cask, floating in a small creek at the bottom of the bay, into which it had been driven uninjured. As soon as it was rolled out, the gimblet was applied and its contents were found to be an inferior sort of claret; here it was instantly determined to pass the night, but as there remained two or three hours of daylight, the party proceeded to examine the other parts of the bay. Not far from the little creek the shore became more abrupt, here a tierce of pork*[19] *was found sticking in a cleft of the rock, where no doubt it had been driven by the surf on the night of our wreck, till now we had only found the pork in pieces, most of which were damaged by beating about amongst the*

17. This proves that the author of the report was Lieutenant Caddy.
18. A boring tool.
19. A barrel of 260lbs (127kg) of pork.

rocks and the pickle being washed out, a great part of it would not keep. The supply of a whole tierce therefore with the pickle in it, was in a manner a reprieve to our fate and our success on this occasion amply recompensed us for a most anxious separation from our friends, whom we longed to gladden with these tidings. Not distant from the place where this great prize was found, in a sudden turn of the coast, lay a considerable quantity of loose pork and half covered by it was found one of the dead bodies, which the sea had given up in a most mangled state. The pork was thrown up above the high water mark and secured; fatigued with the day's work the party returned towards the place they had fixed on for their night's rest, on the way a deal box was discovered on the beach, which on examination was found to enclose a tin case well soldered - it was cut open and the contents though valuable in the great world, were of all others most useless to us; viz a complete set of silver lace for officer's dress of the 2nd Battalion of the 60th Regiment. For a moment the whole was thrown aside but it occurring to Lieutenant Douglas that the tin case would when divided, make two excellent boilers, it was emptied of its contents and a piece of pork taken from the tierce was boiled in it that night. It was but reasonable that on this occasion the party should fare well and in other company than that of the very fellows who had so deliberately and so unfeelingly, left at hazard all our lives, this would have been comparatively a happy time, but as it was we cannot be supposed to have been much at our ease. As soon as day dawned, we set off on our return to the hut, carrying with us samples of the pork and wine as a treat to our friends and an evidence of success; it was impossible to transport all that had been found to the hut, the pork with the pickle in it we determined to keep to the last and to say the truth, we did not wish to have the wine amongst us. From these considerations the resolution was soon formed in a meeting, which was not attended by all the adverse party, to leave the provisions found on the other side untouched for the present, as a store against future wants and the wine to be used only for the sick, till the cold weather should set in. We now proceeded with the finishing and improving our hut, and began to turn our minds to the practicability of snareing [sic] deer, the idea of building a small boat was again brought forward by the discovery of the nails, for want of which the first suggestion of that scheme had been abandoned. From the day the party returned to the hut, there appeared to be some plane [sic] concerting by the foreign seamen, which they carefully concealed from us; but we were at a loss to guess that they had an eye to the provisions on the other side of the bay and we likewise observed they began to intrigue with one or two of our people; the action and reaction of feelings consequent in such a state of society and under such circumstances, did not serve to stifle former resentment and we were continually irritated by the discovery of some fresh injury. One night, things went so far that it appeared advisable to seize the present moment to inflict some exemplary punishment; when suddenly the 2nd Mate joined himself to the adverse part. We knew not how far treason might have spread and therefore thought it prudent to curb our desire to bring matters to a crisis. The utmost exertion of authority, the suggestions of caution or appeals to our melancholy situation, with difficulty hushed the tempestuous torrent of human passions, exhibiting a scene in which our savage neighbours might have blushed for civilised man. The second day after this most distressing affair, the party strengthened by the accession of the 2nd Mate, began to prepare for a journey about an hour before daylight, and one of our soldiers appearing to act in obedience to the signal to get up; Lieutenant Douglas asked him where he was going. He replyed [sic] with great simplicity, that he was going with the seamen; upon being asked whose leave he had, he said he did not think of asking leave, that he was going where they assured him they would be better off. The object of the expedition was now sufficiently evident, yet it was not thought prudent to accuse them of such an intention, or to prevent their departure, but as we could not restrain their villainy we quietly formed our resolutions how to act if they should be hardened enough to commit the crime they appeared to have in contemplation. The soldier was not suffered to accompany them, and they left the hut soon after daylight. In the evening a smoke was seen to ascend from the spot where the wine &c was found on the other side of the bay, and this announced the seizure of that store on which our support was to depend at no distant period. It is not possible to express the mixture of feelings which were excited by the detestable act, the aggravation to our misfortunes which was inflicted by the unnatural state of discord in which we lived. On Friday the 30th it was determined to execute our purpose on the following Sunday [1st] and our plan of proceeding was accordingly laid, in which the great object was to seize at once the most guilty characters; but God's merciful goodness which had been so remarkably manifested towards us, throughout our sufferings now interposed the only event which could quiet such a scene and in powerfully calling forth our gratitude to him.

To this [the flag] we owe our present existence, for on Saturday 31st October, at about 3 o'clock in the afternoon, *when a sudden noise of shouting and hallowing was heard. We who were up the country [gathering cranberries] could not see the flagstaff, nor the sea on account of an intervening rising ground and we therefore ran round the declivity, where we perceived our people running up the hill waving their caps, whilst others were hoisting and lowering the flag and soon a small schooner under sail with a free breeze standing along the shore to the westward. We flew to the hill, where, by the time the whole of our fellow sufferers had assembled and in using every means to attract attention, we suffered some minutes of a more painful stretch of feelings. At length the vessel tacked and stood directly towards us and hove to and the two men forming her crew appeared to be attentively observing us. The wreck strewed on the beach must have explained our situation and when they were convinced that we had not preserved our boats, they came into the bay with confidence and let go their anchor within a few hundred yards of the shore. The little boat was now put out and two men rowed her very slowly towards the shore, where we were all assembled, presenting a most motley group to their astonished view, at length we were asked 'Who are ye[?]'* We were perceived by a small schooner steering along, the Master of which saw our flag and knowing that place to be uninhabited, immediately concluded it was a signal of distress from some people that were cast away. He instantly made towards us, *Lieutenant Douglas replied and in a few words explained our situation; they repeatedly asked if we were Englishmen and seemed to distrust the assurance that we were so and they afterwards confessed, they suspected we were foreigners and that if so, we might seize their vessel to take us to a distant port, they rowed cautiously and by the minute questions they put when close to the beach where they rested on their oars. However, they imperceptibly came so near the shore that Lieutenant Douglas to put an end to suspense by leaping into her, when throwing the painter towards his companions and in a moment the boat was hauled ashore. The alarm this occasioned was soon quieted and after showing them our huts, Lieutenants Douglas, Caddy and Forbes went onboard the schooner where they received for themselves and forwarded to their friends, a biscuit each, and when they remained for the night it was now determined on Monday morning we should leave this scene and be conveyed to a fishing settlement in Fortune Bay about 50 leagues to the Eastward, where we should find a merchant's store and be provided with the means of passing the winter, as it was too late in the season to get to St John's or any of the more distant establishments. We could not leave them [the others] to perish, nor admit them to their society, it was merely intimated to them that they would be received onboard, they came and were treated with humanity, though with the greatest indifference by all the party. On Sunday afternoon we were busily employed in boiling pork for the voyage as the cooking place of the vessel was too small for our appetites; by some mismanagement the slush or grease boiled over, the flame it occasioned in an instant set fire to the roof of the hut [which had] dried with the heat of the fire and in ten minutes our house was laid in ashes. The next morning, Monday 5 November, we left Little Head Bay at daylight and in the evening put into a small creek for the night; in this way not daring to keep the sea at night and in the evening put into a small creek for the night. In this way only proceeding by day in settled weather, we passed 10 days to Fortune Bay where we were to be established for the winter* and on Wednesday the 12th of November, landed us safely at this place, where we are comfortably lodged in the house of Mr Roope, son of Harris Roope Esquire, merchant in Dartmouth,[20] having lost 1st Lieutenant Barclay, 2nd Lieutenant Barnes, 2 gunners, Thomas Coutts and John Grant. When I arrived here, I found it impossible to get to Placentia or St Johns (the season being so far advanced) and accordingly have taken up my winter quarters with the remains of the detachment in this place and shall take the first opportunity in the spring of a vessel to Quebec.

The day after we arrived here, Messieurs Truscott and Bennett went to a place about 7 leagues from hence[21] to be under the cure of a female surgeon *native docteress*, the only medical assistance they could get here, *who amputated their affected toes and performed a wonderful cure.* We have just heard they are recovering very fast. Mr Bennett has lost all the toes of the left foot. *The foreign seamen went to a distant settlement, whence they got a passage to England.*

This place is the residence of a merchant who has in store all kinds of necessaries to sell to the inhabitants here-abouts and therefore the best situation we could be in, as both we and the men were almost entirely destitute of cloaths [*sic*] of every kind, when we came here.

I have got for the men (as you will see by the inclosed account) only what is absolutely necessary in so cold a climate as this, and with regard to their allowance of meat, have also been as economick [*sic*] as possible. *We got a fisherman's house and having provided ourselves with guns, powder and shot we passed the winter like the demi-savages of that country.*

The allowance for one man per week is:

6 pounds of pork]
7 pounds of bread]
2 quarts of flour] which comes to about 7s/6d per week
1 quart of pease]
1 pound of butter]
1 pint of molasses]

The molasses are for the purpose of making spruce beer,[22] which certainly is very conducive to health. As you will see by the inclosed account, I have given the four men here, viz [Gunners] Lockey, Lapsley, Wilson & Stark (Mr Truscott's servant, Jackson, is with his

20. Roope Harris was a Bristol merchant and shipper. He inherited his aunt's estates in 1771 including Greenway House near Dartmouth, for which he had to add Roope to his surname, becoming Roope Harris Roope. His business ran a triangular trade from Dartmouth to Newfoundland and Spain, but he was in trouble by 1791 and Greenway was sold and he filed for bankruptcy in 1800.
21. Probably to the settlement of Garnish.
22. Spruce beer was common in the Colonial United States and the eastern coast of Canada.

master) two large ruggs [*sic*] between them and each of them 7 yards of swan skin, 5 of which made a blanket, and the other two for cuffs to the hands and a kind of covering for the legs, called here buskins.

The measures I have taken will I hope, meet the approbation of General Pattison, to defray the expense of their cloathing [*sic*] and every other expense. Up to the present month, I have drawn upon Messieurs Meyricks[23] for the sum of £73 12s 6d which includes six month's pay for myself, not having drawn any since the 1st of July and 4 month's pay for Lieutenant Forbes, which but you will be good enough to see that Messieurs Meyricks duly answer & when I leave this place in the spring I shall draw for a sum necessary to pay the expense of their living till then from this place.

Our men as well as ourselves, far from being able to save any of our baggage, have hardly been able to save the cloaths [*sic*] on our backs, for which I hope (by an application from General Pattison) the Board of Ordnance will make us as well as them ample allowance. When we were cast away, I had £15 of the men's in my hands, which I hope will not be a loss to me. I shall keep a regular account of every expense of our men and when I get to Quebec submit to the inspection of the officer commanding that place.

Inclosed you have the separate acknowledgement of each man for having received the different articles charged to them and for the payments of which I have got Mr Roope's receipt, which I also inclose you.

We paid John Brine, Master of the schooner which conveyed us here, 30 guineas as a recompense for his going with us more than 50 leagues out of his way, which on account of the season, deprived him of most of his winter's work, the most profitable in this country, for which I hope the Board of Ordnance will make us an allowance, which they will not doubt if General Pattison will be good enough to make an application.

In April 1796 we were taken off by a Government schooner bound for Halifax to St John's to take recruits there for the Duke of Kent's Regiment,[24] *which vessel having been driven in St Piere's Island where a confused account of our misfortune had reached. We were taken to St John's and thence to Halifax, at both of which places we were treated with the greatest kindness and attention by every person, and particularly by HRH Prince Edward. From the latter place we made our way to Quebeck [sic] where we arrived in July, exactly eleven months after our departure from England, and by an odd chance within two hours of the arrival of a detachment of the corps, to which had been added two subalterns, to replace*

23. The Army Agents, Messieurs Meyrick & Porter of Parliament Street, London.
24. The Duke of Kent was Colonel of the 7th Foot.

those we had lost, the Captain of the Phillis having taken Lieutenant Douglas' letter to General Pattison the preceding year by a chance opportunity to England.

Caddy and Forbes join me in desiring you to remember us to all our friends at Woolwich. I am dear Sir, yours &c, Howard Douglas 1st Lieutenant Royal Artillery.

To Lieutenant Douglas, 4th Battalion Royal Artillery[25]

Hill Street, 22 April 1796

Dear Sir,
Your letter to Captain Frazer [sic], reciting all the circumstances of your shipwreck, is a tale of such deep woe and distress as must necessarily make a forcible impression on the feelings of everyone who has read it. I am sure it had a full effect upon mine. It only remains for me to offer you my sincere congratulations on the providential escape which you and your surviving companions most fortunately met with; and whilst I gratefully admire the ways of providence in preserving your lives, I must at the same time pay a just tribute to your cool, firm and undaunted behaviour during the scenes of horror you underwent. I am convinced that the prudent steps you took after getting on shore proved the happy means of your preservation. After the arrival of your letter I lost no time in laying it before the Master General and since that, I made the strongest application to the Board of Ordnance, requesting that they would be pleased to grant you and all the sufferers an indemnification for the losses sustained by that melancholy event, to which I yesterday received an answer and which I transmit enclosed; although you will probably receive one directly from the Board, requiring the affidavit therein specified. Unluckily I had not received this letter from the Board when Lieutenant Kiggell[26] *called upon me yesterday, previous to his departure from London; but I hope this will reach him at Portsmouth before he sails; and that he may have the pleasure of giving it to you at Quebec.*

I desire you will remember me with my good wishes to your young companions in the hour of distress and accept the same yourself from, dear Sir, your very faithful humble servant, James Pattison.

25. The letter of response is also recorded in the Journal.
26. 2nd Lieutenant John Kiggell Royal Artillery (Kane 857) died in Canada on 1 August 1798.

Family and Other Tragedies

1795

Richard and Ann continued to prepare for their move to Plymouth.

> 10 December. Employed all morning in packing up. We dined and spent the day at Colonel Congreve's.[1]

Richard made a loan to his brother Thomas at Manchester; it is unclear what Tom's business was.

> 12 December. Wrote to brother Tom at Manchester inclosing him £200, for which he has given me a bond and is to pay me 5 percent with principal and interest at the death of Mrs Wilkes.
>
> 16 December. Today we had a sale of our furniture &c.
>
> 20 December Sunday. We set off to London to Mr North's where we dined and slept at the inn where the coach goes from.
>
> 21 December. We were up at 3 o'clock and set off at 4 o'clock on our way to Plymouth.[2] Slept at Salisbury.
>
> 22 December. Set off [at] 4 o'clock and slept at Exeter.
>
> 23 December. At 9 o'clock this morning we set off in a chaise and arrived without any accident between 6 & 7 o'clock in the evening at Plymouth.
>
> 26 December. We have been living at the *Fountaine Tavern* in Plymouth Dock[3] till this day, when we dined and supped at

1. Colonel Sir William Congreve Royal Artillery (Kane 260); he introduced rockets into the army. He died at Charlton on 30 April 1814.
2. The Exeter and Plymouth Mail Coach left from The Swan with Two Necks, in Cheapside.
3. The Fountain Inn stood on Fore Street, Devonport, directly opposite the dockyard gates.

Captain Roger's[4] of the artillery and slept at night at our new lodgings.

27 December Sunday. Called at Colonel Davies[5] & Major Laye's[6] with Mrs [Ann] Unett.

Richard was in command of Captain Miller's Company in the Captain's absence, but he was left waiting a long time for his clothes &c.

29 December. Wrote to Lieutenant Spearman, Adjutant 5th Battalion,[7] to get one of the sergeants who is promoted from Captain Miller's company[8] to one at Yarmouth, transferred into it again. I have now the command of Captain Miller's company[9] and I wish to make him my Paymaster Sergeant.

31 December. Dined at the Mess with Lieutenant Fraser.[10]

1796

1 January. We dined and supped at Colonel Davies's.

4 January. Today I come on duty as Captain of the week & as my clothes &c are not yet come by sea, I was obliged to be measured for a suit of regimentals.

5 January. We had company to dinner, viz Captain & Mrs Rogers & Edward Rogers, Lieutenants Fraser, Milbanke and Tulloch of the artillery.[11]

4. Captain Henry Rogers Royal Artillery (Kane 538); he retired on full pay on 1 November 1803.
5. Colonel Thomas Davies Royal Artillery (Kane 228); he died at Blackheath on 16 March 1812.
6. Lieutenant Colonel Francis Laye Royal Artillery (Kane 466); he died at Newcastle in 1828.
7. 1st Lieutenant Alexander Spearman Royal Artillery (Kane 741); he died at Woolwich on 14 July 1808.
8. Captain James Miller Royal Artillery (Kane 540); he died at Charlton on 24 March 1825.
9. Captain Miller commanded No 2 Company 5th Battalion. Miller retained the command, Unett being his second captain.
10. 1st Lieutenant Hugh Fraser Royal Artillery (Kane 798); he died at Colombo on 30 June 1828.
11. 1st Lieutenants Ralph Milbanke (Kane 800) and Alexander Tulloh (Kane 801). Milbanke was killed at St Elmo, Naples on 1 July 1799. Tulloh was a prisoner of war for eight years and went on half pay on 1 August 1800. He died in London on 28 May 1826.

> 6 January. Went to Plymouth and to the citadel &c, which is about 3 miles from [the] dock.[12]
>
> 7 January. Had a letter from my servant Wilson, saying that the vessel had not as yet sailed from London.
>
> 9 January. Had company to dinner, viz Lieutenants Brownrigg, Crawford and Durnford.[13]

Richard went onboard to witness a Naval Court Martial; while the local scandal was of an elopement.

> 11 January. Went onboard the Guard Ship in the harbour to a Naval Court Martial. This morning Lieutenant Tulloch run off with Miss Davies, only daughter of Colonel Davies on a matrimonial trip.
>
> 12 January. Employed all morning at the barracks in examining the arms, clothing &c of the company.
>
> 13 January. Lieutenant West[14] of the artillery who is onboard a bomb [vessel], dined and supped with us.
>
> 14 January. Employed in the morning in looking over the arms &c.
>
> 18 January. This day is the Queen's [Official] birthday,[15] in consequence of which the batteries fired a Royal Salute, as did also the men of war. Walked with Mrs [Ann] Unett to see them fire.
>
> 19 January. Had a bad sore throat, with the rheumatism in my left arm, had it rubbed with hartshorn[16] and oil, found myself much better.
>
> 20 January. Lieutenants Fraser & Glasgow[17] of the Engineers drank tea and supped with us.
>
> 21 January. Went onboard the *Cambridge*[18] to a Naval Court Martial. Dined and supped at the Artillery Mess with Captain Viney.[19]

12. The naval dockyard is at Devonport, not Plymouth.
13. 2nd Lieutenant Henry Fox Brownrigg (Kane 882), 1st Lieutenant Henry Crawford (Kane 864) and 2nd Lieutenant Elias Durnford (Kane 748) Royal Engineers.
14. 1st Lieutenant James West Royal Artillery (Kane 798); he died at Woolwich on 28 November 1821.
15. Queen Charlotte's real birthday was 19 May.
16. Hartshorn comes from the antler of a male red deer.
17. 2nd Lieutenant William Henry Glasgow Royal Engineers.
18. HMS *Cambridge* of 80 guns was the Plymouth Guard Ship.
19. Captain Lieutenant Sir James Viney Royal Artillery (Kane 685); he died at Chelsea on 20 January 1841.

22 January. Was President of a Regimental Court Martial upon one of the 4th Battalion.

23 January. We this day moved into new lodgings as our others were too noisy.

24 January Sunday. Walked with Colonel Davies and called upon General Morris[20] who commands in this district in the absence of Lord George Lennox.[21]

25 January. Came on duty as Captain of the week.

26 January. Was a member on a General Court Martial upon a Captain [Lieutenant] Curling[22] of the Sussex Fencible Cavalry on the prosecution of a Major Worthington[23] of the same corps. Onboard the *Pomona* frigate[24] in the harbour, 20 sailors were struck by the lightning but fortunately no lives were lost. The *Dutton* East Indiaman, one of the West India fleet, which had returned to port yesterday having four companies of grenadiers onboard, ran on shore about 2 o'clock close under the citadel (and is since gone to pieces). There were several sailors drowned and above 20 soldiers. As soon as the ship struck, the soldiers and sailors got below to the liquors and the water rushing through the portholes drowned them, they were most of them drunk.[25]

28 January. Court Martial still continued. Had a letter from my servant, telling me that owing to contrary winds they had been obliged to put into Ramsgate.

29 January. Court Martial still continued from 11 o'clock to 3 o'clock. Dined at General Morris's with a large party of military.

---

20. Lieutenant General Staates Morris.
21. General Lord George Lennox was Governor of Plymouth.
22. Captain Lieutenant Bunce Curling, Adjutant must have lost and left the regiment as he was officially superseded on 8 October 1796. Captain Lieutenant as a rank in the Army at this time, denoted the senior Lieutenant in a battalion, who would be next for promotion to Captain.
23. Major John Worthington Sussex Fencible Cavalry.
24. He must refer to HMS *Pomone* which was a captured French frigate of 40 guns. HMS *Pomona* of 28 guns had been renamed *Amphitrite* in 1795.
25. The *Dutton* East Indiaman ran ashore in a storm in Plymouth Sound with around 600 people onboard. Captain Edward Pellew (despite still suffering from a recent wound) was hauled out to the stricken ship attached to a flimsy line that had been thrown ashore from the wreck with a rescue line wrapped round his body and with the aid of breeches buoys the majority of the crew and passengers were saved. A Jeremiah Coghlan also set out swimming and later by boat and saved about fifty men in total. The troops onboard came from 2nd, 3rd, 10th and 37th Regiments. It is believed that around twenty people lost their lives in this tragedy. Pellew was given the Freedom of Plymouth and the King made him a baronet. Pellew took Coghlan onto his ship and oversaw his rise through the ranks, to eventually die as a Post-Captain.

30 January. Court Martial finished this day. Had a letter from Lieutenant Spearman.

31 January. Employed all morning in making Pay List for February &c.

1 February. The company mustered at 12 o'clock.

10 February. We drank tea and supped at Colonel Mercer's.[26]

16 February. We drank tea at Stonehouse at a Mrs Townshend's whose husband was in the Engineers.[27]

20 February. Called upon Governor Campbell.[28]

22 February. Came on duty as Captain of the Week.

His baggage finally arrived.

24 February. Today our servant arrived with the baggage.

25 February. Was not very well today, having a touch of my complaint in my stomach.

26 February. Have still a little pain in my stomach. We went tonight for the first time to a play, which was acted by desire of Colonel Davies and the officers of artillery. One of my men died this day of a decline.

16 March. Came on duty as Captain of the Week in the room of Captain Sheldrake,[29] who is gone to Torbay with a party to mount guns.[30]

Riots over bread prices were a regular occurrence.

7 April. This morning an express arrived at General Morris's that there was a riot with the tinners in Cornwall on account of the dearness of corn; in consequence of which 400 of the Lancashire Voluntiers [*sic*] with a Lieutenant (Milbanke) of the artillery and 2 three-pounders with 30 men marched at 12 o'clock.

9 April. Attended the funeral of an officer of the East Devon Militia this day, he died suddenly.

26. Colonel Alexander Mercer Royal Engineers was the father of Alexander Cavalie Mercer Royal Horse Artillery of Waterloo fame.
27. The wife of Captain Gilbert Townshend Royal Engineers.
28. Colonel John Campbell, Lieutenant Governor of Plymouth.
29. Captain Lieutenant John Sheldrake Royal Artillery (Kane 628); he died at Tilehurst, Reading on 23 February 1820.
30. A half-moon battery was built at Berry Head in 1795, protecting Torbay, it was armed with twelve 42-pounders.

11 April. Came on duty for the week.

12 April. We drank tea & supped at Mr Shaw's, Ordnance Storekeeper.

13 April. We had company to tea & supper, viz, Mrs & Miss & Lieutenant Landmann,[31] Captain Sheldrake, Lieutenant & Mrs Tulloh and Lieutenant Glasgow.

15 April. Sat [on] a Court Martial.

23 April. This morning an order came from the Duke of York for an officer with 30 men & 2 six-pounders to march immediately into Cornwall, there to be stationed till further orders. The other detachment returned the beginning of the week.

Captured enemy vessels were brought into harbour.

24 April Sunday. Saw two French frigates come into harbour, they are prizes to Sir Edward Pellew.[32]

26 April. Went onboard one of the prizes [*Virginie*] of 44 guns, she is a fine ship and only 2 years old. She had 18 men killed & 30 wounded, is much damaged in her hull, rigging &c. Her mizen mast is shot away, as is also her main-top mast. Had company to tea & supper, viz, Mrs & Lieutenant Durnford, Captain Sheldrake, 2 Mrs Roger's and Lieutenant Anderson of the Engineers.[33]

Finally his Captain arrived to take command.

29 April. This morning Captain Miller arrived, went with him to look out for lodgings.

1 May. The Quartern loaf in London is now fallen to 9½d, it was some little time ago as high as 1s 3d and here it was still dearer. Meat of all kinds is getting very dear in Plymouth market. Roasting 8d per lb, round of beef 7d per lb, mutton the same. Butter has been all the time we have been here at 1s 6d per lb, it is now 1s/3d. Cheese 8d per lb, bacon 1s/1d per lb.

29 May. The men of war in the harbour fired at 1 o'clock, it being King Charles' Restoration.

---

31. 2nd Lieutenant George Landmann Royal Engineers.
32. Commodore Sir Edward Pellew Royal Navy commanded the Western Frigate Squadron, consisting of HMS *Indefatigable*, *Argo*, *Concord*, *Revolutionnaire* and *Amazon.* On 13 April his squadron captured the *Unite* of 32 guns and on 22 April the *Virginie*, a 40-gun frigate.
33. 2nd Lieutenant Henry Anderson Royal Engineers.

With his Captain now in position, Richard and Ann were able to gain some leave.

> 2 June. We set off this morning at 8 o'clock on our way to Southampton and arrived at Exeter to a late dinner.
>
> 3 June. We set off again today at 4 o'clock in the morning & arrived at Salisbury at 8 o'clock in the evening.
>
> 4 June. Set off in a chaise at 2 o'clock [pm] and arrived at Southampton between 5 & 6 o'clock, came through the New Forest, a charming ride.
>
> 11 July. We set off this morning at 6 o'clock on our way to Reverend John Willis' at Pickwick, about seven miles from Bath. We dined at Warminster and arrived at Bath about 6 o'clock in the evening.
>
> 12 July. About 5 o'clock this evening Mrs Willis called and took us with her in their carriage home.[34]
>
> 24 July. I have had for some time a return of my complaint in my stomach, which I fancy proceeds from my having caught cold.

After 11 weeks leave, they returned to Plymouth.

> 17 August. At 6 o'clock this morning we set off on [our] way to Plymouth. Stopped all night at Exeter.
>
> 18 August. Set off at 8 o'clock and arrived at our lodgings between 4 & 5 o'clock in the evening. As the coach was full, I came on the top (as I also did most of yesterday by choice).
>
> 22 August. Called upon Colonel Manley,[35] who is now commanding officer of artillery, who took me & introduced me to Lord George Lennox. Called also upon General Grenville[36] at Stonehouse.
>
> 26 August. This day's newspaper mentions the Quartern loaf having fallen in London to 7¾d which is much lower than it has been for above this twelvemonth.

---

34. The Reverend & Mrs Willis owned Leycesters at Pickwick, but built a new house in its grounds called Pickwick House between 1794–9. It was later renamed Beechfield House. Leycesters was then demolished. It is presumed they stayed at Leycesters.
35. Lieutenant Colonel Orlando Manley Royal Artillery (Kane 337); he died in Dublin on 15 December 1808.
36. Major General Richard Grenville, Colonel 23rd Foot.

He spent a number of days inspecting the various batteries protecting Plymouth Sound.

> 7 September. Was up at half past 5 o'clock and set off at 6 o'clock with a party of 15 men to examine the guns &c at Wester-Ring.[37]
>
> 8 September. Set off at 8 o'clock with a party of 12 men to examine the guns at Staten Heights,[38] returned at 3 o'clock.
>
> 10 September. At 7 o'clock this morning with the [artillery] park marched to Buckland Down[39] by way of exercising the horses &c. Came home at 2 o'clock.
>
> 12 September. Was up this morning at 5 o'clock and before 6 o'clock the three companies of artillery marched with the park, consisting of 4-twelve pounders, 4-six pounders and 2-three pounders. Before 9 o'clock we were joined by the 4 regiments of Militia[40] with the Surr[e]y Fencible Cavalry. Did not come home till between 3 & 4 o'clock. Dined at the Mess.

He also attended a large Field Day with a significant part of Plymouth garrison.

> 21 September. This morning we had a grand field day with all the regiments and a sham fight upon Roborough Down.[41] Took a beefsteak at the Mess.

A dreadful explosion occurred at Plymouth, involving Sir Edward Pellew again.

> 22 September. About 4 o'clock this afternoon a most shocking accident happened in the harbour; the *Amphion* frigate of 32-guns blew up and above 200 souls perished. At 1 o'clock she had fired a salute, it being the king's coronation.
>
> 23 September. It is now said that the frigate had not fired yesterday, but in the morning they had unloaded three or four of her guns at her head and that some of the powder had been through negligence scattered upon the deck and by some accident had taken fire and communicated to what they call the Hanging Magazine, which did not contain more than two rounds a gun; the Grand Magazine remained untouched. She had a few days before completed her

37. The Western King's Redoubt mounted twelve 18-pounder cannon.
38. Actually Staddon Heights overlooking Plymouth Sound, prior to the present Palmerston fort.
39. Now built on in north Plymouth.
40. The South, East & North Devon and North Hants Militia Regiments.
41. It lies 6km north of Plymouth

> powder & had onboard 300 barrels, which had it caught fire, would in all probability have ruined the town and dockyard and destroyed most of the ships in the harbour. She was moored alongside of a sheer-hulk. The explosion blew Captain Pellew, her commander through the cabin window into the hulk, without receiving any injury except his face a little scratched, and what is very extraordinary and what can scarce be believed, the Marine centinel [*sic*] on duty at the cabbin [*sic*] door, was blown into the hulk and lighted upon his feet, without the smallest hurt whatever.[42]

Britain's Continental allies appeared to be succeeding against the French Revolutionaries, but it did not last long.

> 24 September. Yesterday & today we had two Gazettes Extraordinary giving an account of different victories upon the Rhine by the Austrians, the French having lost upwards of 60,000 men.[43]
>
> 28 September. The papers now mention that the Austrian army in Italy under General Wurmser of 70,000 has been totally routed with very great slaughter.[44]
>
> 3 October. Was upon a Regimental Court Martial all the morning.
>
> 17 October. Came on duty as Captain of the week.
>
> 20 October. Wrote to my brother George and also to General Pattison to ask him for the Adjutancy when it becomes vacant by [John] Fraser getting a company.[45]
>
> 24 October. Had a letter from my sister Fanny, telling me of the death of Edward Neve who was a first cousin.[46] I am not very sorry about it as he turned out very worthless and dissipated and too much like his father.

The latest naval success was astounding.

> 7 November. We had this day a Gazette giving an account of ten Dutch ships, three of them men of war with an admiral being taken at

42. Out of a crew of 220, only Captain Edward Pellew, his 1st Lieutenant and 15 men survived the explosion.
43. These refer to the victories of the Archduke Charles over Marshal Jourdan at Amberg on 24 August and Wurzburg on 3 September.
44. This refers to the French victory of Bassano on 8 September 1796.
45. Kane records that his brother-in-law had become a Captain Lieutenant on 30 May 1794 and was likely to gain his Captaincy in the next year, so Richard was trying to lay the groundwork in advance.
46. His Aunt Sarah (Unett) had married the Reverend Titus Neve of Wolverhampton. He clearly did not think much of his uncle.

> the Cape of Good Hope without firing a gun, as also some transports with 3,000 men, they sailed with an intention of retaking the Cape.[47]

General Pattison had sent a positive response but offered a more immediate opportunity, if things turned out as expected.

> 9 November. Had a letter from General Pattison giving me an absolute promise of the Quarter Master-ship of his battalion, in case Captain Lieutenant Fenwick[48] who now has it, should die and he is given over by all the medical people.
>
> 25 November. I set off to Mr St John's at Penny Cross about 3 miles,[49] where I breakfasted; then rode about 8 miles farther with Mr St John & Captain Andrews of the North Hants Militia.[50]
>
> 27 November. Dine with Captain Andrews at the North Hants Mess.
>
> 29 November. Went with 4 men to Western Ring to examine the guns &c.
>
> 5 December. Was up at 7 o'clock and breakfasted at Colonel Manley's at 8 o'clock. A detachment of 2 officers & 40 men, 4 x 12 pounders & 2 howitzers marched into Cornwall. Captain Sheldrake & Lieutenant Fraser [went].

1797

No mention is made of it, but George became a 1st Lieutenant on 1 January 1797.

> 16 January. We gave today 1¾d for an egg, and last week in the market veal was 8d per lb, if you took the whole leg together, but for a pound or two 10d. Cod fish were 8d per lb and for a small pair of soles I gave 4s.

---

47. Fearing that the Cape of Good Hope was under threat, the Dutch government sent an expedition consisting of three ships of the line (*Dordrecht* and *Revolutie* of 66 guns each and *Admiraal Tromp* of 54 guns), four frigates (*Castor* 44 guns, *Braave* 40 guns, *Sirene* 28 guns and *Bellona* 26 guns), a sloop (*Havik* 18 guns) and an East Indiaman (*Vrouw Maria*) with some 500 troops. Not knowing that the British had captured the colony on 14 September 1795, Admiral Englebertus Lucas sailed into Saldanha Bay and anchored on 6 August 1796, desperately short of drinking water. Admiral George Elphinstone's squadron of eight sail of the line appeared on 16 August as the Dutch were about to sail for Isle de France in the Indian Ocean. Hopelessly outnumbered, Lucas surrendered the following day.
48. Captain Lieutenant Thomas Fenwick Royal Artillery (Kane 712); he died at Woolwich on 8 January 1797.
49. Pennycross is now part of north Plymouth.
50. Captain John Andrews North Hampshire Militia.

> 18 January. This being the Queen's birthday, the regiments in garrison and the men of war fired a Royal Salute.
>
> 20 January. Had company to dinner & supper, viz Major Laye, Captain Wildey & Lieutenant Monro of the Hampshire Militia.[51] I gave in the market this morning 7s for a cod fish 16 lbs weight, which was excessively dear.

Poor Fenwick had died and Richard was ordered back to Woolwich as Quarter Master.

> 24 January. Had a letter from Lieutenant [John] Fraser, and another from General Pattison that the Marquis Cornwallis had approved his recommendation of me for Quarter Master, vice Captain Fenwick deceased and ordering me to Woolwich without delay.

But there was a delay.

> 30 January. Expected there would have been a letter today from Colonel Macleod, Adjutant General,[52] to Lord George Lennox, Governor, for my quitting this district, as Lord George has refused me leave till he gets an official letter.
>
> 31 January. Employed all day in packing. Sent part of my baggage onboard an Ordnance ship.
> 1 February. Sent the remainder of my baggage.
>
> 2 February. Colonel Manley had an official letter from the Adjutant General about my having leave.
>
> 3 February. Called upon Lord George Lennox and took leave &c where we staid all night.

Eleven days later Richard Ann could eventually set out for Woolwich to rejoin the 4th Battalion.

> 4 February. At 9 o'clock this morning we set off in chaise on our way to Woolwich; got to Exeter at 4 o'clock in the afternoon.
>
> 5 February. At 4 o'clock this morning we set off in a coach and after travelling all day & all night, we got to London on the . . .
>
> 6 February . . . about 3 o'clock [pm] then took a chaise and arrived at Mrs Godwin's, Greenwich about 4 o'clock, just after dinner.[53]

51. Captain John Widley and Lieutenant James Monro of the North Hampshire (Hants) Militia
52. Lieutenant Colonel Sir John Macleod Royal Artillery (Kane 456)
53. At this period, breakfast was usually eaten about 10am, dinner about 3pm and supper about 8pm, dinner being the main meal of the day.

9 February. Set off in a chaise to Woolwich and breakfasted in the Warren with Captain Godfrey, called upon my brother George and took him with me to London. Waited upon General Pattison to thank him for the Quarter Mastery and to sign the certificates &c for my Warrant [as Quarter Master].

20 February. At 11 o'clock this morning, we set off in a coach to pay some visits at Woolwich and then went to our lodgings upon Shooters Hill.

An invasion scare had shocked the nation.

28 February. The nation for these last few days has been in a dreadful situation; we have had a Gazette Extraordinary that a body of 1,400 French had landed near Milford Haven in Pembrokeshire and yesterday the bank stopped payment in specie. However, the whole of the French laid down their arms & were made prisoners and the London merchants had a meeting and agreed to take paper in lieu of cash, this in some degree [h]as re-established credit.[54] I was this day in orders as Quarter Master, my Warrant is dated the 9 January.

Richard found himself having to act as Adjutant, as his brother-in-law was very unwell.

1 March. The 4th Battalion [Royal Artillery] were inspected by General Farrington. I acted as Adjutant and was in orders to do that duty till Captain [John] Fraser who is very unwell, gets a company. We dined and supped at Colonel Bloomfields.[55]

Another major naval success, brought a certain Captain Horatio Nelson into the limelight.

6 March. We had yesterday a Gazette Extraordinary. Sir John Jervis with 15 sail of the line having beat the Spanish fleet in the Mediterranean consisting of 27 sail & taken 2 of 112 guns, one of 80 guns & one of 74 guns.[56]

---

54. This refers to the landing of 1,400 troops of La Legion Noire commanded by Colonel Tate near Fishguard on 22 February 1797, but they soon surrendered to the hastily assembled local Volunteers and Militia commanded by Lord Cawdor on 24 February.

55. Lieutenant Colonel Sir Thomas Blomefield Royal Artillery (Kane 334); he died at Shooters Hill on 24 August 1822.

56. This was news of the Battle of Cape St Vincent, which actually occurred in the Atlantic. It was here that Horatio Nelson distinguished himself, capturing the *San Nicolas de Bari* of 80 guns and *San Jose* of 112 guns. The others captured were the *Salvador del Mundo* of 112 guns and the *San Isidro* of 74 guns. Jervis became Earl St Vincent for this victory.

Suddenly the family was plunged into despair. Ann had given birth to a daughter Frances Elizabeth on 6 March, but within the week Ann was dead; it is difficult to believe that she died from any other reason than complications after the birth.

> 13 March. This day poor Mrs [Ann] Fraser died, than whom there never lived a more amiable & charming woman; her death in some degree may be attributed to her over anxiety and fatigue with a sick husband who was blind, helpless and bedridden and who had been in a lamentable state of health for a long time. She has left four children to lament her loss. She was buried in a vault at Plumstead.[57]

There are no further diary entries until September and Richard remains virtually silent for the remainder of the year, the reason soon becomes clear.

> We have been staying in lodgings upon Shooters Hill for some weeks, when we went into barracks and remained till the 1 of September, when we took Brooke Hill from Captain Young[58] and went to live there a very pleasant situation.

Five and a half months later, John Grant Fraser finally succumbed and was buried alongside his wife. Richard and Ann Unett took on full responsibility as guardians for the four children, but they were never formally adopted.

> 1 November. Captain [John] Fraser has been gradually getting worse, not being able to get out of bed for some weeks and totally blind; this day it pleased God to release him. We took the children to live with us except the youngest Frances who is at nurse upon Blackheath.
>
> 31 December. We have lived very retired and have mixed very little in company for these some months.

1798

With the new year, Richard began to record events again in his diary.

> 1 January. Came on duty as Quarter Master of the week.

57. *The Environs of London Volume 4* originally published by Cadell & Davies in 1796, confirms that in the graveyard of St Nicholas Church is the tomb of General Goodwin [Godwin] Royal Artillery dated 1786. Later entries make it clear that this vault also includes Mrs Godwin, Captain John & Mrs Ann Fraser with their youngest child Frances Elizabeth Fraser & Mr Thomson whose subsequent deaths are mentioned in the diaries. Unfortunately one of the last V2 rockets to fall on London destroyed the churchyard of St Nicholas and the area around the church was grassed, there is therefore no way of knowing where the vault lies.
58. Captain Lieutenant Brook Young (Kane 615); he died at Bath in 1835.

> 29 January. Set off to London in a coach to Drury Lane to see the new play of the *Castle Spectre*[59] and the *Shipwreck*.[60] Staid all night at Captain Scottowe's.[61]

Patriotic voluntary contributions were all the rage; and the artillery were not exempt.

> 9 February. All the officers of the regiment had a meeting at one o'clock this day and unanimously agreed to give six day's pay as a voluntary contribution to be applied to the exigencies of the state. Books are now opened at the bank to receive the voluntary contributions of corporate bodies and individuals.
>
> 10 February. Marquis Cornwallis was down today and in publick [*sic*] orders returned thanks to the officers & men for their voluntary contribution. The men have given three day's pay.
>
> 28 February. We dined & spent the day at General Phipp's[62] in the Warren.

Richard was given additional responsibilities.

> 10 March. Today it was in orders for me to take the command and payment of the recruits belonging to the four Canada companies of the 4th Battalion.[63]
>
> 24 March. We dined and supped at Captain Ramsey's.[64]
>
> 29 March. Walked to Greenwich and back again to the parade at 5 o'clock.
>
> 1 April. Had company to dinner & supper, viz, Captain Rowley of the Engineers[65] & Lieutenants Morrison[66] and Eliot of the Artillery.[67]

---

59. A Gothic romance by Matthew 'Monk' Lewis. It opened on 14 December 1797.
60. There are few references to a play entitled *The Shipwreck* but there are mentions in 1802.
61. Captain John Skottowe 2nd Dragoon Guards.
62. Major General John Phipps, Colonel of the Invalid Royal Engineers.
63. The four companies of the 4th Battalion in Canada were, No. 2 John Schalch (Kane 535), No. 7 Captain/Lieutenant Edward Trelawney (not in Kane), No. 9 George Hamilton (Kane 497) and No. 10 George Glasgow (Kane 498).
64. Captain Lieutenant George Ramsay (Kane 633); he died at Canterbury in 1834.
65. Captain Lieutenant John Rowley Royal Engineers.
66. 1st Lieutenant William Morrison (Kane 934); he died at Wolverhampton in 1835.
67. 2nd Lieutenant William Granville Elliott (Kane 971); he died near Hastings in 1828.

Home Service 1798–1802

1798

Richard received his first letter from his brother George who had just arrived in Martinique.

> 15 April Sunday. Dressed myself and went to the parade in the evening. Found a letter from my brother George dated 28 February Martinique saying that he had had a pleasant passage out & seemed to like the West Indies pretty well.
>
> 22 April Sunday. Had company to dinner and supper, viz, Captains Wulfe[1] & Dixon,[2] Lieutenant Morrison and Mr Bastard Gentleman Cadet.[3]

Amongst Richard's guest to dinner was one Cadet Alexander Cavalie Mercer, of future Waterloo fame.

> 29 April Sunday. We had company to tea & supper viz, Captain & Mrs Hamilton who are lately married, Lieutenant and two Mrs Adye's, Mr James Adye[4] and Mr Alexander Mercer,[5] both cadets, the latter of whom also dined with us.
>
> 1 May. Wrote a long letter to George in the West Indies; received by Lieutenant Lloyd[6] who left Martinique 10 March, a packet of letters from George, who is in good health and likes his situation.

1. Captain George Wulff (Kane 593); he died at Chatham in 1846.
2. Captain George Dixon (Kane 594); he died at Bath in 1836.
3. Gentleman Cadet James Stokes Bastard (Kane 1082); he died at Charlton in 1871.
4. Gentleman Cadet James Adye (Kane 1047); he died in 1831.
5. Gentleman Cadet Alexander Cavalie Mercer (Kane 1064), famous for his memoir of the Waterloo campaign.
6. 1st Lieutenant William Lloyd (Kane 898); he died at Bermuda in 1831.

11 May. Had company to dinner & supper, viz, Colonels Douglas and Rochfort,[7] Captains Godfrey, Phipps and Skyring.[8]

21 May. Came on duty as Quarter Master of the week.

23 May. We heard today that Mr Sinclair, Commissary & Paymaster to the Artillery at Lisbon and godfather to Alexander [Fraser], shot himself.

1 June. Had a letter from John acquainting us with the death of his little boy,[9] about six or seven months old.

4 June. Being the King's birthday, a Royal Salute was fired with 4 x 12 pounders in front of the barracks. Dined at the Mess and in the evening there was a grand display of fireworks.

6 June. Was up at half after 3 o'clock in the morning to march a detachment off to Bristol with battalion guns.

7 June. Sent a parcel to Captain Macdonnel & Lieutenant Chisholm[10] in Canada.

9 June. We have had lately most dreadful accounts from Ireland; one part of which is in open rebellion.

10 June Sunday. Had company to dinner viz, Captain Lawson,[11] Lieutenants Lloyd, Milbanke, Fauquier[12] and Mr Mercer Cadet.

12 June. Had a letter from George dated 17 April from St Pierre, Martinique, he is very well.

13 June. The news from Ireland most shocking.

14 June. We had a present from Dr Wood of half a kit of salmon; and another from Corporal Atkinson, who is quartered in Sussex of some carp and tench, which owing to the warm weather we were obliged to throw away.

---

7. Lieutenant Colonel George Rochfort Invalid Artillery Battalion (Kane 253); he died on 24 February 1821.
8. Captain Lieutenant William Skyring Royal Artillery (Kane 638); he died in London on 12 September 1806.
9. His son William had died on 25 May.
10. Later entries seem to identify these two officers as Captain Charles Macdonell and Ensign Alexander Chisholm of the 72nd Foot. Chisholm became a Lieutenant on 4 July 1800. However, I can find no evidence for the regiment being in Canada at this time.
11. Captain Lieutenant Robert Lawson Royal Artillery (Kane 731); he died at Woolwich on 23 July 1802.
12. 2nd Lieutenant Henry Fauquier Royal Artillery (Kand 973); he retired in July 1808.

> 24 June Sunday. Had to dinner, viz Dr Mackulloch,[13] and Messieurs Mercer & Bastard Gentlemen Cadets, who also staid [for] supper.
>
> 25 June. Came on duty as Quarter Master for the week. Messieurs Hilliard,[14] Mercer & Bastard drank tea & supped with us.

Another bout of illness struck Richard.

> 2 July. I had the rheumatism so bad this afternoon that I could scarcely sit up.
>
> 4 July. Was in violent pain with the rheumatism.
>
> 7 July. Was in such pain last night that I took 40 drops of laudanum, but could not close my eyes all night. Sent for Dr Irwin this morning.[15]
>
> 8 July Sunday. Had my feet put in warm water last night & took some powders when going to bed, but never closed my eyes, was in great pain all night. Did not get up till dinner time. Messieurs Mercer, Bastard & Hilliard Gentlemen Cadets dined and supped with us. In a good deal of pain in the evening.
>
> 9 July. Got no sleep again last night, was very restless, in much pain. Sent for Dr Irwin.
>
> 10 July. Rested pretty well with what Dr Irwin sent me, very weary. Captain James Grant[16] came down and dined with us. Captain Colbrooke[17] also dined with us.
>
> 18 July. Rode to Town[18] after the Guard mounting and returned to the evening parade.
>
> 23 July. This morning about 4 o'clock, I was awoke with my old complaint, a most violent pain in my stomach, it continued a considerable time. Captain Francklin[19] has been away some days upon leave and stays till the end of the month; so that I am doing

13. Assistant Surgeon James McCulloch (Kane Medical 40); he was appointed Ordnance Chemist in 1806.
14. Presumably he did not last long as he does not appear in any list.
15. Surgeon Gustavus Irwin Royal Artillery (Kane Medical 12); he died at Woolwich in 1828.
16. The only Captain James Grant in 1798 was in the 60th Foot.
17. Captain Lieutenant Paulet Colebrook Royal Artillery (Kane 678); he died at Shooters Hill 29 September 1816.
18. 'Town' was a standard reference for London.
19. Captain Lieutenant Thomas Francklin Royal Artillery (Kane 684); he died at Blackheath in 1851.

> Adjutant's duty. Rode to General Pattison's and gave him the Weekly Returns.
>
> 27 July. Just when dinner was ready, the kitchen chimney took fire and blazed very much. I had a gun fired up, which cleared it.[20]
>
> 30 July. Rode to Blenden Hall[21] to give General Pattison the Weekly Return.

Early reports of the harvest were very good.

> 2 August. Was engaged all morning upon a Court of Enquiry. The harvest is now very general, everywhere good crops.
>
> 9 August. There was a Field day at 9 o'clock.

Richard had been hiring his horse by the week, but apparently also kept a cow for milk.

> 10 August. In the evening I walked home, having left the horse, which I have kept a month this day, at a guinea a week, which is exceedingly high, besides his keep. Sent my cow to Mr Blanch's fields.

George wrote again, complaining that he had not received any letters from the family.

> 15 August. Had a letter from George in the West Indies, dated 25 June, he has never had any of our letters. Wrote him a long letter to go by this day's packet.
>
> 16 August. Have a great deal of pain in arms with the rheumatism.
>
> 18 August. Was in great pain last night and all day with the rheumatism in my arm.
>
> 19 August Sunday. The cow calved this afternoon, I was yesterday offered 15 guineas for her.[22]

Richard appears to have gone alone to Buxton to try the waters as a cure for his ailments.

> 23 August. Set off this evening at 7 o'clock in the mail on my way to Buxton, travelled all night.

20. Firing a blank-loaded gun was a known method of blowing out a chimney fire.
21. Blendon Hall was situated west of Bexley village. It was demolished in 1934.
22. Approximately £900 today.

> 24 August. Breakfasted at Northampton, dined at Litchfield and got to Mr Ward's[23] at 4 o'clock [pm].
>
> 26 August. Did not sleep much with the pain in my stomach.
>
> 29 August. Was very sick in the night, having eat [*sic*] something yesterday that disagreed with me.
>
> 31 August. To Buxton to try the waters for my rheumatism.
>
> 2 September. I was awoke last night with a most violent pain in my stomach, which lasted about 2 hours.
>
> 12 September. I have rode out either on horseback or in a gig every day; drank the waters and bathed every day, which have given me great benefit, though for a few days at the first I thought my pains were much worse, but they gradually went off.

He stayed at The Hall,[24] being apparently much more comfortable than the Eagle and Child[25] he had stayed at previously, but after a further month he had a serious fall.

> 16 October. This evening, about two hours after dinner, I tumbled down in a fit and cut my lip &c exceedingly bad. I was a few seconds insensible. I was put to bed & a doctor sent for immediately, but I would not allow myself to be let blood.
>
> 17 October. I passed a most dreadful night, my nose & upper lip were so cut and full of congealed blood that it was with the greatest difficulty that I could breathe. I had no fever this morning and contrary to the advice of the doctor, I would set off on horseback and rode in very great pain about 40 miles to Acton Hill, where I should have the best advice. My face was so much swelled that my sister Fanny and Mr W[ade] did not know me. I believe it was the Buxton waters & the riding in the heat of the day, that flew up to my head & occasioned the fit.
>
> 29 October. This evening at 8 o'clock, my sister Elizabeth & myself set off in a coach for London; travelled all night and got to Woolwich about 8 o'clock this evening [30 October].

---

23. Robert Ward was a member of the Bar, hence his association with John Wilkes, he later became an MP, being a good friend of George Canning and was on the Admiralty Board until he was appointed Clerk of the Ordnance in June 1811.
24. The Hall was built by the First Duke of Devonshire in 1670 and by 1727 it was functioning as a hotel. It is still a hotel to this day.
25. The Eagle and Child was the dinner coaching stop on the London to Manchester coach route, built in 1760 by the 4th Duke of Devonshire as a spa hotel. It is now known as the Eagle.

From this period onwards, it is noticeable that he made far less frequent entries in his journal. He did, however, record the death of Mrs Wilkes, who it seems had kept the Unetts away from a sizeable fortune.

> 31 December. Had a letter giving me an account of the death of Mrs Wilkes, who died at Froxfield in Hampshire on the 24th instant, after having kept our family out of the estate 40 years.

Anne Wilkes, the sister of Doctor Richard Wilkes the physician and learned historian (the Unett brothers all had Wilkes as their middle name) had married their great-grandfather, George Unett. On the death of his first wife in 1756, the doctor had married again within six months, the widowed Mrs Francis Bendish, sister of the Reverend Richard Wrottesley. The doctor died in 1760 and as he had no children, he left his estate (after his wife's death) to the Unetts. Their father Thomas Unett challenged the will believing that part should be paid to the Unetts immediately, but the lawsuit was decided at Chancery in the widow's favour. Dr Wilkes' widow Francis lived at Froxfield near Petersfield until her death on 24 December 1798 when they finally gained their inheritance. Indeed Dr Richard Wilkes' monument at Willenhall was erected by Captain Richard and John Unett in 1800 after they became his heirs.

1799

> 28 January. This day I went over to Blackheath to the Justices about my house being over-rated in the Parish books and succeeded in getting it reduced from £45 to £25 [per annum].[26]

The estate left by John and Ann Fraser was to be administered by Richard and John Unett as executors, the money to be held in trust for their four children. However, John Fraser's brother Hugh had other ideas and demanded that a sizeable sum be transferred to him. This was to rumble on for a long time to come.

> 14 February. About this time, Mr Hugh Fraser[27] came up from Plymouth. He staid one day & night & then went to London. He came up on purpose to oblige me & my brother John [Wilkes] as Executors to his brother, Captain [John] Fraser, to transfer some money (£1,000[28]) which is now in our names, into his own. But as we have it in trust for the children, I would not do it. He has sent me since a lawyer's letter and I have been obliged to go to another,

26. Approximately £2,500 per annum today was reduced to about £1,400.
27. Brother of Captain John Fraser.
28. About £50,000 in today's terms.

so that the business I suppose will go into Chancery. His behaviour is shameful, after all the trouble & vexation I have had about his brother's affairs.

10 April. Went to the Mess Ball this evening with my brother Tom who wished much to go, otherwise I should not have gone, this being the first Ball & Assembly that I have been at for these two years. Mrs [Ann] Unett would not go.

12 April. Went to London not Mr Stride's, who had written to me to consult about Mr Grant's money.

16 April. Owing to the high winds by which a number of colliers have been lost, the coals have been in London as high as 10 guineas a chaldron, and a favor [*sic*] even to get them at that price.

The three brothers travelled to Petersfield to attempt to get a large sum passed to them, to be evenly distributed amongst the six surviving siblings.

26 April. This morning John, Tom & myself set off in a chaise to Petersfield in Hampshire, near which place the late Mrs Wilkes lived, in order to get a Power of Attorney signed by Mr Andrews & Mr Hamsworth, her two Trustees to transfer the sum of £14,000[29] into the names of John & myself, that we may divide it amongst our brothers and sisters. She has kept our family out of their fortune nearly 40 years.

27 April. About 2 o'clock set off home again, got to Cobham where we slept and was at Woolwich by 1pm the next day.

6 May. Went to London with brother John and after some difficulty we got the Power of Attorney from Mr Andrew's agent, upon our giving him a release, which we had all signed. Went to the bank & had the Power of Attorney registered.

7 May. Went again to London with brother John & had the money (£14,000) transferred into John's & my name.

8 May. Brother John & self, set off again to London & after a good deal of trouble at the bank, we at last settled everything. We sold out of the 3 percent consuls at 55 ¾ and after reserving £566 2s 6d; of which sum we paid my Aunt Godwin at Greenwich £505.0.0. and the rest for other expenses &c we bought the remainder viz £7,802 4s 11d sterling into the new 5 percent at 84 7/8 into seven equal shares, which brings us in £60 15s per annum each.[30]

29. Worth approximately £750,000 in today's terms.

30. Each would receive about £3,000 per annum interest in today's terms.

A new ailment now struck Richard.

> 19 May. I have had for two or three days, a dizziness in my eyes, so that I can scarcely see. This is the first time I had ever anything the matter with them.
>
> 31 May. The doctors have ordered me not to drink any kind of malt liquor or spirits; and to leave off suppers. To drink water with my dinner and one glass of white wine & water after, only.
>
> 1 June. Colonel Douglas drove me in his gig to Dartford, where I went to enquire about a school for James [Fraser],[31] who is to go there after the midsummer holidays.
>
> 4 June. The King's birthday. The whole regiment was under arms & fired a Royal Salute.
>
> 6 June. Butchers' meat is now selling at Greenwich for 10d per lb,[32] roasting and boiling beef. A fore quarter of house lamb 14s. In London Pigeons 1s 3d apiece.[33] A Dorking fowl 14s[34] or £1 8s a couple. A couple of this year's chickens £1 1s!!![35]
>
> 7 June. Had company to dinner & supper, viz, Colonels Manley & Douglas, Captains Quale,[36] Gold,[37] Hayter[38] & Dr Irwin.
>
> 11 June. Had a very restless night, did not get up till between 11 and 12 o'clock. I was very ill all the day and had great difficulty to sit up.
>
> 12 June. Sent for Dr Irwin, who says I have had a good deal of fever with most violent pains in all my bones.
>
> 14 June. Am still very unwell, and in such pain that I can get no sleep in the night.
>
> 18 June. I took last night 40 drops of laudanum but could get no rest. The night before I took 60 drops of ether without any effect. Was in violent pain this morning.
>
> 20 June. Rode out on horseback & though I did not go far, I was not aware how weak I was, for when I came home I was exceedingly unwell.

---

31. The oldest boy.
32. About £2.50 per pound today.
33. About £3.50 today.
34. About £35 today.
35. Equivalent to about £50 today!
36. Captain Lieutenant John Quayle Royal Artillery (Kane 661); he died on 13 June 1810.
37. Captain Lieutenant Charles Gold Royal Artillery (Kane 718; he died at Leamington in 1827.
38. Captain Lieutenant George Hayter Royal Engineers.

23 June. John & William Douglas came and staid the day with us; the latter goes to the same school with Henry Rogers and where James [Fraser] is to go after the holidays.

1 July. The regiment mustered today.

3 July. Today my mare came up from Stafford. I sent Mackintosh the gardener upon a horse to Coventry & he led her from there. He set off from here on the 28 June in the afternoon and left Coventry early on 1 July.

4 July. Had a letter from George dated 22 May, he was very well.

5 July. General Pattison came here today, when the whole regiment were under arms at 2 o'clock; he afterwards saw his own battalion the 4th.

7 July Sunday. Had my mare blooded, about 2 quarts taken away. Two Miss Huddlestone's, Miss & William Douglas, Mr Baynes Cadet,[39] a nephew of Mrs Phipps.

11 July. Received a very large packet of letters from George &c by one of the soldiers, the letters were dated in April. The fleet have had a very long voyage, so that I have had a letter by the packet dated 18 days after these. Had my mare began to be broke today, she threw herself twice upon her back after rearing right up, so that I was afraid she would have hurt herself, she cut her two hind fetlocks. The fall did her good as she was much quieter after it. Hay is £5 5s a load & oats £2 2s per quarter. Bread is risen to 9¼ d the Quartern loaf.

15 July. Came on duty as Quarter Master of the Week. Wrote letter to Mr Stride, attorney in London, in answer to one from him informing me that Lieutenant Hugh Fraser had filed his bill in Chancery against John & myself on account of Mrs Grant's money.

17 July. Went to Town to consult with the lawyer about the answer to the bill in Chancery &c. Took James [Fraser] to Greenwich & left him there to have two of his teeth taken out.

The first letter now extant from George in Martinique spoke of the inheritance they had all shared in following the death of Mrs Wilkes and his double pay, being on the Staff. He was evidently very uncomfortable with the slave trade.

39. Gentleman Cadet Henry Baynes Royal Artillery (Kane 1092); he died at Guernsey in 1844.

Letter from George Unett to Miss [Fanny] Unett, Mr Ward's, Acton Hill[40] near Stafford.

Saint Pierre [Martinique], 20 July 1799

My dear Fanny,
The last letter I received from you was dated 1 March; I am in daily expectation of the second June packet and hope that will bring me another. I wrote to you 29 April and 22 June. The first June packet which arrived a few days ago, brought me letters from [Richard] Wilkes, Bessy [Elizabeth] and Mrs Burne. Our money has certainly turned out full as much or more than we could expect, I had made it out about £50 a year[41] and Wilke's sends me word, it will be £60 15[s] per annum.[42] We shall all be so rich we shall not know what to do with our money. I am already beginning to fix upon some farm that would suit me, thinking myself a man of such consequence as to be able to purchase any estate I may fix upon. Something like old Unett, whose greatest delight as he said, was to purchase '*goud lond che-ap*'. Elizabeth already fancies herself so rich, that she is contriving all manner of ways to get rid of some of her cash, and not content with what she can lay out at Greenwich, she is endeavouring to persuade me to assist her in this country, by getting a portrait of my *most beautiful face* painted and sending it [to] her. She says, as she is now the richest of the family, she can afford it. The painting alone would cost her £10[43] in this country and perhaps not a good likeness then & when it got home it would come to a good deal more to have it set. Altogether it would be much more than the thing is worth and as I am not much afraid of leaving it here, to be picked at by the cockroaches and land crabs. Why, she may have as many copies made of it as she likes for an old song, in England.

This is the last fleet from the Leeward Islands (which you call them at home) until the hurricane months are over, so that there will not be the first of the month packet, which I shall write by very regularly.

I think I have •mentioned to you before that my pay is about double here to what it was in England, yet our messing and everything is so much dearer, that it is with great difficulty I can make the ends of the year meet. But I am determined not to spend more than my pay, but reserve the other for the keep of a horse and [a] couple of dogs on old England, and I trust when I leave the West Indies that I shall be able to say (what I am afraid few military men from hence can)

40. Acton Hill lies 3km south-east of Stafford, near Walton on the Hill.
41. About £2,500 per annum today.
42. Around £3,000 per annum today.
43. About £600 today.

that I left it, not owing a sixpence; or to express it in this country's phase, '*not owing a black dog*'. A dog is a small piece of copper money, about the size of a farthing. Eighteen of these dogs are a quarter dollar, which is called a Moco or by the negroes '*a Damned Moes*', from it having two sides cut, something similar to the teeth in a saw, which is the case with all the negroes that are purchased from the Moco nation, somewhere on the African coast.[44] All their teeth are sawed in this manner when they are young. Cargoes of some hundreds come in here every week and I have been several times to see them sold; though it is the most disgraceful sight to humanity, possibly to be conceived, and nothing but having lived a number of years in this country and being so much accustomed to these sights, could reconcile it. You will see French women going amongst them, with the same indifference, as though they were purchasing a horse or a dog. This letter will arrive in the height of the shooting season and I had intended to say a great deal to Mr Ward about it, but I have somehow or other got into this long rigmyrole [*sic*] story of Mocos and negroes &c &c and have almost filled up my letter with it. [Richard] Wilkes in his letter talks of coming in for a little shooting this year, I hope it will be a great deal, for I am sure it would be of service to his complaint. I should like to be with you all for a few days. What a fagging I would give them both, up some of the large ploughed fields belonging to *Sir Yethart*,[45] but I should certainly make a bargain with Mr Ward, not to begin his story first, for I remember it was in vain for me to say anything after he had told his tale. From the very superior skill and judgement *I* displayed the last day we were coursing together at [Chantley?], I hope he has never since *presumed* to say, that he is anything equal to me, in finding a hare sitting, he cannot forget my finding one he had baulked, no! no! after *my* glorious achievements on that memorable day, he never must enter the Lists with me again, about coursing. Though after all I must confess that my good fortune was chiefly owing to my being at that time very much *down in the mouth*, and not able to *hold my head up*. I never enjoyed better health and my letter will prove, I am in good spirits. Remember me kindly to all and believe me your affectionate brother G[eorge] W Unett.
NB I have written today to [Richard] Wilkes, Bessy & John.

22 July. Today we had in orders an augmentation to the regiment of half a battalion.[46]

44. Mount Moco is the highest peak in modern-day Angola.
45. Presumably he refers to Thomas Anson of Shugborough Hall who owned most of the land around Acton Hill.
46. The formation of the 6th Battalion and raising of four more companies (to total six companies) was authorized on 16 July 1799.

24 July. At 11 o'clock Mrs U[nett] set off in a chaise to take Harry Rogers (who has been staying his holidays with us) and James to school for the first time. Mrs U[nett] took Mary Anne & Alexander [Fraser] with her for a ride.

25 July. We went to see the Woolwich Voluntiers[47] [*sic*] have their Colours presented to them by Mrs Thomas.

30 July. Was up this morning between 5 & 6 o'clock to march Major Burton's company[48] off to Ringmerc[49] in Sussex. I am Captain Lieutenant in the company, but my being Quarter Master prevents my marching with it.

Little Frances was suddenly very unwell, it would not end well.

1 August. Little Frances was so unwell that we sent for Dr Irwin.

2 August. We were engaged to dine at Mr Thomson's, but sent an excuse on account of little Frances being exceedingly ill. Dr Irwin was here twice, in the morning I sent to Greenwich for Dr Mills,[50] but he could not come today.

3 August. Doctors Mills, Rollo & Irwin were here this morning, who agreed that Frances had water in her head & was exceedingly ill. The latter came again in the evening & found her much worse. She has today been quite insensible to everybody & everything.

4 August Sunday. Doctors Mills & Irwin came again this morning & contrary to their expectations found little Frances a good deal better. Last night I took 6 grains of Calomel having a touch of my old complaint in my stomach.

5 August. Was up between 5 & 6 o'clock, when about 400 artillery [men] marched to Gravesend to embark on an expedition, another company was to join them from Canterbury, Colonel Whitworth[51] has the command. Frances still very ill.

6 August. Dr Mills came again with Dr Irwin. Little Frances, Dr Mills thought much the same as on Sunday.

---

47. The Deptford and Woolwich Volunteers; their Colonel was Sir Francis Hartwell.
48. Major John Burton Royal Artillery (Kane 555) commanded No.1 Company of the 4th Battalion. He died on the Isle of Wight in 1830.
49. Ringmer lies about 10km north-east of Brighton.
50. Mr Mills would appear to be a civilian doctor.
51. Lieutenant Colonel Sir Francis Whitworth Royal Artillery (Kane 469) died in London 26 January 1805. He commanded the artillery in the Anglo/Russian expedition to Holland in August 1799.

7 August. Dr Irwin came & found Frances very ill, she continued getting worse until 6 o'clock in the evening when she died. She had suffered great agony with convulsions &c all the day. Her left side she had lost the use of ever since Friday, so that had it pleased God she should recover, she must have been a cripple in all probability for life & perhaps by the affection [*sic*] on the brain, she might have been an idiest [idiot] too. We may therefore be thankful to God that he has released her from all her sufferings.

11 August Sunday. At 10 o'clock this morning, poor little Frances was buried in the family vault with her father & mother at Plumstead, she was 2 years 5 months & a day old. A young gentleman a Mr Rhodes,[52] nephew to Mrs Hartwell of Plymouth Dock brought us a letter from her; he is coming to be a Cadet.

19 August. Had a letter from George in the West Indies, who was very well. The cow calved this morning.

21 August. Had company to dinner, viz, Major Horndon,[53] Captains Waller,[54] Archibald Drummond,[55] Phipps & Dr Macculoch [McCulloch].

28 August. Went in a chaise with Captain Scottowe [Skottowe] down to Greenhithe to dine onboard his ship the *Bridgewater* East Indiaman.[56]

5 September. This morning at 5 o'clock four companies of artillery embarked yesterday evening in the Warren for the same place.[57]

A letter from George to Elizabeth related the 'capture' of Surinam from the Dutch.

To Miss [Elizabeth] Unett, Mrs Godwin's Croom's Hill, Greenwich, Kent

Saint Pierre, [Martinique] 12 September 1799

My dear Elizabeth,
I wrote to Mrs [Ann] Unett on the 3rd of this month, by the *Elizabeth*, a Guinea ship that was going to England, and it being so good an

52. Mr Rhodes does not appear in Kane. Quite possibly Charles Rhodes who became an officer in the Royal Engineers.
53. Major William Horndon Royal Artillery (Kane 557); resigned in November 1800.
54. Captain Lieutenant Charles Waller Royal Artillery (Kane 696); retired in June 1823.
55. Captain Archibald Drummond 16th Foot is the officer of this name in the Army List.
56. The *Bridgewater* was built in 1786 and was commanded by Captain John Skottowe 1796–9. The ship foundered in 1805.
57. These would appear to be Mudge's (1Bn 5 Company), Bowater's (1Bn 7 Company), Riou's (5Bn 8 Company) and Stehelin's (5Bn 10 Company).

opportunity, there is no doubt of her receiving my letter, since which we have had nothing but rejoicings, a vessel having arrived from Cork, which has brought us the account of Lord Keith's victory over the French fleet and of his having taken nine sail of the line and sunk seven; as you may suppose, we are all exceedingly anxious for the arrival of the packet, by which we hope to get all the particulars of the engagement.[58] Indeed, we *poor officers* are the only people that suffer from these victories, a few more will ruin us all, for each one is attended with a dinner which costs £3 14s 8d Sterling[59] and no sooner was the dinner over for the surrender of Surinam,[60] than comes another for drubbing these French scoundrels. It is really quite a tax and being a military man, you are in some measure obliged to attend them. The particulars respecting the surrender of Surinam, you will have long before this arrives, as a vesell [*sic*] was dispatched home immediately with the intelligence. We expect the Commander in Chief &c &c back again in about ten days. The town of Paramarrabo [Paramaribo], or some *out of the way Dutch name*, at Surinam, is described as being very pleasant and well built, the streets very wide and some of them a mile and a half long, foot paths with rows of orange and other fruit trees planted on each side and they [are] paved with a white flat tile (which by the bye, from the reflection of a burning hot sun, must make it very prejudicial to the eyes). Every vessel on its arrival there pays a fruit tax, by which they are entitled to gather as much fruit from these trees as they may want for the use of the crew, all this will sound very pleasant to you at home and I dare say, you would like to gather some of these delicious fruits, which I remember to have heard so much praised, but depend upon it, there is nothing here equal to the commonest fruit at home, even the pine[apple] which are in great abundance, has very little flavor [*sic*]. The town is said to be much larger than St Pierre, though I can scarcely credit it, and the mouth of the river very strongly defended by Fort Amsterdam[61] mounted with 100 pieces of heavy ordnance. The following is the yearly produce, coffee 1,400,000 lbs, cocoa 800,000 lbs, cotton 18,000 bags, sugar 18,000 hogsheads. All the letters I have seen, say they are heartily tired of staying there, it is so abominably hot, with not a breath of wind stirring. I have been telling you a long story, when I might have filled up my paper in a

58. A false rumour.

59. About £200 today.

60. The Dutch island of Surinam surrendered on 22 August to a force under the command of Lieutenant General Trigge; however, it was a subterfuge, the governor and others having secretly agreed to give up the island for a huge sum of money.

61. Fort Nieuw Amsterdam still exists, although very grown over.

much better way, for you will be sure of getting a much better and correcter [*sic*] account from the public papers.

'*Will you hab any sugar barley Sir*', that is all the English, a Mulatto man[62] (who has just been to my door, with a tray full of sweetmeats) can speak, it is a curious circumstance, that this fellow never asks you for any money, meet him where you will and take from him as much as you like, it is all the same; but I fancy he is more *knave* than *fool*, for though I know many Englishmen that take from him whenever they meet him, yet I observe he never allows a *Frenchman* to put his hand into his basket, without the *ready rhino, he knows them too well.* You pay him anything you like, but of course he finds it answers, what he loses by one's not paying him, he makes up by another giving him too much. I wish I could fill my letter full of *sugar barley*, for little *Alesander* and Annie [Fraser] &c to make them not forget *Unco Daws*.[63]

Poor Mrs Beech[64] is again brought to bed of a dead child, this I fancy makes the fifth or sixth, and it never will be otherwise so long as she remains in this climate, it is determined to send her home, so soon as she is in a family way again, for though she has been so many years in the West Indies (now nearly eleven) she suffers as much as one just from home and never is in good health. A man must certainly be mad to bring his wife to this country, if he can any ways avoid it.

I see by the papers that General Martin is dead[65] and I hear that Captain Wilson[66] is obliged to quit the regiment in consequence of the business between him and Major Armstrong of the 11th Regiment,[67] two steps for me. That goes but a short way to 80 [steps], which is what I want to give me a Captain Lieutenancy. What is become of Captain Godfrey [?], he has never written me a word since I left Woolwich. Mrs [Ann] Unett tells me that Miss Phipps was either married or very near being so, wonders will never cease. I had always set her down as an housekeeper for her brother and thought she never would like anyone half as much as him. In some former letters I wrote Mrs [Ann] Unett I asked her to send me out several things, but I forget what they were, so that I cannot be in *very great* want of them and if these victories come so fast, one upon the other,

62. A term for a person of mixed race.

63. Presumably for '*Uncle George*'.

64. There is no officer named Beech shown in the West Indies.

65. Lieutenant General William Martin Royal Artillery (Kane 109) died in London on 12 July 1799.

66. Captain George Wilson Royal Artillery (Kane 475) transferred to the Invalids in 1802 but still gained promotion up to General. He died at Brussels in 1841.

67. Major Andrew Armstrong 11th Foot.

in the manner they have done lately, we fancy in this part of the world, it must bring about a peace and then I shall be coming home, so that I wish you would tell [Richard] Wilkes, except he has an excellent opportunity, not to trouble himself about them. Shirts were what I was most in want of, but I am now pretty well supplied, having made up a piece of linnen [*sic*] and purchased some more at the sale of poor Captain Charles Cameron's effects of the 43rd Regiment, who was shot in a duel here a short time since. Fanny writes me that poor old Crop[68] is still lame and never likely to recover. I wish the next time you write to her, you would desire them to shoot him, for he is only living in misery and a great expense to Mr Ward. I had much rather hear of that, than of his obliged to tail out the evening of his days under some hard master, he has been a witness to some of the happiest days of my love and I never could bear to hear of his being worked hard now. Remember me to Mr Skottowe &c &c &c and love to my aunt and all at Woolwich and believe me dear Elizabeth, your affectionate brother, George W Unett. All's well.

6 October Sunday. Brother Tom & self, set off in the coach for Birmingham, where we arrived about 4 o'clock.

Richard and John again made the journey to the property in Warwickshire.

10 October. Brother John & self rode to Warwick & so to my farm.

12 October. Brother John had his christening this day.[69] Mr Unett of Stone, Miss Letty Unett[70] & myself were sponsors.

He was back in Woolwich in four days.

13 October Sunday. Set off in the coach at 7 o'clock this evening, travelled all night & got home about 8 o'clock this evening [14 October].

28 October. Came on duty as Quarter Master of the week.

12 November. Went to London & attended the lawyer by appointment about Mrs Grant's [Fraser's] money.[71]

68. His horse.
69. The son of John Wilkes christened this day was also John.
70. Letitia Unett was the only daughter of John Wilkes Unett.
71. This would appear to be a simple error by Richard as it would appear he was referring to the money bequested by his sister Ann Grant Fraser to her children.

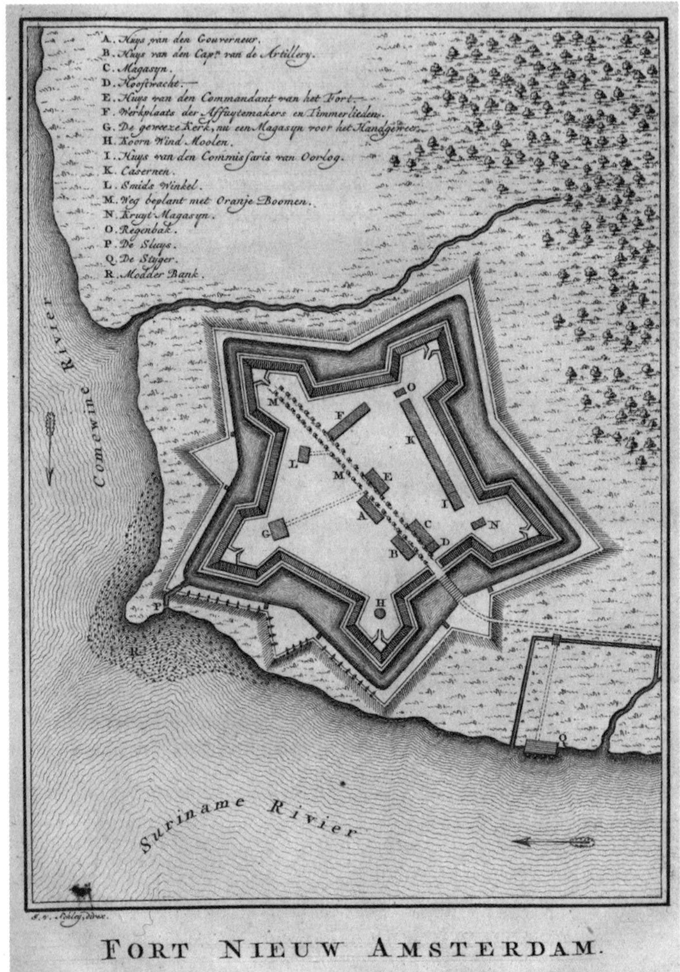

14 November. We had company to tea & supper, viz, Captain & Mrs Adye, Captains Gold & Wulfe, Colonel & Miss Huddleston's & Captain Newhouse[72] were engaged.

2 December. The regiment mustered this morning.

9 December. Dined at the Mess. Came on duty as Quarter Master of the week.

11 December. At sale upon Shooters Hill lately at late Mr Stanley's. Port wine sold by auction at 3 guineas per dozen, madeira at 6½ guineas and rum at 9 guineas per dozen.

72. Captain Lieutenant Charles Newhouse Royal Artillery (Kane 707); he died at Newick in Sussex in 1845.

20 December. We had company to dinner & supper, viz, Colonels Lawson, Manley, Fage,[73] Dr Irwin, Major Scott, Captain Charles Godfrey & Lieutenant Wilmot.[74] General Lloyd[75] & Captain Salmon[76] were asked.

21 December. James [Fraser] came from school today for the holidays with Harry Rogers who is to go for part of them to Captain Meredith's[77] & the other part to Colonel Douglas & to us.

Richard recorded how expensive everything had become in the freezing weather.

24 December. Owing to the frost, coals are got to £4 4s & upwards per chaldron. Potatoes are 3 shillings & 4d per bushel, two bushels make an hundred weight. Turkeys at Greenwich today are as high as sixteen shillings a piece. One turkey was sold yesterday in Leadenhall Market[78] for twenty-seven shillings![79] Fresh butter is sixteen pence halfpenny per lb and salt butter one shilling & 2d. There was beef in the London markets last week which sold as high as 7s 6d per stone of 8 lbs. Eggs are 3d apiece. The price of bread fell last week ¾d, but it is expected to rise again as today in London. The only thing just now which is not dear is sugar, what we gave 1s 3d per lb for a few months ago, we can now buy for 10d per lb. The quantity of forage which is consumed by the horse artillery & the Commissary corps at present at Woolwich, is 150 quarters of oats and 20 waggon loads of hay per week. Oats are £2 16s per quarter & hay is about £6 6s & upwards for a cart load or eighteen hundred weight, so that the Board of Ordnance pay £420 per week for oats alone[80] and about half that sum for hay without reckoning straw &c.

27 December. *Old Jock* my brother George's dog, which he left in my charge, died today.

---

73. Colonel Edward Fage Royal Artillery (Kane 395); he died at Greenwich on 2 September 1809.
74. 1st Lieutenant Edward Wilmot Royal Artillery (Kane 912); he died at Hastings in 1832.
75. Major General Vaughan Lloyd Royal Artillery (Kane 241); he died at Woolwich 16 June 1817.
76. Captain Lieutenant George Salmon Royal Artillery (Kane 655) died in London June 1848.
77. Captain Lieutenant David Meredith Royal Artillery (Kane 649); he died at Halifax, Nova Scotia on 4 March 1809.
78. Leadenhall Market is one of the oldest markets in London, being established in the fourteenth century.
79. About £80 today.
80. £22,000 today.

28 December. I saw today at the Barracks Butcher's Shop, some parts of an ox which was sold in Smithfield Market last week for one hundred guineas![81] The tongue was sold for one guinea and some prime pieces went as high as two shillings a pound!!!

30 December. Had a slight touch of the pain in my stomach.

1800

1 January. The regiment was mustered today.

17 January. Today being James [Fraser's] birthday.

18 January. Had a letter from George dated 3 November 1799.

There still appear to have been issues with John Grant Fraser's will.

29 January. Wrote to Mr Alexander Grant, Edinburgh, & sent him Captain Fraser's probate copy of will.

3 February. Came of duty as Quarter Master of the week.

4 February. Rode over to Greenwich to pay Mr Best's bill for the funeral of little Frances [Fraser].

5 February. Was in the office writing from 11 o'clock till 4 o'clock as it was the packet day for letters. Wrote a very long letter to Lieutenant Alexander Chisholm in Canada, another to George [Unett] and a third to Mr John Brown, Halifax; besides regimental letters to Quebec, West Indies & Newfoundland as Captain Franklin is away.

7 February. We had company to dinner & supper, viz, Major, Mrs & Maria Scott, Captains Salmon, Fisher[82] & Walker.[83] Captain Godfrey was engaged but did not return from London.

8 February. The Duke of York was down today to see some experiments with riffle [*sic*] barrels. He came in forty minutes from the Horse Guards & said he intended to ride back again in thirty-five minutes.[84]

81. Over £5,000 today.
82. Captain Lieutenant George Bulteel Fisher Royal Artillery (Kane 677); he died at Woolwich in 1834.
83. Captain Frederick Walker Royal Artillery (Kane 772); he died in London in 1827.
84. The direct distance between the two is 11.4 miles (18.4km).

11 February. At 9 o'clock this morning attended the funeral of Lieutenant Cashell[85] of [the] 4th Battalion, he died of a decline aged 24 years. Colonel Blomefield, Dr Rollo, two other officers & myself [attended]; he was buried in Woolwich churchyard.

12 February. Lord Howe (late Sir William Howe)[86] was down today to pass some men for invalids.

24 February. Had 9 dozen of wine in from Mr Best at Greenwich, as it is said another duty is going to be put on of 7 or 8 shillings a dozen. The duty on wine is not to take place for the present.

1 March. The regiment mustered today.

3 March. Came on duty for the week.

8 March. We had company to tea & supper viz, the three Miss Huddleston's, Lieutenant & Mrs Deacon[87] and Lieutenants Wallace,[88] Mercer,[89] Durnford, Captain Walker.

12 March. This day was kept as a General Fast throughout the country.[90] Pigeons are 2s 9d apiece!!

17 March. Went in the evening to the Mess club, came home when they sat down to supper as I never eat any. Butter 1s 6d per lb, salt butter 1s 4d per lb, pork 9d per lb, bread 1s 4¼d the Quartern loaf.

9 April. Butter is now 1s 7d per lb, mutton chops 9d per lb, we gave on Monday in Leadenhall Market 10s for a couple of fowls.

10 April. Had in the evening a slight touch of my complaint in my stomach; took just before I went to bed about a spoonful of brandy.

11 April. Have no return of the pain in my stomach.

15 April. Had a letter from George dated the 10 March, he was in good health.

---

85. 1st Lieutenant Samuel Cashell Royal Artillery (Kane 838) died at Woolwich on 7 February 1800.

86. General William Howe was the younger brother of Admiral Richard Howe, 4th Viscount Howe and later 1st Lord Howe, who died in 1799; on which the title of Lord became extinct, but he became the 5th Viscount Howe.

87. 1st Lieutenant Henry Deacon Royal Artillery (Kane 873); he resigned on 15 October 1807.

88. 1st Lieutenant Peter Wallace Royal Artillery (Kane 983); he died in London in 1864.

89. Alexander Cavalie Mercer was promoted to 2nd Lieutenant on 20 December 1799.

90. General (national) Fasts were promulgated regularly by kings at times of poor harvest, drought or disease, as a public day of fast and humiliation, so that the entire nation humbled themselves before God to obtain pardon of their sins and to remove the current threat, in whatever way it had manifested itself.

18 April. This day Captains Wulfe & Robe[91] with 20 gunners of my detachment embarked for Quebec. My eyes very unwell today.

19 April. My eyes still the same, called at Dr Irwin's but did not see him.

20 April Sunday. Called at the hospital, when Dr's Rollo & Irwin advised me to go home again immediately & the latter said he would call upon me, which he did & gave me 10 grains of calomel. He brought with him his instruments to cup me, but my pulse were [*sic*] so low that he did not think it prudent to take any blood from me. He advised me to leave off meat for a few days & to live very low.[92]

21 April. The dizziness before my eyes not quite so bad.

25 April. I went to the parade this morning, my eyes are got well. I have never tasted meat or drank anything but Imperial[93] since this day week.

27 April. Came on guard &c in the Warren. As there are so few captains at Woolwich, now the Quarter Masters are to mount the Guard with the others until further orders. In going my rounds between 12 & 1 o'clock the rain was so heavy that I got much wet.

28 April. Every necessary is now so extravagantly dear that a riot is expected every hour in London. Beef is 1s & 1s 3d per lb. Rump steaks 1s 6d per lb, mutton in Woolwich is 1s per lb, fresh butter 1s 7½d per 1b. A butcher in Woolwich that used to kill forty sheep and upwards a week, now only kills five or six, the times are dreadful.

1 May. The regiment had a field day this morning.

5 May. I saw some cherries in Covent Garden Market today & upon enquiring the price learnt they were £1 11s 6d per lb.[94]

9 May. Came on Guard today.

15 May. I was engaged to dine at the Mess but came home after the parade at eight o'clock.

18 May. Came on Guard.

26 May. Came on duty as Quarter Master of the week. Mr Barry from the West Indies called upon me when I showed him the Warren; he brought us letters [dated] last autumn from George.

91. Captain Sir William Robe Royal Artillery (Kane 654); he died at Woolwich 5 November 1820.
92. Eat little and then only bland foods.
93. Still water.
94. About £80 in today's terms!

> 4 June. Came on Guard. There was a very handsome display of fireworks at 9 o'clock.
>
> 14 June. The chickens are now selling for 7s 6d a couple, we gave yesterday for a couple of ducks 8s. Bread is 1s 5½d the Quartern loaf.
>
> 17 June. Came on Guard.
>
> 21 June. James [Fraser] & Harry Rogers came from school for the holidays. I have had at times lately pains in my head and Dr Irwin has ordered me to leave off my single glass of wine & water, which I used to take after dinner. I have therefore tasted nothing but water for these three weeks.
>
> 26 June. Have had for these four days a touch of the pain in my stomach, with headache.

Richard was off to a camp on Bagshot Heath.

> 30 June. Set off in Captain Godfrey's chaise with him to the camp at Bagshot,[95] where we arrived about 3 o'clock.
>
> 1 July. This morning there was a field day of three brigades, amounting to between 5 & 6,000 men. The king, queen &c were present.
>
> 2 July. Left camp at 11 o'clock. There were about 20,000 altogether encamped. Harry Rogers was with me as I took him to join his regiment, he having an Ensign's commission in the 85th Regiment.[96] He came home with me having got leave again to the 14th instant.
>
> 6 July. Had a letter from George.
>
> 8 July. Came on duty as Quarter Master for the week.
>
> 13 July Sunday. Harry Rogers went this morning to Windsor to be present on the 14th, when the Returns for the fortnight are given in.
>
> 14 July. Yesterday afternoon, one of the clerks in the office hung himself with his silk handkerchief in a tree not far from my house. He had been absent without leave for three days & I suppose his fear of punishment made him commit the crime.

95. Bagshot Heath was regularly used in the summer months for large-scale encampments.
96. Henry Rogers was already enrolled in the Armagh Militia. He was appointed as Ensign without purchase in the 85th on 18 March 1800 and became a Lieutenant in the 85th Foot by purchase on 28 August 1800. He transferred to the 2nd West India Regiment as a Captain on 20 July 1805 and transferred as a Captain into the 6th Foot on 26 March 1807, serving at Walcheren, the Peninsula (wounded at the Bidassoa and Orthez) and North America. He became a Major in the 6th Foot on 12 August 1819.

17 July. After dinner Harry Roger's came back, having got six months leave to continue at school.

23 July. Harry Rogers went to a school in London, which was fixed yesterday.

30 July. About ten days ago at Cirencester Market in Gloucestershire, oats were sold £4 4s a quarter. Owing to the great crops and the fine harvest weather they are down at *£1 11s 6d.*

9 August. Came on duty.

25 August. Had a letter from George dated 26 June, he was then in good health. Captain Charles Godfrey came in from camp this evening and as he had not got his baggage, he drank tea, supped & slepped [*sic*] at my house.

30 August. Came on Guard.

7 September Sunday. Came on Guard. The price of bread about a fortnight ago had fallen to 1s 2d the Quartern loaf, it is now risen to 1s 3d, there have been riots in many places in consequence.

12 September. Had a letter from George dated 17 July, he was then in good health & speaks of coming home soon. The newspapers are full of riots in different parts of the country, viz Nottingham, Coventry, Birmingham, Poole &c on account of the extravagant & shameful price of all the necessaries of life.

15 September. Our man servant Wilson has been gone a week to Scotland to see his relations, so that we are without a servant.

16 September. Came on Guard.

17 September. For these few days there have been riots in London on account of the dearness of bread.

20 September. This evening there was a disturbance in Woolwich on account of the high price of every article of life. The horse artillery were parading the streets all the night, some windows were broken, but nothing serious happened.

29 September. Came on duty as Quarter Master of the week.

3 October. Had a letter from George.

4 October. We had company to dinner & supper, viz, Captain & Mrs Gold, Captain & Mrs Eveleigh,[97] Mrs Meredith and Captain Charles Godfrey.

97. Captain Lieutenant Henry Evelegh Royal Artillery (Kane 747); he died on the Isle of Wight in 1859.

13 October. Came on Guard. At a confectioner's shop in Piccadilly they ask a shilling & eight pence apiece for pears!!! And two shillings apiece for peaches!!!

22 October. Our man servant returned last night from Scotland. Bread rises again tomorrow to 1s 4½d the Quartern loaf. I yesterday in Town asked the price of pork, the loin was a shilling a pound!!

23 October. The regiment had a field day. Came on Guard.

24 October. I had the rheumatism so violently last night in my left leg & thigh that I never once closed my eyes all the night. I have had it flying about me lately. We were engaged to spend the evening at Major Scott's, but my leg &c pained me so much I was obliged to send an excuse.

25 October. Last night again I was in so much pain that I never closed my eyes though I took forty drops of laudanum. Sent for Dr Irwin who has given me to take 12 grains of Dover's Powders[98] and two of Dr James Analeptic pills.[99]

26 October. Had a good night, did not get up till between 1 & 2 o'clock.

27 October. Had a good night having taken the pills & powders &c.

31 October. Was not so well today.

1 November. This morning early I was in most violent pain &c in my belly. At 8 o'clock I took a table spoonful & half of Castor Oil. At times during the morning I had frequent pains, but they became better towards night.

2 November Sunday. Found myself very well.

5 November. A detachment of several officers & 100 men embarked at 1 o'clock at the Warren Wharf to the West Indies.

9 November. About 1 o'clock [pm] there was one of the most tremendous storms I ever remembered; indeed, I heard one of our officers say that he did not recollect such another since the violent hurricane at Barbadoes in 1780.[100] It lasted about two hours.

98. Dover's Powder was a traditional medicine used for colds and fevers by inducing sweating. It was in use up until the 1960s.

99. Dr James Analeptic Pills were sold as a remedy for rheumatisms, indigestion, lack of appetite, giddiness in the head and flatulence.

100. The Great Hurricane of Barbados in 1780 is the deadliest Atlantic hurricane on record, with an estimated 22,000 people being killed.

> 10 November. The storm yesterday has done an astonishing deal of damage. There is scarcely a house that has not lost some tiles, chimneys &c. A number of houses & out-houses are completely down; a great number of trees are blown up [*sic*] by the roots and wherever there was any old wooden garden paling it is entirely laid down.
>
> 20 November. Last week a cow keeper at Woolwich gave for four cows out of a drove that were going over Shooters Hill one hundred guineas![101] And a Mr Harden, a farmer here gave fifty guineas for two others.
>
> 22 November. Have got the rheumatism in my left thigh & arm.
>
> 25 November. Came on Guard.
>
> 5 December. Came on Guard.

Richard went to apply for a position in the Horse Artillery for George.

> 11 December. Rode to Blenden to ask General Pattison to make application for my brother to get into the Horse Artillery, which he promised to do.

Richard underwent some form of electric shock treatment for the numbness in his arms. He also recorded a highway robbery nearby, he with some artillerymen captured them.

> 13 December. Went to the hospital & was electrified, having a numbness in both my hands.[102] About 10 o'clock am a chaise with three gentlemen going between Blackheath & Shooters Hill was stopped by three footpads with crapes[103] and pistols & robbed of two gold & one silver watch and upwards of £80 in money & notes. The alarm was given, the horse & foot artillery were sent in every direction & in about an hour they were all three taken. I saw them searched, they had no less than six brace of pistols, all except one loaded with ball & slugs; the watches, crapes, money &c found upon them.[104]
>
> 17 December. Rode to General Pattison's as he had appointed me to wait upon him today at one o'clock. He showed me a letter that he had in answer to his application for my brother to get into the horse

101. About £6,000 today.
102. Probably based on Galvani's and Volta's experiments.
103. Black silk masks, used to disguise themselves.
104. The Annual Register records that an eyewitness to the robbery saw the robbers retire into a wood between Charlton and Woolwich; he then informed the commandant of Woolwich, who sent out horse artillery to patrol the skirts of the wood, while the foot artillery drove through the wood. They were apprehended without resistance.

artillery. He is to be appointed on his arrival from the West Indies. Bread is risen to 1s 7½d the Quartern.

20 December. Came on Guard.

1801

2 January. Came on guard.

6 January. Wrote a long letter to Colonel Laye in the West Indies.

8 January. Had the pain in my stomach.

9 January. Took some Calomel last night & did not go out all day. A Bombardier who is with a regiment with Battalion guns at Shrewsbury, sent me a brace of hares.

18 January. Have had a bowel complaint for these two days, took some Calomel.

21 January. Rode to Town; called at the bank to receive the half year's dividends upon £1,000 belonging to the children, but could not get it, as there was no subpoena put on it by Chancery at the [laws]suit of (that I could almost say rascal) Hugh Fraser their uncle, who so far from assisting them, does everything he can to ruin them by law. At this time therefore, the three children do not receive the annual income of a single sixpence from their father; and was it not for their poor mother's fortune, which happened luckily to be settled upon them, they would have had nothing to support them but their pension of £10 per annum each.

I have had for five or six days a bowel complaint which has plagued me a good deal; this morning in London I was in very great pain, which lasted till I came home to a late dinner. I had difficulty in riding home.

22 January. Went to the Warren, though my bowels are still out of order.

23 January. Captain Evelegh is gone upon leave for a month, so that I must attend all the parades as Adjutant.

24 January. The Quartern loaf within these three weeks has been as high as 1s 9½d the Quartern, fresh butter 1s 8d per lb, veal this week was 1s 3d per lb, pork above 1s per lb. For some peas to fatten a pig I gave a few days ago no less than 11s a bushel!!!

26 January. The Public Funds are falling very much on account of this Northern Confederacy between Russia, Sweden & Denmark against this country.[105]

105. The formation of the League of Armed Neutrality, which threatened British trade routes through the Baltic.

29 January. Walked a good deal in Town so that when I came home I was attacked with the complaint in my bowels.

2 February. Came on duty as Quarter Master of the week.

12 February. Borrowed Major Scott's gig & went to London to my lawyer & took with me all the vouchers for the money, which the late Captain [John] Fraser paid away as Executor to his elder brother. This business arranging has cost me a great many, many evenings.

23 February. *I have dreamed that George was married to Miss Twiss.*[106]

11 March. Came on Guard.

13 March. Rode to Dartford to see James [Fraser].

16 March. Came on duty as Quarter Master of the week. Last week at Orford Market wheat sold for the enormous price of *28s a bushel!!!!* All kinds of meat is now 10d per lb, veal cutlets as high as 1s 6d per lb.

27 March. Meat is getting enormously dear. Veal cutlets *1s 6d & 1s 8d* per lb, beef & mutton scarcely any under *a shilling per pound!!!!*

28 March. On Wednesday last, the 25th, the three footpads which were taken by the soldiers on the 13 December last for robbing a chaise, with three gentlemen it, were hanged on Shooters Hill.[107] They were old offenders, though one of them was only 19 years of age & another 22 years old. They confessed having shot several people on the road &c. It is supposed there were not less than fifty thousand people to see them executed. Six of the artillery soldiers who took them, went over to Maidstone to prosecute them, had their expenses paid them & received each a £10 note.[108]

2 April. Fowls are now 11s a couple, asparagus 17s a hundred, cucumbers 2s 6d apiece, pigeons 2s each. Mutton and beef none under 10½d or 11d a lb, veal cutlets 1s 4d per lb. There are dreadful riots on account of the dearness of provisions.

4 April. Had a letter from George dated 16 February, he was very well.

---

106. Presumably he refers to Miss Katherine Maria Twiss, daughter of Colonel William Twiss Royal Engineers. However, he could also refer to one of the four daughters of Francis Twiss and Frances Kemble (the former actress Fanny Kemble). Actresses were often viewed as little more than whores at this time.

107. The hanging at Shooters Hill on 25 March actually saw the execution of four men for highway robbery; they were Richard Sheppard, Richard Morley, James Seamans and Patrick Summers.

108. Worth about £500 today.

9 April. Came on Guard.

17 April. Today I received orders to hold myself in readiness to go in a few days to Ireland, to join my company, as by the junction of the Irish with the English artillery I shall get promoted.[109]

18 April. Came on Guard. I went my rounds.

19 April. It has now been notified to me, that I do not go so soon as I expected to Ireland but must wait for further orders.

1 May. The regiment had a field day at 8 o'clock this morning. A few days ago I sold my cow for £9 9s, we had had her ever since we came to this house in September 1797, I then gave £12 for her, but she had a calf with her which I sold a few weeks after for £3 10s, so [by] that reckoning three other calves which I have sold since, viz in 1798 for 18s, in 1799 for £1 3s [&] in 1801 about two months ago for £3 3s, I have been no loser by her & am now very sorry to part with her. I am told I have sold her too cheap.

4 May. Rode to the *Green Man*[110] upon Blackheath to attend the Commissioners of the Income Tax, where I had been summoned, on account of my not returning any income by reason of my being ordered out of the kingdom. They were extremely polite, so I thought it best to make a merit of necessity and returned my income to them whilst there. I was in hopes to have escaped paying it.

6 May. Came on Guard.

8 May. Last night I took a Calomil[e] pill of 8 grains & did not go out today.

Finally Richard had gained his full captaincy. He officially transferred from the Royal Irish Artillery into the Royal Artillery on 18 April 1801 and was given command of No. 8 company in the newly formed 7th Battalion Royal Artillery. This company was already in the West Indies and it is unclear which company he commanded at Woolwich before he was sent out to the West Indies to join them in the autumn.

9 May. Today I was in Orders as Captain of a Company, my commission being dated 18 of April.

11 May. Had a letter from George dated the 23 March, he was then well.

---

109. The Royal Irish Artillery existed as a completely separate arm of the artillery from 1755 when it was formed, until the Act of Union of 1801, when they became part of the 7th Battalion of Royal Artillery.

110. Ye Green Man public house stood where Inverforth House stands today.

> 13 May. Spent the evening at Major Scott's to meet the Godfreys. Mrs U[nett] & Elizabeth declined going, but insisted upon my going as the Godfrey's are to set off very soon to Ireland, Captain John Godfrey[111] being appointed Chief Fire Master in Ireland.
>
> 16 May. Came on Guard.
>
> 22 May. Wrote a long letter to Fanny & inclosed her the half of a £20 note.[112]
>
> 24 May. Poor Mr Thomson died this afternoon between 6 & 7 o'clock; we had sent about 5 o'clock just before I set off in order to acquaint Mrs Godwin how he was; but when we arrived, she had that instant got an account of his death.
>
> 30 May. Mr Thomson was buried at 8 o'clock this morning in the vault which Mrs Godwin made in Plumstead churchyard for all her family. There are already buried in it, General Godwin, Captain & poor Mrs Fraser with their youngest child Frances Elizabeth Fraser & now Mr T[homson].

Around June 1801 George was sent to Curacao. The year before, French troops from Guadeloupe had landed on the island, but the Dutch governor had refused to surrender the island to them. When HMS *Nereide* unwittingly sailed into view on 15 October 1800 while the Dutch and French troops were firing on each other, the Dutch governor promptly surrendered the island to the *Nereide*, who with the crews of three other frigates sent to her aid took formal possession of the island. Captain Walter Tremenheere of the Royal Marines was initially given the post of Lieutenant Governor by Vice Admiral Hugh Seymour, but General Sir Thomas Trigge wanted to replace Tremenheere with Lieutenant Colonel William Hughes 87th Foot. Tremenheere refused to give up his position with the approval of Vice Admiral Hugh Seymour. However, on the death of Seymour in 1801 Trigge successfully installed Hughes as Governor on 1 June 1801 and George Unett was made his Military Secretary. Hughes was superseded by Colonel Arthur Whetham 1st Foot Guards from October 1801 to August 1802, when Hughes was reinstalled and he remained until the island reverted to the Dutch on 13 January 1803. George seems to have remained at Curacao throughout both their tenures.

> 4 June. The regiment was under arms & fired a Royal Salute in honor [*sic*] of the King's birthday. In the evening there was a Mess Ball.
>
> 5 June. Came on Guard in the Warren.

111. Captain John Godfrey Royal Artillery (Kane 607); he died at Purfleet in 1831. Kane shows him as having resigned on 7 November 1798.
112. It was quite common to send half banknotes in two separate letters by the mail, as they could only be redeemed once brought together again.

> 7 June Sunday. I had a touch of the rheumatism yesterday in my right arm, but last night it was so bad that I could not sleep, I was in so much pain.

The electric treatment had been resumed.

> 9 June. The regiment had a Field day. I have been for these two days past *Electryfied* at the hospital for the rheumatism, which has been of service to mc.
>
> 11 June. Went to the hospital to be *Electryfied.* Today I had a return of the dimness in my eyes.
>
> 12 June. My eyes are worse; but the rheumatism in my arms is rather better.
>
> 14 June Sunday. *My eyes* were very bad yesterday & today.
>
> 15 June. Went to the hospital & my eyes rather better.
>
> 17 June. My eyes are considerably better, so is my rheumatism.
>
> 18 June. Took the Practise this morning for Captain Colebrooke.
>
> 19 June. Bacon is now selling for 1s 6d per lb; ham that has been boiled 2s 2d per lb; beef & mutton 10d per lb, chickens at the poulterers 10s 6d a couple.
>
> 21 June. Came on Guard for Major Scott.
>
> 22 June. Came on duty as Captain of the week.
>
> 2 July. Came on Guard.
>
> 11 July. Went with Mrs U[nett] and James [Fraser] in Major Scott's gig to London to take James [Fraser] to a dentist when he had two teeth taken out.

They were off to Birmingham again.

> 12 July Sunday. We have been very busy all day in packing for our journey to Birmingham & Staffordshire. Today we had a new patent pianoforte [which] came from London/ Mrs U[nett's] harpsichord went back in exchange. She had originally paid eighty guineas for it & could now with difficulty get allowed eight guineas. The harpsichords are now out of fashion; we gave thirty guineas for the pianoforte.[113]
>
> 16 July. We set off a little after 6 o'clock for Birmingham in a chaise.

113. About £2,000 in today's terms.

> 17 July. We came yesterday as far as Towcester 60 miles from London where we slept. Set off again this morning at 6 o'clock & got to Birmingham by 3 o'clock to dinner.
>
> 18 July. John's youngest child little Thomas has been all day very unwell, so that they sent for the surgeon this evening; it is his teeth &c.
>
> 24 July. Went again to Stafford. Saw Colonel Judgson,[114] Captain Augustus Frazer,[115] Lieutenant Lloyd[116] & Macdonald[117] of the Horse Artillery. To the latter I have lett [*sic*] my house at Woolwich.

An invasion scare led to immediate orders to return alone to Woolwich.

> 28 July. When we came home I found a letter from the Adjutant General's Office, Woolwich, ordering me to Woolwich immediately on account of the threatened invasion.[118]
>
> 29 July. At 7 o'clock [pm] I set off in the coach, travelled all night . . .
>
> 30 July . . . got to Woolwich at 5 o'clock [pm] today & dined at the Mess. Slept at Captain Charles Godfrey's.
>
> 31 July. Went to my house & got a bed &c for my barrack room.
>
> 3 August. Came on Guard.
>
> 6 August. Went to my new house with a bricklayer about some alterations &c.
>
> 11 August. Was out with my brigade of 6 medium 12 pounders from 10 till 12 and from 2 till 4 o'clock.
>
> 12 August. Out with my brigade 4 hours.
>
> 13 August. Out with my brigade.
>
> 14 August. Come on Guard. Went my rounds at 12 o'clock [pm].

---

114. Lieutenant Colonel Thomas Judgson Royal Artillery (Kane 522); he retired on full pay in December 1805 and died at Rothbury in 1835.
115. Captain Lieutenant Sir Augustus Frazer Royal Artillery (Kane 765); he commanded the Horse Artillery at Waterloo and died at Woolwich in 1855.
116. 1st Lieutenant William Lloyd Royal Horse Artillery (Kane 922); he was mortally wounded at Waterloo and died at Brussels on 29 July 1815.
117. Actually Captain Lieutenant Alexander Macdonald Royal Horse Artillery (Kane 785); he commanded the six RHA troops attached to cavalry brigades at Waterloo; he died at Leamington in 1840.
118. This fear had led to a naval attack with fireships on Dunkirk on 7 July 1800, but it achieved little.

17 August. Came on duty as Captain of the week. At 1 o'clock [pm] the whole regiment was under arms to receive for the first time, our new Master General, the Earl of Chatham.[119]

23 August Sunday. Today accounts came of the death of Lieutenant Colonel Thomson in Egypt, he was wounded the 10 May, had had an amputation of one of his legs & was doing exceedingly well. Was removed to Rosetta and died the 8 June.[120] His loss is a severe blow upon the regiment, he was an excellent officer, a sensible man & sincerely regretted by all his acquaintance[s].

25 August. Owing to the great crops of everything & the fine harvest weather, corn & potatoes have fallen in price most wonderfully. Came on Guard.

2 September. Came on Guard.

11 September. At 8 o'clock [am] I rode out with Major Scott & his troop to Dartford,[121] where they encamped for a few hours, came back between 4 & 5 o'clock.

12 September. Came on Guard.

14 September. Had out my brigade & encamped for the day upon Plumstead Common.

15 September. Encamped upon Plumstead Common & had a sham fight with Captain Godfrey with his brigade of 6 guns, long 6 pounders. Mine are medium 12 pounders. It had a pretty effect, staid [*sic*] out till after 5 o'clock.

Finally Richard was ordered to join his company in the West Indies; Ann, probably because of the three children, would not go with him.

17 September. Today I was in Orders to hold myself in readiness to join my company in the West Indies.

18 September. Encamped &c as yesterday. Today I paid £240 for a house &c[122] in Woolwich.

19 September. There was no brigade exercise today.

---

119. John, Earl of Chatham, became Master General of the Ordnance on 18 June 1801, replacing the Marquis of Cornwallis.

120. Lieutenant Colonel Henry Thomson Royal Artillery (Kane 505).

121. Major George Scott (Kane 558). Laws does not show him allocated to any particular company or troop.

122. About £13,000 today.

Now that they had a new house, Richard went to Birmingham to collect Ann and the children.

> 21 September. At 5 o'clock set off with Wilson[123] in their gig to London to go by the Mail at 7 o'clock [pm] for Acton Hill. Travelled all night . . .
>
> 22 September. . . . and got to Mr Ward's by 5 o'clock, in the afternoon, where I found Mrs [Ann] U[nett] and the two children.[124]
>
> 13 October. Tonight the town of Stafford &c was illuminated, bonfires were lighted and nine sheep were roasted whole at them in honor [*sic*] of the preliminaries of peace being signed with France.[125]
>
> 15 October. At 8 o'clock [am] we set off in a chaise to Birmingham on our way home, got there to dinner.
> 16 October. We got up at 5 o'clock & at 6 o'clock we set off, slept at Benson[126] 73 miles.
>
> 17 October. Set off again about 6 o'clock and got home about 4 o'clock, 59 miles.

It seems that Ann knew nothing of the new house and he does not record her reaction.

> 18 October Sunday. Employed all day in our new house, which I have lately bought and have been building an addition to it of a cellar, a sitting & bedroom. I made [purchased] this building when I was at Woolwich & had left Mrs U[nett] in Staffordshire. I did not mention it to her, so that she was surprized on her arrival.

---

123. His servant.

124. Presumably Mary Anne and Alexander as James would be at school.

125. The preliminaries of the Peace of Amiens were signed in London on 30 September 1801, but it was not ratified until the signing in Amiens on 25 March 1802.

126. Benson is a village in South Oxfordshire lying about 12 miles south-east of Oxford.

The West Indies, 1802–1803

Finally Richard was ordered to leave for the West Indies.

> 20 October. Today I was ordered by Colonel Macleod Adjutant General[1] to go to the West Indies, the ship now lays at Deptford.
>
> 10 November. Went to London in the coach & then onboard the *Trojan* West Indiaman about 400 tons,[2] Captain Mann, in order to arrange things with him. She is a very fine ship, coppered & sails well. She drops down to Gravesend the end of the week.
>
> 12 November. This evening I was attacked with pains in all my joints & limbs.
>
> 13 November. Was very hot last night & in a good deal of fever; was in great pain at times during the day with sharp darting pains all over me. Sent to Dr Irwin who has ordered me to take some of Dover's powders tonight at going to bed.
>
> 14 November. Was a little better. Baggage onboard the *Trojan*.

A surprise visitor brought some very good news.

> 15 November Sunday. Was surprized today by a visit from Captain James M Grant who brought with him Hugh Fraser, who has dropt [*sic*] the lawsuit and wishes to have everything between us settled amicably, he now will hear reason.
>
> 17 November. Went to Town & was employed all the day with Hugh Fraser in settling the late Captain John G[rant] Fraser's accounts &c.

---

1. Lieutenant Colonel Sir John Macleod (Kane 456) was Deputy Adjutant General of the Royal Artillery from March 1796 until April 1807. He died at Woolwich in 1833 as Colonel Commandant.
2. The *Trojan* was built in 1795 and was originally chartered by the East India Company. However, having returned from India in 1797, she became a West Indiaman. She went ashore on Deal beach in December 1802 and although she showed on the Lloyd's Register until 1807, her information was not updated from 1801.

> 19 November. Found myself so unwell that I went to bed directly.
>
> 20 November. Found myself better.
>
> 21 November. Went to London again and employed all the day about settling the late Captain [John] Fraser's affairs whilst he was acting Executor to his oldest brother James Fraser &c.
>
> 22 November. At 1 o'clock set off in a chaise to Gravesend to embark to join my company in the West Indies.
>
> 23 November. After dinner Captain Waller, Lieutenant Stanwix[3] & myself embarked onboard the *Trojan* West Indiaman, Captain John Mann.
>
> 25 November. Anchored in the Downs about 10 o'clock this evening.
>
> 26 November. Wrote a few lines to Mrs U[nett].
>
> 27 November. About 12 o'clock we had a terrible storm came on which lasted till towards 5 o'clock in the morning. It had blown pretty fresh all the day, we dragged our anchor & were obliged to let go the best bower.[4] A number of ships near us cut their cables & went to sea, some have lost their masts &c,[5] others are on shore.[6] One brig is totally gone to pieces and about 13 or 14 people have lost [their] lives. Captain Mann who has been at sea above 40 years, says he never experienced such a night at anchor.

Richard took a chance and disembarked to get to London urgently to settle these legal affairs for the children.

> 1 December. Still at an anchor in the Downs waiting for a fair wind. This evening I got a letter from Mrs U[nett] desiring I would come to Town immediately as the Executors of late Mr J Baillie[7] would not pay the children's legacy to any person but myself. I went on shore at Deal & sat up . . .

---

3. 1st Lieutenant Robert Stanwix Royal Artillery (Kane 1091) died at Barbados on 24 September 1802.
4. The two anchors carried at the bow were called the bowers. To differentiate them, the port anchor was denoted as the 'Small Bower' and the starboard anchor as the 'Best Bower'.
5. The Swedish East Indiaman *Sophia Magdalena* was wrecked off deal on this day.
6. The *Duke of Clarence* sailing to St Kitts was driven onshore at Deal on this day, but was successfully refloated in December and taken into Ramsgate.
7. This may well refer to James Baillie (1737–93) of Ealing Grove, Middlesex who was a West Indian merchant. A share of his estate may well have gone through his daughter Hannah Baillie who had married a James Fraser.

> 2 December . . . until 3 o'clock the next morning, when I set off in the coach and arrived at Woolwich about 4 o'clock in the afternoon.
>
> 3 December. At 8 o'clock set off in a chaise to London with Mrs U[nett] & James [Fraser]. James went & had three teeth taken out whilst I went to the Counting House of Messieurs Lang &c[8] and to the office of Messieurs Kaye & Winter attornies[9] [*sic*] &c.
>
> 4 December. I went to Town again & arranged everything, did not receive the money but signed a receipt &c, it will be paid by three instalments to anybody authorized by me & upon showing my receipt, for which purpose I have left it with Mrs U[nett]. Did not return to Woolwich, but set off in the coach at 6 o'clock in the evening to Portsmouth, to meet the ship.

Richard rushed to Portsmouth to meet the ship, but as luck would have it, he had to wait eleven days for it to arrive because of contrary winds. He seems to have enjoyed his enforced wait.

> 5 December. Got there at 9 o'clock. The wind remained contrary until the 16th when the *Trojan* arrived at Spithead. Captain, Mrs Waller &c came on shore when we all dined at the *Crown Inn*[10] & paid very extravagantly for our dinner. We all went onboard in the evening. During my stay at Portsmouth I became an honorary member of the Artillery Mess. I also dined several times onboard a ship, viz the *Carysfort*,[11] *Deseree*[12] & *Trent*[13] frigates.

It took over ten days of bad weather to fully clear the English Channel, but then Richard enjoyed a pleasant passage to the West Indies.

> 17 December. At 3 o'clock we set sail with a fair wind, which only lasted us two days, when it became contrary. We tacked about with very bad weather . . .
>
> 25 December . . . till Xmas day, when it blew a hurricane, which lasted all day & night & the next day when it moderated, fortunately we did not suffer much damage. We were in the chops of the

8. Lang, Turing & co were West Indian merchants.
9. Winter & Kaye were the antecedents of the modern law firm of Freshfield's; they advised Sir Richard Arkwright.
10. The Crown Inn stood at 34–36 the High Street, Portsmouth. Its guests included Marshal Blücher in 1814, but it ceased trading as an inn in 1818.
11. HMS *Carysfort* was a 28-gun frigate.
12. HMS *Desiree* was a French frigate of 36 guns, which had been captured on 8 July 1800 during the raid on Dunkirk.
13. HMS *Trent* was a 36-gun frigate.

Channel[14] & the waves were really dreadfully high. I may say I never [really] saw the sea until this time.

26 December. The wind continuing contrary, we bore away to get into either Scilly or Plymouth.

28 December. This morning we were in sight of land, but a fair wind springing up, we tacked & had upon the whole a pretty good passage to Martinique . . .

1802

. . . where we came to an anchor about 6 o'clock in the evening on Wednesday 21 January. On the 21st I had the misfortune to sprain my right anckle [*sic*] which gave me a great deal of pain. I was afraid I could not have got my shoe on to come onshore. I was not able to put it to the ground for three or four days.

Finally Richard got ashore on Martinique when his ankle had eased a little.

29 January. We all dressed ourselves *en militaire* & came on shore at 8 o'clock this morning. I continued to hobble pretty well with a large stick. We met Colonel Laye who introduced us to Sir Thomas Trigge.[15] We all dined at Mr Hall's Ordnance Storekeeper, here I slept &c. Lieutenant Rogers, Engineers,[16] lent me his horse when I rode up to Fort George & dined at the Artillery Mess. When the French were in possession of this island, this fort was called Fort Bourbon. It stands upon a very steep hill, is very fatiguing to ascend in the heat of the day, but the prospect from it is grand & picturesque. As my baggage was not come up I went with Dr MacArthur[17] & slept at the redoubt.

30 January. Had my baggage brought up by a parcel of negroes, it cost me three dollars.

31 January Sunday. The surgeon sent me his horse to ride to breakfast &c, my leg still lame.

1 February. I have got up these few days at guns firing & gone to bed a little after. I intend for the future to pursue this plan. The regiment

14. The western entrance to the English Channel, where it meets the North Atlantic.
15. General Sir Thomas Trigge was Commander in Chief in the West Indies. He had been instrumental in the capture of Dutch Surinam in 1799 and the Swedish and Dutch dependencies of St Martin, St Bartholomew, St Thomas, St John and St Croix in 1801.
16. 1st Lieutenant Edward Rogers Royal Engineers.
17. I cannot find any record of a Dr MacArthur or MacCarthy (he spells it either way).

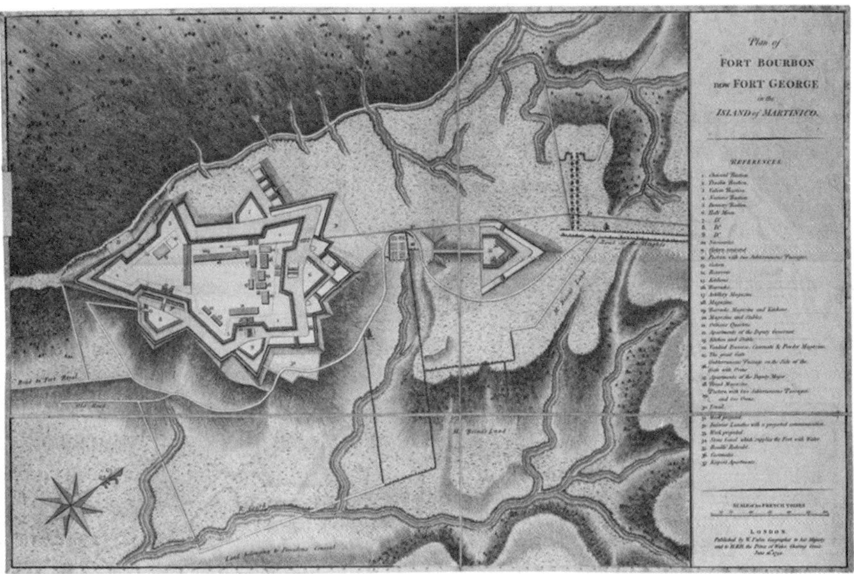

were mustered this morning at 6 o'clock. Wrote a long letter yesterday to Mrs U[nett] which I sent off this morning. At 4 o'clock this afternoon, the 11th Regiment[18] in garrison here, were reviewed by Brigadier General Maitland,[19] they made a fine appearance.

Richard was asked to numerous social events but avoided most.

2 February. Was asked to dine at Sir Thomas Trigge's but sent an excuse.

3 February. The officers of artillery were asked to a Ball in Fort Royal given by one of the Commander in Chief's adc's. Some of them went, I did not.

5 February. The regiment & garrison was under arms at 6 o'clock this morning to receive the Danish Governor of Santa Cruza [St Croix], who came to see Fort George &c, he was saluted with 15 guns. My anckle [*sic*] is still swelled.

10 February. The artillery were asked to a Ball in Fort Royal, some of the officers went, I did not go. The thermometer today was only at one time 71 degrees [Fahrenheit – 22°C].

18. The Devonshire Regiment was to spend six years in the West Indies.

19. Brigadier General Thomas Maitland.

12 February. Rode out this morning with Lieutenant Rogers. The country is most delightful & pleasant early in the morning. I had on my greatcoat and did not find it too much, as it was rather cool.

15 February Tuesday. Lieutenant Rogers sent me a horse this morning, rode down to Fort Royal, met him & took a pleasant ride.

17 February. All the officers were invited to a ball this evening at a French lady's &c. I did not go.

19 February. Lieutenant Rogers sent me a horse, rode out & then breakfasted with him in Fort Royal. He introduced me to Colonel Shipley,[20] who asked me to dinner, which I declined. Returned at 10 o'clock & was President of a Brigade Court Martial. Captain Leech 40th Regiment[21] called in upon me to show me a humming bird's nest which he had just taken, it had one egg of a reddish tinge; the egg seemed to be much larger in proportion to the size of the nest, which was not bigger in diameter than a shilling, it only lays two eggs.

20 February. Rode down to Fort Royal with Colonel Laye & breakfasted at Mr Hall's, staid [to] dinner there. Went into the warm bath before dinner.

Richard was under orders for the Island of St Vincent.

21 February Sunday. Was in Orders a few days ago to hold myself in readiness to go to St Vincent at the shortest notice.

22 February. Breakfasted with Captain Hely 11th Regiment.[22] Rogers lent me his horse to ride down. Sent my baggage in a cart & at 10 o'clock got into a canoe; Wilson with some of my boxes in another & set off for St Pierr's [Saint Pierre] on my way to St Vincent; arrived there about 1 o'clock [pm]. Dined with Dr Innes[23] and the General Hospital Mess, slept at Dr James Johnston's[24] who invited me to his house &c. Mrs Johnston is sister to Mrs Beech, they are particular friends of George's.

23 February. Walked out &c. Called and left my name at Government House. Dined at a Mr Cruden's with 16 gentlemen, a most superb dinner.

---

20. Lieutenant Colonel Charles Shipley Royal Engineers.
21. Captain Thomas Leach 40th Foot.
22. Captain George Hely 11th Foot.
23. Purveyor George Innes (no. 884 in Johnston).
24. I can find no record of this doctor.

24 February. Rode out this morning. Received a card from General Keppel the Governor,[25] asking me to dinner today. It was dated yesterday; sent an excuse, as I was engaged to a Mr Wade's, a costly dinner, three courses and a desert, this dinner could not have cost less than £50 & upwards.[26] The company 17 gentlemen. Weather exceedingly hot.

25 February. A terrible rowing night with rain. Went to the shore, where there was still a most tremendous surf; a number of vessels on shore, some of them dashed to pieces & many lives lost; many ships cut & drove out to sea. Fortunately the wind came from the land, otherwise the loss would have been much greater. Dr Johnston had company to dinner.

26 February. Dined at the famous *Patty Chollet's* with Mr Barry, who arrived yesterday from Antigua. We had an excellent dinner & most capitally dressed; but the charges are infamous; not less than 5 or 6 dollars each for dinner. I am told it is quite impossible to live there under a *Joe* per diem; that is £1 17s 4d, if so little.

His orders to St Vincent were rescinded.

28 February Sunday. Rode out in the evening and saw in the country a negro dance. This evening I received orders from Colonel Laye not to proceed to St Vincent, but to join him again at Fort George immediately.

1 March. I tried all day but could not get a canoe &c. Was engaged to dine at Mr Sayer's the Pay Master General but sent an excuse as I was not quite sure about getting a boat.

The canoe trip was boisterous and Richard prepared for the worst.

2 March. About 10 o'clock [am] set off in a canoe for Fort George. The wind was rather high with a great swell, so that I expected every instant to be upset. I therefore took off my coat & sword &c & prepared to swim onshore; arrived without any accident. Called upon Lieutenant Rogers, who lent me his horse, rode up to Fort George to dinner. There was a Ball given by Mr Hall, Ordnance Storekeeper, to which all the officers were asked, but I did not go,

4 March. Rode to Fort Royal & breakfasted with Rogers. Called afterwards upon Captain & Mrs Francklin who are here on their way home from Jamaica.

25. Major General William Keppel was Colonel of the 3rd West India Regiment.
26. Over £2,500 per head today!

He records a death, but also recalls with delight the high esteem in which everyone seemed to regard George.

> 6 March. Came on duty as Captain of the Day for the Garrison. Last night, as one of the French negroes was going from this fort to the town (Fort Royal) he was stung by a snake and this morning he is dead. When I was at St Pierres it gave me much pleasure to hear my brother George spoken off [*sic*] (in a number of large parties) in the highest terms imaginable.
>
> 7 March Sunday. We had Divine Service in the Garrison, which was performed by Reverend Hugh Williams under one of the galleries.
> 10 March. Came on Garrison Duty as Captain of the Day.
>
> 13 March. Wrote a very long letter to Mrs U[nett], to brother John & to my sister Fanny, by Captain Newton[27] who has got leave to return to Europe & sails tomorrow.
>
> 14 March Sunday. Came on Garrison Duty as Captain of the Day. Was asked to dine at Brigadier General Maitland's but sent an excuse.

Richard got his first attack of fever.

> 15 March. This evening I was attacked with the fever; in two days I became so weak I could scarcely stand.
>
> 22 March Monday. Am pretty well again, though rather weakly. Had a ride before breakfast. Received a letter from Mrs U[nett] dated the 19 January.
>
> 23 March. Rode out with Colonel Laye. Was asked to dine at Sir Thomas Trigge's but sent an excuse.
>
> 25 March. The brigade was out at gun firing.
>
> 26 March. The brigade was out at gun firing and fired. Came on duty as Captain of the Garrison. Rains hard in the evening.
>
> 27 March. Admiral Campbell with 7 sail of the line anchored in the bay.[28] Admiral Totty saluted him with 13 guns.[29]
>
> 28 March Sunday. Had Divine Service today. Rode with Colonel Laye. Six more men of war anchored. The packet arrived but I had no letters (2 February packet).

---

27. Captain Lawrence Newton Royal Artillery (Kane 603); he died at Woolwich in April 1805.
28. Admiral Sir George Campbell took command of the Jamaica Squadron in 1802.
29. Rear Admiral Thomas Totty was to die of yellow fever on 2 June 1802. His body was preserved to be buried at Portsmouth Garrison Chapel.

31 March. We had another field day this morning at gun firing with 4 six-pounders & fired &c. The Sergeant Major's wife was brought to bed on Saturday last; this morning the guns firing waked the infant & frightened it till it had a locked jaw, it died in the afternoon.[30] Rode in the evening with Colonel Laye. Wrote to Mrs U[nett] by [the] packet.

1 April. The regiment mustered at 6 o'clock this morning. In the afternoon the artillery were reviewed by Brigadier General Maitland (who dined at our Mess). I was the Exercising Officer; we had 5 six-pounders & fired twenty rounds per gun. The regiment looked & performed exceedingly well & much to the satisfaction of General Maitland. Between 40 & 50 men of my company arrived from Curacao. Had a long letter from George who remains behind with the Governor to whom he is Military Secretary until the island is given up, when he goes to England.

2 April. Came on duty as Captain of the Garrison.

3 April. Rode with Colonel Laye to Fort Royal and breakfasted with Lieutenant Rogers. Very warm. As there are only three captains in the garrison doing duty beside myself, I come on Garrison duty every fourth day.

10 April. Came on Garrison duty. Have rode out several times lately upon Colonel Laye's horse. Some of the soldiers today killed in the fort a serpent about 6½ feet [2m] in length; a shocking looking animal. Its bite is death in a few hours.

11 April Sunday. Showery all the day. Dined at Brigadier General Maitland's &c.

15 April. This morning at 6 o'clock we were reviewed by Sir Thomas Trigge &c. We had eight 6-pounders and about 150 men with drummers &c. There have not been so many artillery at Martinique since the year 1795. His Excellency was very well pleased with their appearance, I was the Exercising Officer. We had afterwards a public breakfast in the Mess room. It has rained a good deal lately.

Richard saw the results of a mutiny on Dominica.

27 April. We have had rain more or less almost every day lately. This morning at 6 o'clock the whole garrison were under arms together with part of the 1st, 4th & 10th West India Black Regiments from Port Royal to put in execution the sentence upon seven men of the 8th West India Regiment who have been ordered to be shot by a General Court Martial for the mutiny & murdering [of] three

30. Fright is unlikely to be the cause of death!

of their officers viz Captain Cameron,[31] Lieutenants Mackie[32] & Wasteneys,[33] as also the Commissary Mr Lang, the Clerk of Cheque, some of their own sergeants & a gunner, James McGill of the artillery. They murdered Lieutenant Wasteneys in a most cruel manner and ravished Mrs Mackie. She swore to no less than fifteen who did it following each other & they were all put to the bayonet by order of General Johnstone,[34] she has been deranged ever since.[35] The seven black prisoners arrived in the fort yesterday afternoon. I was Captain on Garrison duty & therefore had *the charge of them*, till their execution. They seemed very unconcerned & when I went my rounds at night, I found them all fast asleep and snoring. They were shot about 7 o'clock, first three, then two & two. Extremely hot yesterday and today.

---

31. Captain Alexander Cameron 8th West India Regiment.
32. Lieutenant William Mackay 8th West India Regiment.
33. Actually Ensign Edward Wastneys 8th West India Regiment.
34. Brigadier General the Honourable A Johnstone was Colonel of the 8th West India Regiment.
35. The mutiny occurred at Prince Rupert's Bay on Dominica on 9 April 1802 following a rumour that the regiment was to be disbanded and the soldiers sold into slavery on the plantations; they rose and killed five officers and some men and then secured themselves within the fort. Johnstone brought together a force of 1,300 men including the 68th Foot and Marines from two ships anchored in the bay. Preparations were made to storm, but representatives from the regiment offered to surrender unconditionally at 5 pm, when the regiment would be found formed on the parade ground. Johnstone agreed to this and upon entering at the appointed time, he found the three surviving officers at the head of their troops, who seemed to have resumed military discipline and order. Johnstone did not order the troops to ground their weapons immediately, but began to harangue them, despite the fact that many could not understand him. This caused unrest and realising the situation was deteriorating, he now ordered them to ground weapons. Rumours of treachery caused the black soldiers to hesitate and Johnstone had his men open fire, causing the rest to disperse, but they were hunted down and captured. About fifty men were killed and fifty wounded. Seven men were identified as the ringleaders and court-martialled. The regiment was transported to Martinique, where the executions took place as described by Richard Unett. A subsequent Court of Enquiry reported to the Secretary of War which highlighted a number of irregularities in the men's pay. On 24 May 1802, another Court of Inquiry was convened at Barbados, where the regiment was now stationed, found that Johnstone had contributed greatly to the mutiny. A number of others were court-martialled and executed and 148 others who took an active part were sent as pioneers (effectively engineers) in other regiments to be worked to death. The remainder were transferred to other regiments, but the 8th Regiment continued, the 11th being renumbered. Johnstone was court-martialled for 'irregularities'; he was acquitted but was passed over for promotion and his career was effectively over. He resigned and got involved in various nefarious businesses and was implicated alongside Admiral Sir Thomas Cochrane in 1814; while awaiting trial he disappeared and was never heard of again.

1 May. Today I was President of a Garrison Court Martial at Fort Edward[36] upon a black Sergeant Major of the 1st West India Regiment for insolence &c.

The fever struck violently this time.

2 May Sunday. I went to bed last night about 9 o'clock in perfect health, but in the middle of the night I awoke with a severe ague fit upon me. About an hour after I had a violent burning fever upon me. I then burst into a most profuse perspiration, so that the sheets & mattress were as wet as if they had been dipped in water. This perspiration certainly was of great service to me in carrying off the fever. Was rubbed all over twice during the day with lime juice.

5 May. Yesterday & the day before, I drank a great quantity of cool drinks made with sour oranges & gros syrop[37] [*sic*] & this morning I took a dose of Castor Oil &c and am pretty well. Went to the Mess again.

Finally the news they all wanted arrived; peace was declared.

9 May Sunday. A few days ago a sloop of war arrived from England with an account of the definitive Treaty of Peace, being signed on the 27 March last;[38] it was immediately given out in the General Orders.

13 May. The weather for some days past has been exceedingly hot. I heard a merchant who has been a number of years in the West Indies say that he had never found the weather warmer than it has been lately. Had a letter from George inclosing one from Mrs U[nett] to him of 2 March, she and the children were all well.

25 May Tuesday. Was a member of a General Court Martial which began sitting in Fort Royal upon two officers of the 7th West Indian Regiment & upon a Lieutenant of the 39th Regiment. Was asked to dine at Colonel Shipley's but declined.

26 May. Went down to the Court Martial at 9 o'clock, dined at Colonel Shipley's

36. Fort Royal was renamed Fort Edward during the British occupation of Martinique.

37. Gros sirop is a pure sugarcane syrup.

38. The Peace of Amiens was officially signed by France, Spain, the Batavian Republic and Britain.

> 4 June. Dined at Sir Thomas Trigge's, all the Field officers & captains in garrison.
>
> 5 June. Received a long letter from Mrs U[nett].
>
> 7 June. Received a long one from George.
>
> 8 June. This day we finished our Court Martial, but the court was not dissolved until the 12th.
>
> 13 June. Wrote to Mrs U[nett] by the packet.
>
> 15 June. For some days I have had the dysentery upon me. Last night I got up about 9 different times &c. Today I drank a glass of port wine after dinner with port and water at dinner

The next day he reported a strong earthquake.

> 16 June. My bowels have been a great deal better, owing I imagine to the wine as it is the first I have ever drank in the West Indies &c. About 9 o'clock this morning, we had a severe shock of an earthquake. I was sitting on a chair in a gallery, which shook very much under me. It lasted many seconds, another one was felt the night before last. I heard some persons say that they thought the shock lasted a minute and a half, there was a good deal of damage done to different houses, but I heard of no lives being lost. I heard General Maitland say that he was walking across the courtyard of his house & that it affected him just as if he was in liquour, making him reel to and fro; others it caused to vomit &c.
>
> 20 June Sunday. We have had thunder most days this last week, with violent rains. I am now got pretty well again, though a good deal pulled down.

With peace normal formalities were resumed on the arrival of a French warship.

> 22 June. This morning, a French ship of 74 guns came into the harbour; she saluted when she came to anchor [near] the Admiral's ship with 15 guns & had 13 in return. She afterwards saluted Fort Edward & had a return of gun for gun.
>
> Came on Garrison duty. I yesterday heard a melancholy accident. A French girl a few miles from here went into a hen house, a snake leeped [*sic*] from the ceiling & bit her, she died in half an hour.
>
> 2 July. On the 1st of this month Captain [Francis] Rey sailed from here for England onboard the *Tamar* frigate[39] with about 100 artillery, belonging most of them to the 3rd Battalion, others who are sickly

39. HMS *Tamar* of 38 guns.

to the 7th Battalion. Had a letter by the packet from Mrs U[nett] yesterday, wrote a long letter to her by Captain Rey.

A few days ago we had a most terrible night with rain, thunder & lightning, such that I never heard before. Two of the men of war were struck by the lightning & lost their main-top mast shivered to atoms from top to bottom.

8 July. Captain Massey[40] & Lieutenant Dennis[41] went home with some more artillerymen.

French delegates arrived announcing that French troops would soon arrive to take possession of Martinique, which was being handed back as part of the peace treaty.

9 July. This morning a French corvette arrived in 23 days from L'Orient, having onboard two French generals and the *Prefect.* They bring accounts that 15 days after they sailed, the ships with the troops to garrison the West India islands were to sail. We are to evacuate this island on their arrival, the sooner the better.

11 July Sunday. Wrote to Mrs U[nett] by the packet. The French officers &c have dined these two days at the Commander in Chief's, but their insolence & filthiness at his table beggars all description.

17 July. There was another very sharp shock of an earthquake yesterday morning about 3 o'clock, but I did not feel it. Wrote to sister Fanny and to John, also to Mrs U[nett] by Major Foster of the 11th Regiment[42] who was to sail tomorrow in a Liverpool ship.

18 July Sunday. Had a letter from George dated 3 July.

Richard showed a French captain over Fort Edward, delivering up all the military stores.

19 July. Had a letter from Mrs U[nett] by the packet. This morning at 6 o'clock the French artillery captain came up to the fort, when I went round the works & delivered up to him all the guns, shot, powder stores &c.

20 July. Last night I scarcely slept any, on account of the rheumatism in my left arm. I have been very free for some months of it.

---

40. Captain Lieutenant George Massey Royal Artillery (Kane 853); he died at Canterbury on 15 April 1812.
41. 1st Lieutenant John Cripps Dennis is shown in the Irish Artillery in the Army List of 1801 but then disappears. He is not in Kane.
42. Major James Forster 11th Foot.

He records an accidental death.

> 26 July. We have had for some days very heavy rain, with violent thunder & lightning. This morning one of the light infantry 11th Regiment in cleaning his gun which was loaded accidentally shot his comrade in the barrack room; the ball went in at his back & out again near his left nipple & so into the ceiling of the room. He lived about twenty-four hours in sad agonies; he forgave his comrade.

Richard had to make a return of stores at Fort George, but he also received orders to move.

> 29 July. This morning I was ordered with a Lieutenant to go round Fort George and give a Return of the gun carriages &c, whether serviceable or unserviceable. Received orders to hold myself in readiness at the shortest notice for Barbadoes [*sic*] to take the command of the artillery &c and to be *Commissary of Horse*[43] in the room of Lieutenant Taylor,[44] who is going to England.

George wrote a long and lively letter home as he awaited the ending of the British occupation of Curacao and his hopes of returning home for a long period of leave.

> Letter from George to John Wilkes Unett, Square, Birmingham
>
> Curacao, 1 August 1802
>
> Dear John,
> It is more than probable this will be the last letter you will receive from me from this part of the world, at all events, even if we remain longer, that at present we have reason to expect there will not [be] another opportunity occur for some time to come & on account of the commencement of the hurricane season; all vessels are obliged to be under weigh on this day, otherwise their insurance is forfeited.
>
> I yesterday wrote [to] Fanny by a brig bound to Glasgow and a few days previous I wrote Mrs [Ann] Unett and Elizabeth, I am almost tired repeating the same thing over and over again. The constant burden of my song is; that we are still in daily expectation of the arrival of the Batavian troops,[45] when we immediately evacuate this island, and sail direct for old England. I think I mentioned to you

43. The Commissary of Horse was responsible for inspecting the condition of all the artillery horses.
44. 1st Lieutenant John Taylor Royal Artillery (Kane 1029), he retired in 1825.
45. Holland had been renamed the Batavian Republic by the French revolutionaries.

Officer of the Royal Irish Artillery 1790.

Royal Artillery 1799.

Leith Races by William Thomas Reed.

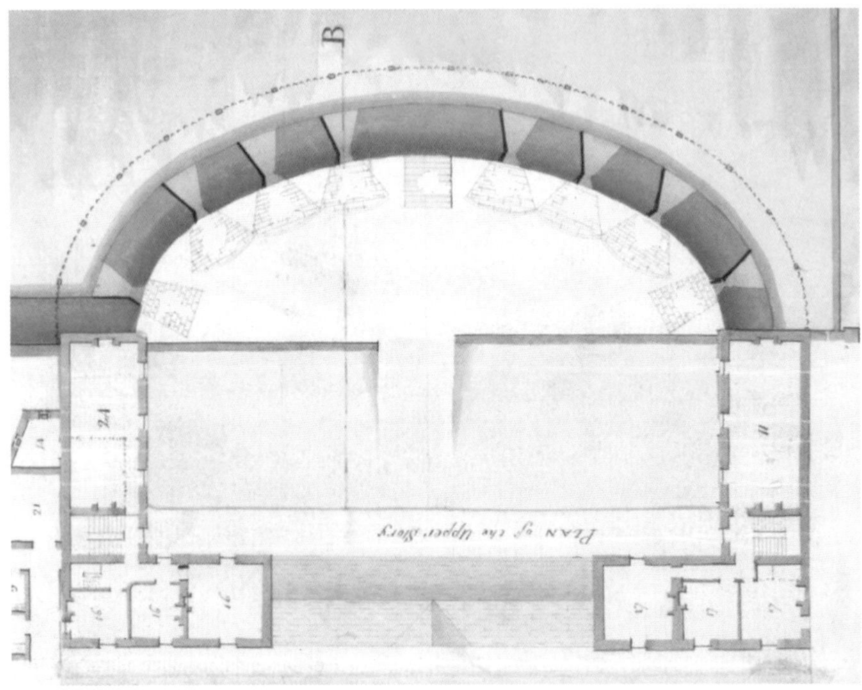

Plan of Leith Fort 1785.

Review of the London Volunteer Cavalry and Horse Artillery, Hyde Park, 1804.

Gowrie Castle Barracks.

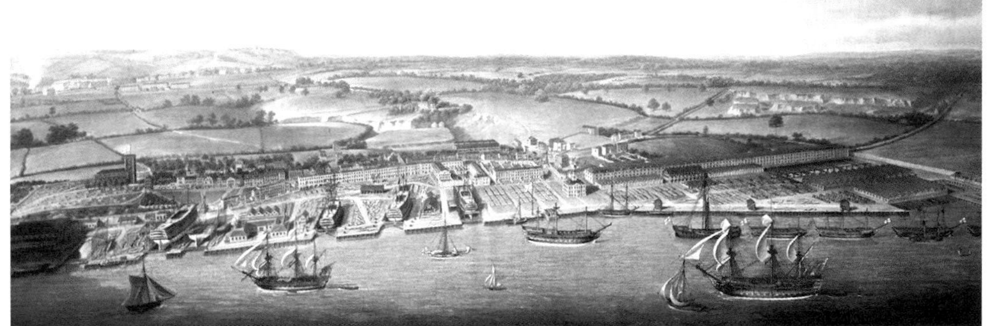

Woolwich Dockyard.

Blendon Hall 1900.

Bombardment of Copenhagen 1807 – Danish depiction.

Bull baiting by Ibbettson.

General John Manners Kerr.

General William Grinfield.

General Lord Adam Gordon.

Colonel Fitzroy Maclean.

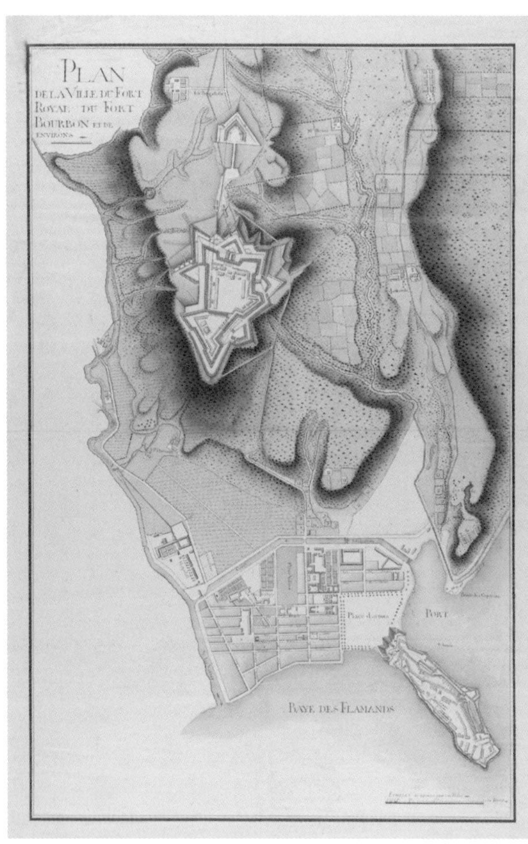

Left and below: Fort Royal and Bourbon plan and view.

The wreck of the *Dutton*, Plymouth 1796.

The capture of Martinique 1809.

Officers of the 7th Fusiliers 1813.

Officer of the 52nd Foot.

Church of St Nicholas, Plumstead.

before, that I had permission either to remain with Colonel Hughes as Military Secretary, until the giving up of the island, or to go home when and in what manner I liked best. We have a man of war in the harbour (the *De Ruyter*[46]) ready to take us onboard as soon as ever the Dutchmen arrive, but they are not the most active people in the world and we may yet be kept in this state of uncertainty some time. If they are not already sailed, probably they will not attempt it until the hurricane months are past, but you yourself will better judge of my arrival from the newspapers informing you of their sailing, to take possession of their colonies in this country.

Our headquarters ere this, are removed to Barbados, consequently when you write to [Richard] Wilkes, you had better direct to him there. I have not heard from him [for] some time, his last letter mentioned his having been twice attacked with fever, but he had quite recovered, this is all in his favor [*sic*]. The greatest danger is always apprehended in the first attacks and I am in hopes he will now be somewhat accustomed to the climate and be able to *battle* against it for a short time very well. As for me, I am as well in this *burning sun*, as out of it and can walk & shooting [*sic*] the whole day through, without any inconvenience. [tear – There is?] a cricket match, which begins on Mon[damaged – day nex]t. I am afraid I shall not be able to attend, my time is so very much taken up in my office, I never quit it till three o'clock. I should not enjoy such good health, if I did not constantly ride out every evening, Colonel H[ughes] and myself scarcely ever let one pass without doing it. We take our *full allowance of old madeira*, mount our horses and generally go eight or ten miles in the course of the hour. If we did not ride fast, we should not get sufficient exercise, there being no twilight it is very soon dark in this climate. You ought to ride; make it a point and on no account whatever to swerve from it, not to do any business after dinner, which I would so strictly adhere to, that I would send away the best client I had if he came at that time. You ought to do as we do, drink your bottle of wine every day and take a great deal more exercise on horseback and do not so constantly *bother* your *brains* over a parcell [*sic*] of *musty* old parchments, or quit the unhealthy profession at once, and turn *farmer*, as I mean to do some day or other, when I can find some rosy cheeked damsel, who will take a fancy to the cut of my jib and is not too fine a lady to be above looking after a dairy. I fancy I shall be now rather difficult to please. I have seen too much of the world and suffered too much to be easily *caught. Recollect you are not to show Mrs U[nett] the last line.* Most of our officers are returned to England, I am almost the only one (of those that are

46. The Dutch 68-gun *De Ruyter* had been captured in 1799 and taken into the Royal Navy as a store ship.

to be relieved) remaining. I know not where my company will be on my arrival, most likely at *Woolwich.* I wish most sincerely *our first interview was over*, for I very much dread *it.* They certainly cannot refuse me six months leave of absence, after five years in this cool country, to spend amongst you and my friends at Henley, Acton Hill &c. I shall certainly make you go both a shooting and hunting too with me. As far as *money* goes, I mean to have the best horse in the country. A short time now will attach Captain to my name.

I shall add nothing at all about the young Bartling's, you may have half a dozen for all that I know to the contrary, as you have not written me a line [for] I don't know how long. I shall only beg to be kindly remembered to Mrs [Elizabeth] Unett and all at Stowe. Believing me always your affectionate brother G[eorge] W[ilkes] U[nett].

I shall be very much in want of a good spaniel, when I return, I wish you would look about, if he is not all perfection, don't mind him and never mind the fire, if he [costs?] I will repay you.

Richard sailed for Barbados but managed to go without his manservant.

4 August Wednesday. At 8 o'clock this morning I embarked onboard the *Start* schooner of 90 tons for Barbadoes. Was to have sailed yesterday evening, but the ship could not get out of the careenage.[47] Wilson went onboard with my baggage, but this morning he went on shore for something, so that we sailed without him.

Came to Carlisle Bay about 11 o'clock on the 7 August Saturday, dressed myself & waited upon General Kerr.[48] Went out to dine in the country at a Mr Radish's &c.

8 August Sunday. Dined at Mr Savary's the Storekeeper's. Called yesterday upon the Brigadier General (who commands the district) Kerr. Went to the evening parade and fell in with the detachment of artillery. Was introduced to Colonel Fitzroy Maclean[49] who commands the garrison. Made an apology to him for not calling in the morning, as I understood he was in the country.

9 August. Employed all morning in giving directions &c about the stores &c. Went into the water, very fine sea bathing. Was asked to dine at the Mess of the 2nd Battalion 60th Regiment. Rode out in

47. A location where ships could be safely turned on its side, to allow the hull to be repaired and cleaned.

48. Brigadier General John Manners Kerr was Commander of the Forces in Grenada, Dominica, Barbados and St Vincent from 1801–4.

49. Lieutenant Colonel Sir Fitzroy Jeffreys Maclean 60th Foot.

the evening, met General Kerr who took me home with him to tea. Mrs Kerr a pleasant woman.

10 August. For several days past we have had some heavy showers of rain. Rode to town in the morning and called upon Lord Seaforth,[50] employed about the stores &c that are landing from the schooner. Dined at Mr Savary's. As soon as dinner was over, came home and wrote to Mrs U[nett] by Lieutenant Taylor, who embarks at gun firing tomorrow morning. Rode to town in the evening. Heavy rains at times during the night with thunder.

11 August. Employed all morning in writing to Colonel Laye & sending Returns &c. Breakfasted at Lieutenant Rogers. Was admitted an Honorary member of the 60th Regiment & dined there. Rode out in the evening.

12 August. Was up at 4 o'clock to a garrison punishment. Went into the sea. Took a long ride in the evening. Busy all morning at home.

13 August. Thunder last night with heavy rain. Employed all morning in examining into the Horse department, dined at the Mess. Called in the evening at Lieutenant Rogers & staid [for] tea. Came home at 8 o'clock, then dressed and went to a Ball at Colonel Maclean's about thirty couple of dancers. Did not dance, nor stay [for] supper.

14 August. Did not get up till very late. My servant arrived from Martinique, brought me a letter from Mrs U[nett] and another from sister Elizabeth. I had also one from George, but of an old date. Took a long ride in the evening.

15 August Sunday. Attended Divine Service this morning at 6 o'clock with the garrison. Bathed at 7 o'clock, dined at Mr Savary and drank coffee, attended parade at sunset. Showery.

Richard was yet to know it, but a hurricane had just landed. General Grinfield was renowned as brave, but also a harsh disciplinarian. He was determined to knock the troops into shape.

16 August. Breakfasted at Lieutenant Rogers, went through all the stores at the arsenal with the storekeeper. Called at Colonel Macleans. Our new Commander in Chief, General Grinfield,[51] arrived here

50. Colonel Francis Mackenzie, 1st Baron Seaforth was Governor of Barbados from 1800 to 1806.

51. Lieutenant General William Grinfield had been appointed Commander in Chief of the Forces in the Windward and Leeward Islands on 5 June 1802.

this morning from England onboard the *Chichester* 44 guns,[52] he was saluted by Fort Needham[53] with 19 guns. Was asked to dine at General Kerr's, as also by two officers of the 68th Regiment at their Mess but refused the three. Rains very much with lightning most of the day. Drank tea at Lieutenant Rogers.

17 August. Waited upon General Grinfield &c who asked me a number of questions &c. Wrote to Colonel Laye. Took a ride in the afternoon.

18 August. The whole line were under arms this morning at 6 o'clock & inspected by General Grinfield. He found fault with almost everybody & everything. Breakfasted with Lieutenant Rogers.

19 August. The whole line under arms again at 6 o'clock. On account of there being so many Ordnance stores now exposed to the weather &c, I this morning waited upon General Grinfield and stated to him the above circumstance & that the fatigue party of the 8th West India Regiment had been taken away from us to attend field days; and that if the artillery were obliged to be at all field days, a great loss would attend the Board of Ordnance &c. Dined and drank coffee at Mr Savary's then rode out with Lieutenant Rogers.

20 August. Yesterday it was in orders that on account of the multiplicity of business in their own department, the detachment of artillery would not attend field days, except one day in the week (the Inspection day) and on a Sunday unless particularly ordered. There was also a fatigue party of 50 men of the 8th West India Regiment to assist in carrying stores. Was President of a Board of respective officers, about stores &c, the minutes of which were laid before General Grinfield. General Grinfield sailed this morning for Martinique, he returns in a few days. Took a long ride in the evening.

21 August. General Kerr called upon me at 7 o'clock this morning and asked me to dinner. He said he wanted to consult me about the detachment of the line which is ordered to be attached to us to learn the gun exercise.[54] I have found the weather much hotter here than

52. HMS *Chichester* is recorded as having been a 44-gun frigate but had been converted to a store ship in 1793 and reduced her armament to 20 guns. Her log records having a small refit to carry General Grinfield and his suite. The ship sailed from Spithead with the General onboard on 14 July 1802.

53. A fort had been built at Needham's Point on Barbados in 1650 to protect Bridgetown. It was renamed Charles Fort in 1660, but it is clear that the old name stuck.

54. Battalion guns were to be allocated to infantry battalions, to be worked by a detachment of infantrymen.

at Martinique. I am covered all over with the prickly heat, which is very unpleasant & itches dreadfully; it is a sign of good health. Rode to the parade with General Kerr and then home again with him to coffee &c. Mrs Grinfield was there & came home about 9 o'clock, *very chatty & agreeable.*

22 August Sunday. Attended Divine Service at 6 o'clock, breakfasted at Lieutenant Rogers'. Asked after the parade at sunset into Colonel Maclean's; came home at 8 o'clock. The *Start* schooner arrived from Martinique with more stores & brought me two letters from Colonel Laye.

23 August. Was out at drill at 6 o'clock with the detachment of the 60th Regiment consisting of one lieutenant, 1 sergeant, 1 corporal & 15 men to be taught the 6-pounder exercise. Brought the lieutenant home to breakfast with me. Rode in the middle of the day & called upon General Maitland. Dined at Colonel Maclean's with a large party, in the evening there was a Ball, but I did not dance, or stay supper and came home at 11 o'clock. The company about sixty.

24 August. Wrote to Colonel Laye by the return of the schooner. It rained hard in the afternoon; no parade. Walked with Captain Robertson 2/60th[55] to look at a house to rent for Colonel Laye. Called upon the Assistant Quarter Master General & made application for quarters in the barracks, but there are none empty.

25 August. Rains hard most of last night and all morning. Was up a little after 5 o'clock for the Inspection day; the wet morning prevented our being under arms. Breakfasted with Lieutenant Rogers. Wrote to Mrs U[nett], rode in the evening. Was in the arsenal in the morning & seeing the stores packed &c.

26 August. Rains hard most of last night. Went in the morning & took a house for Colonel Laye, scarcely a house to be had for any price. Rode & called upon General Kerr. Dined at the Whist Club in Bridgetown; played two rubbers & won 2½ guineas.[56] Came home about 8 o'clock.

27 August. Got up between 5 & 6 o'clock; went to the drill of the men at the gun exercise. Sent Colonel Laye's baggage to his house. The packet arrived. Rode out in the evening.

28 August. Wrote to Colonel Laye. Rode to town, put my letter in the packet which sails tomorrow for Martinique. Rode out again in the evening. Drank tea with Rogers. Rains very hard in the evening.

55. Captain John Robertson 2/60th Foot.

56. About £140 today.

29 August Sunday. Was up at 5 o'clock. At 6 o'clock went to the Church Parade, breakfasted with Rogers. Attended parade in the evening, took a dish of coffee at Mr Emery's.

30 August. Rode out at 6 o'clock, saw my drill; came back at half past 7 o'clock to breakfast. My eyes rather bad with the reflection of the sun upon the white sand &c. Rode out again in the evening; went afterwards to Rogers', came home at 8 o'clock. Saw my drill after dinner, before I rode out. The lightning very livid in the evening.

31 August. Showery in the morning, continued at different times during the day. Rode out in the morning & took a cup of coffee at Mr Savary's.

1 September. Was up at 5 o'clock, it being the Inspection day when all the garrison are under arms; but the wet yesterday prevented our being out. Got on horseback at half past 5 o'clock, rode till about 7 o'clock, then breakfasted with Rogers. Was afterwards obliged to ride into the country about forage for the horses; came back again to the arsenal, then rode to town and called upon Mr Glasford Commissary General,[57] Mr Sayers Paymaster General, Dr Gordon Inspector General[58] and Dr George Innes Purveyor. Excessively sultry, everybody you met was complaining of the heat & I heard a number of people who have been long in the West Indies say, they thought it the hottest day they had ever felt. There was a very large party dined at the 60th Regiment Mess. Came home between 6 & 7 o'clock. Bought a horse, gave £30 currency, that is *£22 8s sterling*.[59]

2 September. Yesterday morning being bad, we had the Weekly Inspection today. Was up at 5 o'clock, between 6 & 7 o'clock it rained very hard, which drove the regiments home again. Got wet through, came home & changed. Went in the afternoon with Rogers to call upon Mr Radish (the Controller of the Customs) who lives about two miles off, drank tea & staid [*sic*] the evening, came back about 11 o'clock. Heavy showers in the afternoon. Went to the drill after dinner. Very hot again.

3 September. Before I rode out, breakfasted with Rogers. General Grinfield arrived from Martinique onboard a frigate. On leaving the ship she saluted him with 17 guns. Dined at General Kerr's, came home at 8 o'clock, very hot.

57. Commissary General John Glassford.

58. Inspector of Hospitals Theodore Gordon (Johnston 1189).

59. About £1,250 today.

4 September. Got up at 6 o'clock, wrote to Colonel Laye by the *Castor* frigate[60] & then rode to General Kerr's to breakfast. Called after upon General Grinfield. Went after dinner to the drill of the artillery &c.

5 September Sunday. Up at 5 o'clock, went to the Church Parade at 6 o'clock. Rode out in the afternoon after the Evening Parade, very hot. Drank tea at Rogers'.

6 September. The schooner arrived with more stores from Martinique. Rode in the morning to call upon General Kerr & Colonel Murray, the Adjutant General.[61] Excessively hot. Dined in the country at Mr Radish's with a large party. Came home at 11 o'clock. Mr Radish is half-brother to the celebrated Mr George Canning MP.[62]

7 September. Very hot. Dined at General Grinfield's with all the commanding officers of regiments & corps & came home between 5 & 6 o'clock to the Evening Parade. Was up at 5 o'clock for the Inspection. At 10 o'clock General Grinfield went round the barracks, he found great fault with almost every barrack room, amongst the rest with my men's barracks; gave me *chocolate* &c. Very hot indeed. Wrote to Colonel Laye by the return of the schooner. Went after dinner to my drill, rode for an hour afterwards.

9 September. Attended my drill at 6 o'clock this morning. I have now got another detachment of the 68th Regiment came into barracks today. I have been paying rent for a house since my arrival here. Dined at Dr Austen's Ordnance Surgeon.[63]

10 September. Very hot. Attended the drill after dinner, when General Grinfield ordered the two guns to fall in with their regiments and marched us about with the regiments till it was dark. I had my horse & intended to ride, but he kept us so late that I could not. Went into Colonel Maclean's for an hour after the parade.

11 September. Dr Austen breakfasted with me. Very hot. Attended drill in the morning & evening. Rode out in the evening for half an hour.

12 September Sunday. Dr Toosey[64] breakfasted with me. Attended Divine Service with the garrison at 6 o'clock. Rode to headquarters

60. HMS *Castor* of 32 guns.

61. Colonel George Murray Adjutant General in the West Indies.

62. George Canning was to become Foreign Secretary from 1807–9 and again 1822–7. He was also Prime Minister for four months in 1827.

63. I cannot find any record of a Dr Austen in the Ordnance Medical Department.

64. Apothecary George Toosey (Johnston 2008).

in the middle of the day to speak to the Adjutant General. Extremely hot. A Garrison Parade in the afternoon.

13 September. Out with the drill before 6 o'clock, breakfasted with Rogers. Rains hard most of the day, no drill in the afternoon. Went to Colonel Maclean's in the evening. A great deal of thunder & lightning.

14 September. Thunder with very vivid lightning last night & early this morning. Up before 6 o'clock & had my horses with the new harness to draw the guns &c to try them. Dr Austen breakfasted with me. Was a member upon a Garrison Court Martial. Rains hard almost the whole day from 7 o'clock in the morning. The lightning extremely vivid.

15 September. The whole garrison out, it being Inspection Day. Had all the horses in the field harnessed when General Grinfield inspected them and asked me a number of questions. The ground so wet that it was in some places nearly over the shoes. Several men of the line taken ill with standing on the wet ground, carried off the field. The Commander in Chief visited the arsenal for the first time, gave me a number of directions. Also the barracks, said my barracks were now very clean. Dined at the Mess of the 68th Regiment. Rode out for half an hour in the evening.

16 September. Got up at ¼ before 6 o'clock and bathed. The packet arrived, I had a letter from Mrs U[nett] dated 4 August. Was invited to spend the day & dine at Sir John Birnie's[65] about six or eight miles off but sent an excuse as I cannot be absent from parades without asking General Grinfield himself, which I do not think it worthwhile to do for a dinner. Had a card some days ago to dine at Lord Seaforth's on Saturday next but sent an excuse on that account which I mentioned in my answer.

Richard was obviously finding General Grinfield somewhat challenging.

17 September. Was out with the drill before 6 o'clock; had also a 6-pounder with two horses and the artillerymen at drill at the same time. All the men of the artillery now at Barbados belonged to the late Irish Artillery and I am sorry to say that I found most of them this morning very awkward indeed. Ordered them out again in the evening.

Rode to town to call upon General Maitland about negroes &c. Very hot. Dined at Mr Savary's to meet the new Storekeeper Mr Langley. At 5 o'clock went to the parade, when General Grinfield marched us

65. I cannot find any record of a Sir John Birnie.

about till half past 6 o'clock. Came back and drank coffee on my own. In the different movements of the guns, General Grinfield always calls out to me & says, *is it not so and so* &c. I must own that some of his manoeuvres are new to me and I think not correct, but I make it a rule never to contradict him. I know in the end the weakest must go to the wall. I therefore *always say yes!* To everything.

18 September. Got up before 6 o'clock and bathed. Read most of the morning. At 5 o'clock went to the parade when General Grinfield marched us about with the guns till nearly dark.

19 September Sunday. Attended Divine Service with the detachment at 6 o'clock. Called in the morning at Mr Savary's, found Mr Langley, went with him to the arsenal. Dined at Mr Savary's at a quarter before 5 o'clock went to the Garrison Parade. Marched about till dusk. Went there again, drank coffee.

20 September. Wind rather high last night. Out in the morning before 6 o'clock with the gun drill. Mizzling rain in the morning. Attended the Evening Parade & marched till dark with the two six-pounders.

21 September. Got up before 6 o'clock, rode out for 2 hours. After breakfast rode to town and found Colonel Laye & Lieutenant Dubourdieu[66] there very unexpectedly. Martinique was evacuated on the 15th instant. Dined at Mr Savary's to meet Colonel Laye. Went at 5 o'clock to the Evening Parade. Heavy thunder with livid lightning. Excessively hot today.

22 September. Inspection day; the garrison under arms at 6 o'clock; horses out in harness. Heavy rain about 10 o'clock. Colonel Laye & Lieutenant Dubourdieu breakfasted with me. About 12 o'clock set off to ride to town, but the rain drove me back.

23 September. Out at 6 o'clock with the gun drill. About 7 o'clock the artillery (about 60) landed with the 2nd Battalion 68th Regiment. Lieutenants Brown[67] & Dubourdieu breakfasted with me. Lieutenant Stanwix was brought on shore last night very ill of a fever. Dined at Mr Savary's. At 5 o'clock went to the parade, were marched about till it was dusk. Above 20 men died in two days onboard the ship in the passage from Dominique [Dominica] to this place.

24 September. Poor Stanwix died this morning. Sent to Bridgetown & ordered furniture &c for his coffin. Crape, a hearse & two chaises to be at the Artillery Hospital exactly at 5 o'clock. General Grinfield

66. 1st Lieutenant Saumarez Dubourdieux Royal Artillery (Kane 1001); he was killed at the siege of San Sebastian on 21 July 1813.

67. Probably 1st Lieutenant James Browne Royal Artillery (Kane 995) who resigned at Jamaica in February 1812.

visited the barracks. Came on duty as Captain of the Day (not Garrison Duty). Attended the funeral; quite a private one. Called in at 7 o'clock at Mr Savary's & drank tea.

25 September. Extremely hot. At 6 o'clock bathed. Rode in the morning & called upon Colonel Laye. Wrote to Mrs U[nett] & to John. Had a letter from the latter, the first.

Richard to John Wilkes Unett Esq, Square, Birmingham

Barbados, 25 September 1802

Dear John,
I have this moment received your *only* letter dated 18 July; it had been to Martinique. A vessel sails this morning for Liverpool, I have therefore no time to write you a long letter. I arrived here on the 7 August to command the artillery & a pretty fagging business I have had of it. To the surprize [*sic*] of everybody, the French troops arrived at Martinique on Sunday 12th instant; the British flag was struck at 12 o'clock on Tuesday [14 September 1802]. The next day, the English troops embarked & arrived here two days ago. Colonel Laye now commands, to my great comfort. Our new Commander in Chief, General Grinfield plays the very devil with everybody and everything; a more foul-mouthed dog I never met with. He gave me to drill 2 lieutenants and 35 men of the 60th & 68th Regiments. I have been out with the guns every morning at daylight and again in the evening at 5 o'clock till it was dark. As commanding officer of the artillery, I am very often obliged to ride in the middle of the day to his house, nearly two miles off, through a hot burning white sand, the reflexion [*sic*] of which nearly blinds me. Exercise is certainly good, even in the middle of the day in this country; for since I have been obliged to stir about, I never was better than I am at this moment. We buried yesterday afternoon Lieutenant Stanwix of the artillery (a very fine young lad who came out to this country with me) after three days illness. I am going this morning to take an inventory of his things, that they may be sold by Vendue;[68] there is a sad ugly fever here, the artillery are healthy, but the 2nd Battalion 68th Regiment that disembarked two days ago are very sickly. I *cannot tell you how many are dead within these 48 hours*, when they came on shore, one died in the boat & three were left on the wharf in the last agonies. Our garrison is now above 2,000 men, so many coming at once has put us into dreadful confusion; my heart aches for what I see going on. I never was cut out for a soldier and I wish to God I had done

68. A West Indian phrase for a public auction.

with it. I have not time for more. God bless you my dear John and your wife & family. Remember me to all and believe me, yours affectionately R[ichard] W Unett.

I fancy George won't be at home till the spring. I wrote to you on the 17 July, I will write again soon. I have written to Fanny[69] about the money, it is her *loss of memory.*

26 September Sunday. Attended Divine Service at 6 o'clock with the garrison. Very hot. Came on duty. All the garrison under arms at 5 o'clock in the event &c. Drank tea & spent the evening at Mr Savary's.

Richard reported that a serious fever had broken out, probably brought with the troops from Martinique.

27 September. Rained very hard last night and this morning. A very bad fever in the garrison, a number of soldiers dying daily. Took an inventory of poor Stanwix's effects.

28 September. Intended to ride this morning but Mr Langley the Storekeeper had my horse. I had given him leave to send for him at any time when he wished, he is recovering from a fever. Very hot. Came on duty. Went in the evening & drank tea at Mr Savary's.

29 September. Up before it was light. The whole garrison under arms, it being Inspection day. The prickly heat very troublesome. On the 27th Lieutenants Brown[e], Dr Midford[70] and Captain Dick[71] dined with me at the 60th Mess. Yesterday Colonel Laye dined with me. Lieutenant Dubourdieu has breakfasted several times with me lately. Five or six men are dying daily. Above 400 sick today in the garrison. Rode to Bridgetown and dined at Dr Austen's. Came home at 7 o'clock & drank tea at Mr Savary's. Was asked to a Ball at Colonel Maclean's (who is moved to Bridgetown) but did not go.

30 September. Very hot. Rode out this morning. Employed in making my Muster Rolls. Dined at Mr Savary's.

1 October. Mustered this morning at 6 o'clock. Employed all morning about my horse department. Several soldiers died of the 68th Regiment and one woman of my company.

69. Their sister Frances.

70. Assistant Surgeon William Midford Ordnance (Kane Med 55); he died at Sevenoaks in June 1807.

71. Captain Lieutenant Patrick Dick Royal Artillery (Kane 792); he died in London on 21 October 1803.

2 October. Showery. Came of duty. Dined in Bridgetown with Colonel Laye at Nancy Clarke's Hotel.[72] Rode out in the evening.

3 October Sunday. Rains hard in the night & again this morning. Up at 6 o'clock to the Church Parade. Rains most of the day, so that there was no Evening Parade. Dined & staid the evening at Mr Savary's. *The fever not so bad in the garrison.*

4 October. Up before 6 o'clock and bathed. Rode to town. Extremely hot. Took a long ride in the evening. Came on duty. Saw a gentleman from Martinique who told me that the French buried 100 men the first week after their arrival. They were now burying from 20 to 25 a day. The 11th Regiment now at Dominique [Dominica] lost 10 men the day after they landed. They are still very sickly.

5 October. Rode out before 6 o'clock, very hot. Wrote to the 60th Mess to thank them for their civility & attention to me while I have been a member of their Mess. Breakfasted at Dr Macarthur's. Joined the Artillery Mess again today. Went to the parade at 5 o'clock.

6 October. The whole garrison under arms as soon as it was light. Rains at 11 o'clock; dined at General Grinfield's & in the evening there was a ball. Did not dance. About 70 people came home at 9 o'clock.

7 October. Lieutenant Dubourdieu breakfasted with me. Very hot. Rode to town in the middle of the day. Rode out in the evening. Captain Dick & self on duty every other day.

8 October. Came on duty. Sat on a Brigade Court Martial. Out at the evening parade with the guns.

9 October. Rains hard last night & this morning with thunder. This day was appointed as a Fast instead of the 10th tomorrow, it being Sunday on account of the dreadful hurricane that happened here on the 10 October 1780. The garrison attended Divine Service. Rains almost the whole day. No parade in the evening. Colonel Laye breakfasted with me. Had a letter from George dated 25 August. Rode out in the evening with Colonel Laye. Went and drank tea at Mr Savary's.

10 October Sunday. Rains very hard in the night with thunder. Attended Divine Service. Lieutenant Rogers breakfasted with me. Wrote to George. Dined at Mr Savary's. After evening parade returned there to tea.

72. Nancy Clarke was a free woman of colour and ran the Royal Naval Hotel at Bridgetown, Barbados. She moved to London later and lived on Duke Street, where she died in 1812.

11 October. Was so hot & so uncomfortable all last night with the prickly heat that I did not sleep a wink. Up at gunfire to our regimental drill. Very busy all morning. Excessively hot. No evening parade. The packet arrived; had a letter from Mrs U[nett]. Rode out in the evening with Colonel Laye to town. Called as we returned, drank tea at Mr Savary's.

12 October. Bathed at 6 o'clock. Excessively hot; I heard some natives of the island say that they thought yesterday and today the hottest day they had ever felt. Came on duty, dined at Mr Savary's. Attended the parade & drill of the guns. Very busy all morning with my accounts.

13 October. Up before gun firing. All the garrison under arms. Dr Midford breakfasted with me. Employed with my accounts. About 11 o'clock it rained exceedingly heavy for two hours. Had a letter from my sister Fanny; dined at Mr Savary's. Rode in the evening to Mr Radish's and drank & spent the evening there.

14 October. Up before gun firing when the garrison were under arms for two hours for a punishment. Lieutenant Stone[73] breakfasted with me. General Grinfield visited the barracks at 11 o'clock. Very hot. In the evening, attended the parade & marched about till it was dark. General G[rinfield] very savage.

15 October. Excessively hot. Employed all the morning with my accounts. Rode out in the evening. Called in at Mr Savary's & drank tea.

16 October. Very hot. Employed in settling poor Stanwix's affairs. Came on duty. Out with the guns in the evening.

17 October Sunday. Attended Divine Service at 6 o'clock. Lightning very vivid last night. Rode in the middle of the day to Ormond Fort.[74] Dined at Mr Savary's. At a ¼ before 5 o'clock went to the parade. Lord Seaforth there and received with every honor [*sic*]. Returned to Mr Savary's to tea. Exceeding hot. Could not sleep last night. A good deal of lightning last night.

18 October. Up before 6 o'clock to the drill. Came on duty. Employed about Stanwix's accounts, all his things have been sold by Vendue, except a few small articles, such as a toothpick case, housewife &c, which his sister had packed up for him. These I have reserved and packed up to be sent to England to his family. He was an only son and soon, very soon, cut off. Had he lived, he would have made a fine

73. 1st Lieutenant Henry Stone Royal Artillery (Kane 965); he died in Persia in 1812.

74. Ormond's Fort stood close to Fort Needham.

character. Thank God! The fever has now almost left us. Attended the evening parade, was marched about till it was dark.

19 October. Up before 6 o'clock & bathed. Lieutenants Stone & Dubordieu breakfasted with me. Rode to town. Excessively hot. Took a long ride in the evening.

20 October. The whole garrison under arms at gun firing, it being Inspection Day. Dr Midford breakfasted with me! Mr Langley, Savage & Lieutenant Rogers dined with me. Took a long ride in the evening.

21 October. Employed all morning about late Lieutenant Stanwix's affairs &c. Rode out in the evening, the packet arrived. Excessively hot.

Richard wrote again, he was desperate to come home and was hoping an exchange might achieve it; but he also indicated that George might not get away from Curacao until the following January.

Barbados, 21 October 1802,

Dear John,
The last two letters that I wrote you were written on 17 July & 25 August.[75] It gave me pleasure to hear at last from you dated 18 July. I am sorry you give such bad accounts of your wife, I trust she is before this time fully re-established in her health.[76] Your letter found me at this island; I was ordered here the beginning of August to command the artillery. Embarked on the 4th of that month I arrived here the 7th.

On the 1 August, I was appointed *Commissary of Horse*, 8 shillings per day additional pay, besides a few *candle ends & cheese parings of office.* I am rode by ___ ___,[77] in 2/3 of the perquisites, otherwise it would be an excellent thing, notwithstanding I contrived altogether, that my pay with &c &c amounted for August to about £50 sterling, £30 of which I saved, as I drink no wine, beer or ale, or spirits of any kind, my expenses are trifling. I am resolved to *make hay, while the sun shines.* I sent my wife in July, two drafts for £81 13 shillings and I enclose her by the opportunity which takes this, a bill for £100 sterling. A man deserves everything he can get in this diabolical country; mine is literally got my [*sic* – by] *the sweat of my brows*, for at this moment

75. He means 25 September.
76. She lived until 1860.
77. Purposely left blank in the letter, but he complains about Grinfield openly. Colonel Laye?

the perspiration is running down me in torrents in every direction. The weather has been and still is excessively hot. I have heard some of the natives say lately, that they never felt the weather so warm. I declare in riding out in the middle of the day, which I am often obliged to do, the sun almost melts one alive. When I came to this country, it was understood that there would be a General Relief of the companies in the West Indies this Xmas, this plan is now dropped, there being not artillery *sufficient* in England to furnish the Relief this year. I have however two strings to my bow and if I possibly can, I most certainly will return next summer. My object is to effect an exchange with another captain; if I can accomplish this, I think I shall get to England in the spring. We have had a terrible fever here, which carried off eight or ten soldiers in a day; sometimes only after one day's illness. Poor Lieutenant Stanwix of the artillery who came out with me, caught the fever on his passage from Martinique, was landed here one day; the next we buried him after three days sickness. Thank God, it has now subsided in this island, though at Dominique [Dominica], Martinique, Trinidad & Guadeloupe, the mortality is dreadful. The French have lost at the latter island in three months, out of *3,500 men, 3,300 men!!!* only about *200 men* alive about a month ago; in all probability those are dead by this time. At Martinique they buried one hundred men the first week, they have buried by the last accounts in this country *forty three General & Field officers out of seventy!!!* The French captain of artillery to whom I delivered over all the guns, ammunition &c &c at Martinique, died a few days after the evacuation of the island; he complained very much of the heat. No talk about Curacao being given up; reports say that will be next January. I had a letter from George dated 25 August. I wrote him a long letter a few days. If I get home safe from this infernal country, *I never will again if I possibly can help it, return.* A burnt *child dreads the fire*, and sure enough I am broiling daily from morning till night and from night till morning. I never was so harassed as since our new Commander of the Forces arrived, General Grinfield, he is a very devil. He finds fault with everybody and everything; he has certainly *relaxed a little* from his first plans, it is still bad enough.

Thank God, I am in good health. Kiss all your children, tell them their uncle has sent them *his burning* kisses each. Remember me to my family, to your wife and believe me ever your affectionate R[ichard] W Unett

22 October. A good deal of thunder in the morning and again in the evening. Wrote to Mrs U[nett], to Elizabeth, to John & to Fanny. Out with the guns in the evening. Extremely hot.

23 October. Employed all the morning in finishing my letters to go to Woolwich by Dr Midford. Rains exceedingly hard in the middle

of the day. Rode in the morning & again in the evening. Called & drank tea at Mr Savary's.

24 October Sunday. Attended Divine Service in the morning. Dined at Mr Savary's. Went to the evening parade. Returned & drank tea at Mr Savary's. Dr Midford breakfasted with me.

25 October. Rode in the morning with Colonel Laye to Bridgetown & breakfasted at a Mr Cohen's, a Jew. Very hot. Rode again in the evening. The packet arrived, had a letter from Mrs U[nett]. Employed in the morning &c.

26 October. Bathed this morning. Very hot. Employed all morning about my Muster Rolls &c. Came on duty. Attended the Evening Parade with the guns. Wind very high last night. Lightning very vivid this evening.

27 October. Up at gun firing. The Inspection Day. Wrote to Mrs U[nett] by the packet. Rode in the evening. Very hot.

28 October. Employed all morning &c. Out in the evening with the guns. Rode afterwards to Mr Radish's & spent the evening. Came home at 12 o'clock. Excessively close.

29 October. Employed with my horse accounts. Was President of a Board of Survey upon some clothing. Breakfasted at Rogers'. Showery. Drank tea at Mr Savary's.

30 October. Very hot. Attended Divine [Service] this morning at 6 o'clock. Out in the evening to the Parade.

1 November. The artillery mustered at 6 o'clock this morning. Rode to town. Extremely hot. Asked to dine at Mr Cohen's but refused. General Grinfield has been confined for eight or ten days with the gout in his foot, he was this morning out again & visiting the barracks with Captain Stopford[78] Commodore &c. Very hot. This evening I saw one of my company in the hospital in a high fever & quite delirious &c; he died in half an hour after. He brought on the fever by intemperance.

2 November. Rode out early this morning to see about grass &c. Breakfasted with Dr Macarthur. Very hot. Rode out again in the evening. Drank tea at Mr Savary's.

3 November. Up at gun firing, it being Inspection Day. Lieutenant Stone breakfasted with me. Was asked to dine at Mr Cohen's, but

78. Captain Robert Stopford, commanded HMS *Excellent* of 74 guns. He served as Commander-in-Chief of the Leeward Islands station in 1802.

refused as I invited Dr Burke,[79] Mr Sayers and Dr Innes to dine with me. An excessive heavy shower of rain in the middle of the day. Rode in the evening with Mr Savary & Rogers, went to Charles Fort and drank tea at Captain Hardy's.[80] Very hot.

4 November. Excessively hot. Employed about my men's accounts. Dined and drank tea at Mr Savary's.

5 November. Yesterday my horse had a little running at the nose & a slight cold. Gave him in the morning a physic ball, which worked him very much, was very sick & would not eat. Last night he died to my great surprize and loss. Was up this morning at gun firing. Went to Bridgetown with a party of me & the devil carriage,[81] brought a 24-pounder iron gun. Breakfasted at Colonel Shipley's then rode to Colonel Laye's. Excessively hot. Came on duty.

6 November. Bathed this morning at 6 o'clock. Sat upon as Court Martial at 10 o'clock, then walked to Colonel Laye's with the proceedings. Employed after with my accounts. Excessively hot; the weather for this week past much hotter than usual. Attended parade at 5 o'clock then rode out in the evening.

7 November Sunday. Attended Divine Service at 6 o'clock. Employed all the morning about my accounts &c. Dined at Mr Savary's. Went to the parade at 5 o'clock, returned to tea. Very hot.

8 November. Employed with my company's accounts from breakfast to dinner without ever getting up from the table. Was engaged to dine in the country at Mr Radish's, but could not go, on account of our having a punishment at 5 o'clock. Rode there after 6 o'clock, did not come home till 11 o'clock. Exceedingly hot.

9 November. Employed all day as yesterday in paying my men & dined at Mr Savary's. Out in the evening with the guns. Excessively hot.

10 November. Up at gun firing, it being Inspection Day. A shower of rain between 6 & 7 o'clock. Was invited to dine at General Grinfield's & at Lord Seaforth's. Sent an excuse to both of them. Employed all morning in paying my company. Extremely hot. Took a long ride in the evening.

79. Apothecary William Augustus Burke (Johnston 1752).

80. Captain Lieutenant Thomas Hardy Royal Artillery (Kane 846); he died at Jamaica in 1814.

81. A devil carriage was able to transport a large garrison carriage with the gun tube attached.

11 November. Up at 5 o'clock with a fatigue party &c to go to Bridgetown to bring away another of the 24 pounders, but neither the sling cart or devil carriage was repaired &c. Rode out & called at Colonel Laye's & staid [for] breakfast. Dr Innes dined with me. Out in the evening with the guns, marched about till it was dark. Very hot & close. Asked to a Ball & supper at General Maitland's but sent an excuse.

12 November. Employed all morning about my accounts. Very hot. Took a long ride in the evening with Colonel Laye.

13 November. The packet arrived. Wrote to Mrs U[nett]. A smart shower about 7 o'clock. Breakfasted at Dubourdieu's. Had a letter from Mrs U[nett], Mary Anne [Fraser] has been very ill, is now got well again. Rode out in the evening. Drank tea with Rogers. Rain with thunder & lightning at 8 o'clock.

14 November Sunday. Attended Divine Service at 6 o'clock. Employed in the morning in making Muster Rolls for the horse department. At Evening Parade a quarter before 5 o'clock, Colonel Laye sick.

15 November. Up at gun firing when the artillery had a field day & fired with small arms. Showery. Out in the evening with the guns & marched about till nearly dark.

16 November. Up again a gun firing & had another field day with small arms &c [in] preparation to our being reviewed. Rode out in the evening. Lieutenant Stone breakfasted with me.

17 November. Up again at gun firing &c as yesterday. Colonel Laye & Lieutenant Dubourdieu breakfasted with me. Slight showers of rain.

18 November. Up before gun firing; rains hard between 5 & 6 o'clock, but cleared up. We were reviewed &c afterwards General Grinfield inspected our books &c he said mine were very correct & neat. We all breakfasted with Colonel Laye in the Mess room. The general expressed his satisfaction at our appearance &c. Showery most of the day. Had a letter from George dated 27 October.

19 November. Rains most of the morning. Had another letter from George dated 20 October. Was President of a Court Martial. A great sickness at Antigua. Captain Armit[82] of the Engineers & Lieutenant Fisher of the Artillery[83] dead.

82. Captain Lieutenant George Armit Royal Engineers.

83. 1st Lieutenant John Fisher Royal Artillery (Kane 1017) died at Antigua on 8 November 1802.

20 November. Up this morning at gun firing. The artillery under arms for a punishment of two of my company. Wrote to George. Captain Dick breakfasted with me. Rode out in the evening. Showery the day.

21 November Sunday. Attended Divine Service at 6 o'clock. Showery. Not quite so hot as it has been lately. At the Evening Parade drank tea afterwards at Mr Savary's.

22 November. Rained very hard early this morning. Was President of a Court Martial. Rode after dinner.

23 November. Up at gun fire to a field day of the 60th Regiment. The additionals of that regiment fired for the first time. Rained very hard early this morning. Out in the evening to a drill of the artillery with 4 x 6-pounders.

24 November. Up before gun firing, it being Inspection Day. Ground very wet. In the barracks most of the morning upon a survey of hammocks & blankets. Lieutenant Lynch 11th Regiment[84] breakfasted with me. Out in the evening with 4 x 6-pounders with the artillery.

25 November. Out at gun firing to drill with the artillery &c. General Grinfield visited the barracks. A heavy shower of rain at 10 o'clock. Lieutenant Devon 68th Regiment[85] breakfasted with me. Out at drill in the evening. Drank tea at Mr Savary's.

26 November. Rained hard last night & this morning no drill. Have got the rheumatism in my back & shoulders &c. Out in the evening to the gun exercise. Had my shoulders &c rubbed well with Opodeldoc[86] at going to bed.

27 November. Up at gun firing &c. Asked to dine at Mr Savary's but did not go. Went in the evening to Colonel Shipley's who gave a Grand Ball & supper. Almost everybody there. The supper very super, did not come home till nearly 12 o'clock.

28 November Sunday. Up at gun firing, but it rained, which prevented Divine Service. Employed all the morning in a review of necessaries &c and his making Muster Rolls.

29 November. Up at gun firing with the artillery to a punishment. Employed about the horse accounts &c. Out at drill at half past 4 o'clock.

84. Lieutenant John Lynch 11th Foot.

85. Lieutenant George Devon 68th Foot.

86. A medical camphorated liniment.

> 30 November. Up at gun firing & rode out for an hour. Breakfasted at Colonel Shipley's.
>
> 1 December. Was obliged to get up at 3 o'clock, having a touch of the dysentery. Rained hard last night & this morning Inspection Day, though it had rained so much, yet at a little after 5 o'clock General Grinfield was at the barracks. He inspected the troops on their private parade. Colonel Laye was sick. After the different inspections the general sent to me to meet him in the arsenal, he went into every store &c. Rained most of the morning. The brigade mustered at 10 o'clock. Drank tea at Mr Savary's.

Richard had yet to get home and now there were rumours of war again.

> 2 December. Up at 5 o'clock. My bowels rather out of order. Rains in the morning no drill. Very warm. Went into the sea. Yesterday a sloop of war arrived from England, out [in] 45 days. She brings accounts that there is a prospect of another war taking place between England & France immediately. I am sorry for it. General Grinfield sent for Colonel Laye. As soon as he came back, he sent for me to say that General Grinfield had directed him to order me to Antigua tomorrow and asked me if I should like it. I answered by no means, if I had a choice. I therefore hope to get off going. Out at drill in the evening.
>
> 3 December. Caught cold yesterday in bathing, have got pains in all my limbs. The general and Lord Seaford came round the barracks. Mr Langley breakfasted with me. Employed all morning with my accounts. Out at drill in the evening.
>
> 4 December. Employed all morning with my accounts. Rode out in the evening with Colonel Laye. Very close and warm.
>
> 5 December Sunday. Attended Divine Service at 6 o'clock with the garrison. Wrote to Mrs U[nett] by Lieutenant Dixon of 11th Regiment.[87] At the parade in the evening at half past 4 o'clock.
>
> 6 December. Employed all day in paying my company. Very vivid lightning in the evening. Out at the Garrison Parade at 5 o'clock.
>
> 7 December. Rode out before breakfast. Employed all the morning in paying my company. Out with the guns at the Evening Parade.
>
> 8 December. Up at a little after 4 o'clock; the whole line out, it being Inspection Day. The line fired. Dined at General Grinfield's. In the evening was the Weekly Ball, came home about 9 o'clock.

87. Lieutenant Manley Dixon 11th Foot.

9 December. Lieutenant Dubourdieu breakfasted with me. Employed in the morning in paying my company. Asked to dine at Mr Savary's but did not go. Out with the guns in the evening. After the parade, drank tea at Mr Savary's.

General Grinfield ordered some extraordinary movements which ended in disaster.

10 December. Showery, very warm. Rode to Bridgetown. In the evening the whole garrison were under arms for a field day & fired; the line fired a volley & then charged, in consequence of which Lieutenant Henderson of 2nd Battalion 60th[88] was thrown down & the gun going over his thigh, broke it in two places. Nobody but General Grinfield would ever think of making the guns charge in line with the battalions, when the artillery men are all exposed to the enemy & without any defence for themselves & must inevitably be all cut off. The general does not know artillery movements. Was asked to dine at Captain Hardy's at Charles Fort, but could [not] go until after the Evening Parade, staid till nearly 1 o'clock.

11 December. Up at a little after gun firing to a Regimental Parade. Showery & very warm. Rode out in the evening with Colonel Laye.

12 December Sunday. Up at gun firing, when it rained & there was no church service. Dined at Mr Savary's. Attended the Evening Parade at a quarter before 5 o'clock. Went again after the parade & drank tea.

13 December. Up at gun fire; was ordered to examine and give in a report to General Grinfield of the state of the guns in the Colonial Batteries and forts &c. Had a party of 2 non-commissioned officers, 12 gunners & 12 negroes &c. Began this morning at Ormond Fort; breakfasted with Lieutenant Rogers. Went there again at half after 4 o'clock, came home at a little after 6 o'clock. Wind high with showers.

14 December. Rains hard with high wind last night and this morning at 6 o'clock, so that I sent my party to their barracks again. Cleared up towards 7 o'clock, when I went off with my men, breakfasted at Colonel Shipley's. At half past 4 o'clock pm went to Charles Fort & drank tea after at Captain Hardy's, the Captain Gunner of the fort. Showery.

15 December. Up before gun firing, it being Inspection Day. The line fired. Breakfasted with Dr Burke. Captain Bover[89] (of the *Blenheim*

88. Lieutenant Thomas Henderson 2/60th Foot.

89. Captain Peter Bover Royal Navy died suddenly on 14 December 1802.

74 guns,[90] Commodore Hood[91] who arrived from England this day week) was buried with military honours at 1 o'clock. The ship fired minute guns, I did not go. Went in the evening with my party to Charles Fort to examine the guns &c. Went afterwards and drank tea at Mr Savary's.

16 December. A very boisterous blowing night, with rain & continued during the day &c. At gun firing went with my party to Willoughby Fort.[92] In the afternoon went to Rickett's Battery.[93] Drank tea at Mr Savary's.

17 December. A very boisterous night. Wind high in the morning. Went at gun firing to Grenville Fort &c. Made out my report this morning to General Grinfield and another for Colonel Laye. Very busy all the morning. Rode out in the afternoon. Wind high with showers.

18 December. Wind very high. Up before gun firing to a punishment. Made another report out for Lord Seaforth. Employed all morning with my company's accounts. Dr Innes & Toosey dined with me.

19 December Sunday. Wind high last night with showers. Up at gun firing; attended Divine Service with the garrison. Very busy all the morning with my accounts. At the Evening Parade we fired 13 guns as a salute to Lady Seaforth. The whole line marched past & saluted her. Showery. Had pains in my limbs and back, Dr Burke gave me something to take at bedtime.

20 December. Did not get up till after 6 o'clock, found myself free from pain. Employed all the day with my paylists &c. Showery. Out in the evening with the guns & drank tea at Mr Savary's.

21 December. Up at gun firing. Employed all day as yesterday. The packet arrived. Wind high with rain. Out in the evening with the guns &c.

22 December. Up nearly an hour before the gun fired, Inspection Day. Rained very hard, when everybody got wet through. The other packet arrived; had a letter from Mrs U[nett] but no date. Rode out in the evening with Colonel Laye. Called in [&] drank tea at Mr Savary's. Wind very high.

90. HMS *Blenheim* was originally of 90 guns, but was razeed to 74 guns in 1801.

91. Captain Samuel Hood Royal Navy arrived as a Commissioner in Trinidad.

92. Fort Willoughby stood at the mouth of the River Constitution in Bridgetown on the eastern bank.

93. Rickett's Battery stood opposite Fort Willoughby on the western bank.

23 December. Showery with high wind. Up before gun firing to parade for a punishment. General Grinfield went round the barracks. Employed with my company &c. Out with the guns in the afternoon.

24 December. Close and warm. President of a Court Martial. Employed with my accounts. Lent Mr Savary 500 dollars.

25 December. Xmas day. The whole garrison under arms with Colours, guns &c for Divine Service. But the rain prevented us just after the square was formed & the clergyman had begun. Got wet through. Dined at Mr Savary's. Busy with my accounts.

26 December Sunday. A great deal of rain with high wind last night, no church service. Rains hard all the morning. Lieutenant Stone breakfasted with me. Dined again at Mr Savary's. Came to the parade at a quarter before 5 o'clock, but it began raining very hard & so continued; no parade. Went back to Mr Savary's.

27 December. Rains very hard most of the day. Rode in the evening, no General Parade.

28 December. Rained very hard last night. Very busy all yesterday morning and again today in making Muster Rolls.

29 December. Was up before gun firing, but it had rained so much, that we had no Inspection, began raining very hard afterwards. Cleared up a little in the middle of the day. Employed all morning. Had a letter from George dated 7 December, answered it. Dined with Dr Innes at the Staff Mess. Came home about 8 o'clock when I got completely wet through and through.

30 December. Rains very hard all the day and all last night. Four sailors at 8 o'clock this morning were hanged in the bay onboard the *Excellent* man of war for mutiny. Asked to dine at the Whist Club but refused. Very busy all morning.

Some of his men were ordered to Trinidad, but he was not perturbed.

31 December. Rained very hard all last night and the morning. The 5th Battalion of the 60th Regiment landed from Surinam.[94] A detachment of 24 artillery embarked for Trinidad, 12 of them my company; most of them great vagabonds. Drank tea at Mr Savary's.

94. The 5th Battalion 60th Foot had been in Surinam since 1799, but handed it back to the Dutch as part of the Peace of Amiens.

1803

1 January. Rains hard most of last night and again most of the day. The artillery mustered at 6 o'clock in the morning.

2 January Sunday. Rains hard last night and again most of the day. No Divine Service in the morning, nor any parade in the evening. So much rain was never known before in this island as there has been this year in Barbados 1802.

3 January. Rains hard almost the whole day with wind. Employed about my accounts. No General Parade owing to the weather.

4 January. Rains very hard most of last night, again most of the day. Drank tea at Mr Savary's. No parade &c.

5 January. Up before gun firing. The ground so exceedingly wet, no going on it, but General Grinfield came up & saw us upon our own private parades. The packet arrived yesterday; had a letter from Mrs U[nett]. Lieutenant Rogers breakfasted with me. Rode to town. Colonel Rogers[95] arrived to relieve Colonel Laye.

6 January. Rains very hard almost the whole day. Asked to dine at Mr Savary's to meet Colonel Rogers', but did not go. Went there in the evening.

7 January. Today was fine, except an occasional shower. Brigadier General Beresford was buried at 1 o'clock with military honours.[96] I had the command of 5 six-pounders & marched from the barracks at 10 o'clock to the front of the King's House; had 15 men with three horses to each gun. I fired minute guns during the ceremony which lasted 46 minutes, afterwards fired three vollies [*sic*] of five guns each. General Grinfield was pleased with my firing. Drank tea at Mr Savary's.

8 January. Rains in the morning & again in the evening. Rode out in the afternoon. Drank tea at Mr Savary's.

9 January Sunday. Rains hard in the morning, no church service. Employed in paying my company all morning. Employed yesterday from 9 o'clock to 3 o'clock in taking a Remain of Clothing.

10 January. Showery. Employed in paying my company. Rode out in the evening. Drank tea after at Mr Savary's. Received my parcel today from home. Showery.

11 January. Showery &c. Employed about my accounts. Drank tea at Mr Savary's.

95. Brevet Lieutenant Colonel Henry Rogers Royal Artillery.

96. Brigadier General Marcus Beresford died on 6 January 1803.

12 January. Up before gun firing, it being Inspection Day. A heavy shower of rain at 5 o'clock am. The line out, but the ground so we that the guns were nearly up to their axle trees &c. Employed all morning about the horse accounts.

13 January. The general visited the barracks. Not very well yesterday & today. Both my hands feel numbed & my head dizzy, took 3 Analeptic pills[97] about 11 o'clock and at 1 o'clock a bason [*sic*] of broth. Eat nothing but broth for dinner. Showery.

14 January. Was a member upon a General Court Martial which began sitting today; nine officers of 5th Battalion 60th to be tried.[98] Took a long ride in the evening. Took a long ride at Mr Savary's.

15 January. The Court Martial sat again at 9 o'clock & broke up at 2 o'clock, this to continue till finished, without any adjournments. Dr Burke gave me something to take at bedtime & tomorrow morning. My head &c unwell. Rode out in the evening. Went to the Whist Club which we have just formed, to meet at each other's quarters &c. Tonight at Colonel Shipley's my hand gave me great pain. Came here early.

16 January Sunday. Gave in my name sick today. Rained very hard last night. Asked to dine at Mr Savary's but did not go. Had my feet put in warm water and took some whey at going to bed. Showery.

17 January. Am pretty well today. The whole line under arms in the evening & fired 17 guns, then a feu de joye [joie] down the line; then another salute of 17 guns, afterwards a feu de joye &c. This as a kind of rehearsal for tomorrow.

18 January. At 10 o'clock the line under arms. At 1 o'clock we fired a salute of 21 guns down the line, then a feu de joye [joie] &c. Was asked to a Ball & supper at Lord Seaforth's but sent an excuse. Took a long ride in the evening. Dr Burke sent me a draught to take at going to bed.

19 January. The General Court Martial sat again. Rode out in the evening. Called in, drank tea at Mr Savary's.

---

97. Analeptic pills stimulate the central nervous system.

98. The president of the court martial was Colonel Maclean of the 2nd/60th. Captain Hillerich was tried for challenging and fighting with Lieutenant Koch; he was acquitted. Lieutenants Michael de Wend, Adam Krein and John Herbert were tried for acting as seconds; these were also acquitted. Lieutenant Ellert was charged with drunkenness and acting in an unofficer-like manner to Captain de Wend. He was found guilty of some of the charges and sentenced to be cashiered. A further trial commenced immediately afterwards on Lieutenants Koch, John Herbert, John Zuhleke, William Johnson and Alexander Mackenzie, on charges of conspiring to cause dissension by attempting to exclude Hillerich from the Mess. The five were acquitted, but the court highlighted Koch as the main protagonist and he was suspended from rank and pay for six months

20 January. The Court Martial sat again. Out in the evening with the guns. The packet arrived, but had no letters. Have not been very well these some days.

21 January. The Court Martial sat again. Out with the guns in the evening.

22 January. The Court Martial sat again. Took a ride in the evening with Colonel Laye.

23 January Sunday. Up before gun firing, the whole garrison out to Divine Service. Out again in the evening.

24 January. The Court Martial sat again. Dr Burke has given me something to take morning & evening. Rode out in the evening with Dr Burke. Very warm.

25 January. The Court sat again. Rode out in the evening.

Because of his continued illness Richard was advised to request a Medical Board to send him home.

26 January. The whole line under arms at gun firing. The Court did not sit today, the Judge advocate being particularly engaged. Dined & spent the evening at Mr Savary's. On account of the dimness in my eyes and the numbness in my fingers, Dr Burke has strongly recommended me to apply for a Medical Board & go to England. That a cold climate is absolutely necessary to brace me &c.

27 January. The Court sat again. Was asked to dine at Colonel Maclean's (Lord Seaforth to be there) but declined. There was a Ball in the evening. Rode out after dinner & got caught in the rain.

28 January. The Court sat again. Rode out in the evening. Called in at Mr Savary's and drank tea. Colonel Rogers at present lives there, he has been very unwell for these five days, he is a little better. Rains in the evening and during the night.

29 January. The Court sat again. Dr Burke has strongly recommended me to go to England, that this hot climate might prove of very serious consequences to my health, from the dizziness in my eyes and the numbness in my fingers he was apprehensive I might either have a stroke of the palsy, or an apoplectic fit and said it was absolutely necessary that I should go without loss of time to a cold climate.

I therefore wrote to the Commanding Officer to request Lieutenant General Grinfield would order a Medical Board to report upon my case. I was this day before them (for a very few minutes) and they have given their opinion that I should go to England immediately for the recovery of my health. My head aches very much, with a violent pain across my eyes. Rode out in the evening, then back to the Whist Club, of which I am appointed Tresurer [*sic*]. Rains in the evening.

England Beckons

1803

Richard was duly ordered home on leave.

> 30 January Sunday. Gave in my name sick and did not go to the parades. Rode out in the evening. Drank tea at Mr Savary's. Today I was in General Orders for 6 month's leave to go to England for the recovery of my health from 1 February.
>
> 31 January. The Court sat again. Rode out in the evening. Called and drank tea at Mr Savary's. Colonel Rogers lives there, he is better.
>
> 1 February. The artillery mustered at 6 o'clock [am]. The Court sat again. Rode out again in the afternoon.
>
> 2 February. The Court met again for a short time, when [we] were dissolved &c. Captain Dick sailed in the *Warrior* transport for England. My head has ached very much with a violent pain across my eyes. Rode out in the evening.
>
> 6 February. I have not attended parades for some days; have rode out every afternoon. My head has pained me a good deal, with a numbness in my hands.
>
> 7 February. Rode out in the evening. Drank tea at Mr Savary's.
>
> 8 February. This morning at gun firing, the whole garrison were under arms, when a soldier of [the] 68th Regiment was shot for desertion. Two others were pardoned.
>
> 9/10 February. Cool & pleasant, rode out each day in the afternoon.
>
> 11 February. Have agreed for my passage to Liverpool in the ship *Venerable* Captain Lewlas, for which I am to pay for my passage & board & my servant's passage only *£72 16s 0d*, or 312 Dollars![1]

1. About £3,600 today.

> 13 February Sunday. I have rode out every day lately, as I attend no parades.
>
> 14 February. Rode to town in the morning about settling some business for George. Rode out again in the evening and drank tea at Mr Radish's.
>
> 15 February. Have been employed several mornings in settling the accounts of the horse department and with Mr Savary and Mr Langley.

Finally Richard set sail for England. Why Rogers went home with Laye when he was his replacement is not clear, but he did retire in the September on getting his lieutenant colonelcy confirmed.

> 16 February. A few days ago a detachment of artillery arrived from Woolwich, with my Captain Lieutenant Keane.[2] Embarked this afternoon onboard the *Venerable*, with Lieutenant Colonels Laye and Rogers. We found everything in great confusion &c & that she would not sail until the morning. Went ashore again & slept at Nancy Clarke's Tavern in Bridgetown.

Landing at Liverpool, Richard sped home via Stone and Acton Hill.

> 17 February. Sailed between 11 & 12 o'clock. After a middling passage & meeting with some very blowing weather, landed at Liverpool on Sunday morning 3 April.
>
> 4 April. Set of at 4 o'clock in the afternoon, got to Stone at 5 o'clock the next morning.
>
> 5 April. Then took a chaise and arrived at Acton Hill about 7 o'clock & surprized my sister Fanny very much, as she did not know that I was coming home.
>
> 9 April. Set off in a chaise. Arrived at Birmingham about 2 o'clock; it is astonishing how much I improved by my few days at Acton Hill.

He arrived at Woolwich to find that George had also returned from the West Indies only a few days earlier.

> 10 April Sunday. Set off at 7 o'clock in the evening, arrived in London about 2 o'clock [pm] the next day. Took a chaise & was at Woolwich to dinner, where I found my brother George, who had

2. Captain & Lieutenant Charles Keane Royal Artillery (Kane 825); he died at Barbados on 14 January 1813.

arrived about ten days before from Jamaica. Found Mrs U[nett] & Mary Anne [Fraser] very well.

19 April. Major & Mrs Phipps,[3] Major & Mrs [George] Dixon & Lieutenant Carthew[4] dined & supped with us.

23 April. Had company to dinner & supper. Captain & Mrs Close,[5] Captain & Mrs Howard Douglas, Lieutenant Taylor & Captain Massey. Alexander [Fraser] met with an accident at school by tumbling downstairs a few days ago. He is now pretty well again; I called upon them but Alexander did not know me.

29/30 April. Went to London both days. Called upon Messieurs Lang & Co about the children's money. We dined & spent the day at Colonel Douglas'.[6]

1 May Sunday. Brother George set off this evening to join his company at Canterbury.

18 May. We dined & spent the day at Captain [Henry] Deacon's. Very cold weather.

19 May. Major [Scott] with Edmund & John Scott have slept and breakfasted with us for these four or five days; they are just come up from Canterbury, he having got an appointment in the Warren.

27 May. Showery & with high winds. The regiment was reviewed by the Duke of York.

Belatedly Richard recorded the resumption of war with France.

29 May. We are now at war again with the French.[7]

31 May. Went to London, came home at 5 o'clock, was so unwell that I was obliged to go very early to bed. Have been confined to the house with a rheumatic cold &c & did not go out until Tuesday 7 June.

11 June. Set off in a chaise with Mary Anne [Fraser] to bring the boys home for the holidays. Left Mary Anne at Greenwich, went

---

3. Major George Phipps of the Infantry Royal Military Academy Woolwich.
4. 1st Lieutenant Robert Carthew Royal Artillery (Kane 946); he died on his passage from Corunna on 22 January 1809.
5. Captain Lieutenant John Close Royal Artillery (Kane 878); he died at Hastings in 1857.
6. Lieutenant Colonel Robert Douglas Royal Artillery (Kane 424); he died at Woolwich in 1827.
7. War was actually declared on 18 May 1803.

> round by Camberwell, took the boys to Town &c. Called as we came back & drank tea at Mrs Godwin's.
>
> 12 June Sunday. Captain Macdonell & Gwynn[8] came down & dined unexpectedly. Captain Gwynn came a few days ago from Scotland.

Richard's company had remained at Barbados and Captain Gother Mann[9] exchanged to take command there, Richard taking Mann's company (8 Company 5th Battalion) who were stationed at Waterford in Ireland.

> 15 June. Today I was ordered to hold myself in readiness to go immediately to Ireland.
>
> 14 July. A few days ago I was ordered to march to Ireland with one hundred recruits, they are not yet sufficiently drilled, but will be ready to march [in] the beginning of August. The Prince of Wales came down & reviewed the regiment &c. He dined afterwards at General Drummond's in the Warren.
>
> 15 July. Today I was ordered to proceed without delay *direct to* Waterford, being appointed to command a brigade of artillery at that place.
>
> 17 July Sunday. My servant (Wilson) embarked with my baggage at 2 o'clock onboard a transport with some of the horse artillery for Cork.

Richard's Journals end here, but it is clearly annotated that the next one would begin on 19 July, but this unfortunately is not extant, nor any later journals.

The family correspondence also virtually disappears from June 1803 until September 1807, with George stationed in the Home Counties and Richard in Waterford, Ireland.

From an odd note in the files, it appears that his sister Elizabeth had arranged for some goods to be sent to Richard who was still at Waterford in June 1805. In fact, Richard's company was stationed at Waterford continually until 1 February 1808, when Richard was promoted a Major and he handed the company over to Captain Frederic Glubb.[10]

---

8. The only Captain Gwyn I can discover in the Army List is Captain William Gwyn of the 45th Foot.
9. Captain Gother Mann Royal Artillery (Kane 749) went out to the West Indies in place of Richard Unett in 1803, but on his return passage on 4 December 1804 he died.
10. Captain Frederic Glubb Royal Artillery (Kane 925); he retired in July 1813.

To Miss [Elizabeth] Unett, Mrs Godwin's Croom's Hill[11] Greenwich

Newbridge Street, [London][12] 14 June 1805

C Graham presents best compliments to Miss Unett & acquaints her that the box for Captain Unett is at last shipped in the *Anna*, Captain George Paynter for Waterford. C Graham is sorry he has not had an opportunity of shipping it sooner. He hopes Miss Unett will now soon hear of its arriving safe and in good condition.

Mr & Mrs North & Mrs Graham desire best compliments to Miss [Elizabeth] Unett, they also desire to be kindly remembered to Captain [Richard] & Mrs [Ann] Unett when Miss Unett writes to Waterford & hope they were well when Miss Unett last heard from them. Mr North is pretty well recovered from his gout, the rest of the family well.

11. Crooms Hill is a residential road in Greenwich to this day. Records show a Mrs Jane Goodwin of Crooms Hill in 1822.

12. New Bridge Street runs north from Blackfriars Bridge.

Copenhagen, and the West Indies Again

The next letter we have is from George, whose company went on the expedition to Copenhagen in 1807, in a pre-emptive strike by the British before Napoleon took the Danish fleet, then the fifth largest in the world. The Danes were forced to surrender after a three-night bombardment which devastated parts of the city and the fleet was taken to Britain a few months later.

George to J[ohn] W[ilkes] Unett Esquire, Square, Birmingham

Within 400 yards of Copenhagen, 5 September 1807

Dear John,
I have now been landed three weeks and have not had time to write a line to anyone. I have been constantly until yesterday with my guns at the advanced posts and so near the enemy that I have either been engaged with them most mornings or else kept constantly on the alert and turned up in the night half a dozen times with '*Captain they are a coming*', they have only continued out two or three times and have met with such [a] reception that they will not attempt it again.

The bombardment has commenced and been continued very briskly for two days. The largest church was burnt down this morning[1] and the town is now on fire in several places, whether this will make them surrender I know not, as they make a determined resistance *behind their works*. We have got upwards of 2,000 prisoners with several pieces of cannon &c &c; but we must be quick in our operations, or we shall not be able to return if we wait until the frost setts [*sic*] in, they know this and will consequently hold out as long as possible.

I perceive the newspapers have given us the place without any difficulty, but I assure you we have something to do yet. We are a

1. The steeple of the Vor Frue Kirke (Church of Our Lady) became a prominent mark for the British artillery; almost every Danish image of the Copenhagen attack depicts the destruction of this spire.

good deal annoyed by their gunboats; our last resource is to storm,[2] this must be done & soon, for we never can show our faces in old England if we do not take it, limited as we are to time.

We have lost a good many men and officers, but I am in good health & spirits and mean to spend my Christmas amongst you all and knock down a few partridge. If you write to Fanny, tell them I am very well, and will write when we get into Copenhagen & I can get a little quiet. The nights are getting cold and a clean pair of shirts would be a great luxury after sleeping so long upon straw in ditches and under hedges. Remember me to all and believe me your affectionate brother, G[eorge] Unett.

George gained his Captaincy on 1 February 1808 and he was given command of 10 Company of the 7th Battalion which was stationed in Barbados. George took passage in the beginning of November to the West Indies and he took command of his company from Captain Charles Waller.[3] He was immediately placed on the Staff of Sir George Beckwith and wrote on Christmas Day, as they prepared to embark to attack Martinique.

George to Miss [Fanny] Unett, Mr Wards, Aston Hill near Stafford.

Barbados, 25 December 1808

My dear Fanny,
I wrote to [Richard] Wilkes immediately upon my arrival here and hope he would mention it in case any opportunity offered. I should also have written [to] you and John, but do assure you I had not time, not even to say one [or] two lines that we had a good passage out and arrived within the five weeks. The night previous to our making the land, we fell in with the packet and it being dark and not being able to distinguish what she was, we turned up all hands to make ready for action. I was for some time without any cloaths [*sic*] on and finding myself thirsty, drank off a quantity of porter. The next morning I awoke with a headache, which was made much worse by my landing and being under the necessity of immediately reporting my arrival to the Governor who lives at a good distance. This, with meeting several friends and all asking you a thousand questions and being obliged to be so much in the sun, gave me a light fever which lasted me two days, but not being a *Johnny*

2. Preparations had begun for storming the defences before the city surrendered.
3. Captain Charles Waller Royal Artillery (Kane 696) was a contemporary of his brother Richard and was promoted Major the same day. He retired by the sale of his commission in 1823.

Newcome[4] and not easily frightened away from the good things of this world. I got perfectly well and have since been employed most incessantly in the embarkation of stores, not having been once into Bridgetown (about a mile distant) though I am in want of several things. From the number of troops collected here, there is no room in barracks, but I have been fortunate enough to [a]light on my legs at my own Commandants (General Stehelin's[5]) at whose house I am now staying.

We shall finish embarking our guns &c &c in a day or two and are looking out hourly for Sir George Prevost,[6] who is coming with about 3,000 troops and some artillery from Halifax, when we proceed to attack Martinique, which has now been blockaded by our squadron for several weeks, though not with success; several vessels with troops and provisions having got in and amongst others a frigate about four days since, with flour &c and 170 artillerymen. She compleately [*sic*] out-manoeuvred our squadron laying to in the very centre of them the whole night (being taken for our own) and as soon as daylight appeared, she made a push and got through the whole of them.[7] The *Express* brig[8] very gallantly endeavoured to run her onboard in [torn – an attempt?] of [disabling?] her, but without effect, passing about [a few yards?] astern of her; wherein she fired a Royal Salute.

The French Commander in Chief (Villaret[9]) has sent General Beckwith[10] word how much obliged to him he is, for having given him so much time to make all his preparations, and I have no doubt he will give us a little more to do than we had at Copenhagen, however the more difficulties the greater honor [*sic*]. I have a light brigade

4. A fictional character whose trials and tribulations as a young officer were written by an officer of the Army and illustrated delightfully by Thomas Rowlandson and published in 1815. A second adventure with him similarly joining the Navy was written by Alfred Burton, an ex-Royal Marine officer, in 1818. It is clear that the term 'Johnny Newcome' was already in use as a term for a newbie.
5. Brigadier General Edward Stehelin (Kane 534) commanded the artillery in the West Indies 1809–14.
6. Major General George Prevost was Lieutenant Governor of Nova Scotia.
7. The French frigate *Amphitrite* of 44 guns was the only ship that successfully breached the British blockade. When the British landed on the island *Amphitrite* was scuttled.
8. HMS *Express*, a schooner of 12 guns.
9. Vice Admiral Louis Villaret de Joyeuse was appointed Capitaine General of Martinique and Sainte Lucie [Saint Lucia] in 1802 and retained this position until the British captured Martinique in 1809.
10. Lieutenant General George Beckwith commanded the troops sent from Barbados, Vice Admiral Sir Alexander Cochrane commanding the fleet.

and shall land with the First Division, I have been fagging in the sun from morning to night for several days in compleating [*sic*] it.

28 December. Everything is now onboard, our preparations are on a large scale and I am sorry to say, we have lost several men in compleating [*sic*] them, for our poor fellows work like horses. Four of those who came out with me are dead & several more sick. Now I am on this dismal subject, I am very sorry to acquaint you of the death of poor General Hughes at Surinam,[11] it was the first thing I heard on landing; but adieu to this melancholy subject. I will give you the first information I am able of our operations against Martinique. Another frigate with troops &c, has escaped our blockading squadron & got in safe. Everyone of course blames the admiral.

I had nearly concluded my letter without informing you that I have some hopes of returning to England as soon as the expedition is over, as an officer in this place whose company is at Colchester, wishes to remain here and I shall most certainly indulge him. Remember me very kindly to all at the Hill and let me hear from you as often as you can. Believe me dear Fanny, your affectionate brother, George W[ilkes] Unett

4 January 1809. Sir George Prevost is arrived with his army, but owing I fancy to some misunderstanding between him and General Beckwith, our operations are suspended *for some time*. Anything is at a standstill for the present. Some obstacles have arisen to my exchange, in my next I may be able to say more about it. I am in good health and getting flush every day. G[eorge] W[ilkes] U[nett]

PS Tom Thompson[12] is at Barbados and going with us.

George also wrote to John at the same time.

Barbados, 28 December 1808

My dear John,
I may say (not as a common excuse) but with great truth, that I have not had time to write you a few lines since my arrival. I found this place the greatest scene of bustle imaginable, in making preparations for an attack on Martinique, and I have since been fagging in the sun all day long in embarking Ordnance Stores &c our preparations are on a very large scale, as we expect to meet with great resistance from Villaret, who is the Commander in Chief, and has *politely* sent us word that he is very much obliged to us for having given him

11. Brigadier General William Carlyon Hughes, then Governor of Surinam, died at Surinam on 27 September 1808. George had worked with him in Curacao seven years before.
12. Staff Surgeon Thomas Thomson (Johnstone 1719).

so much time to make his arrangements. We are now quite ready and are anxiously looking out for Sir George Prevost who is coming from Halifax [Nova Scotia] with three regiments and some artillery.

By some mismanagement or other, we have not been able to prevent supplies of both men and provisions from being thrown into the garrison, though the whole of our fleet have closely blockaded the island for several weeks. A few days back a frigate with 170 artillerymen onboard, got in. The captain of whom deserves great credit, he fell in with our squadron in the night, tacking as they did and laying with them, and as soon as daylight appeared, made a push for it and got in. The *Express* brig, though so much inferior, endeavoured very gallantly to run her onboard and disable her, though she probably would have gone down herself in doing it. She passed her astern by a few yards. I have met with a good many acquaintances at this place, but am sorry say, the first death I heard was poor General Hughes. Poor fellow, I am sure I have reason to regret him, for he was a staunch friend of mine. He had been unwell for some time previous to his death, but was not able to get home, though he had the Duke of York's permission, as there was no one to relieve him. Now I am on the subject, I am in hopes of returning myself as soon as the expedition is over, a captain of ours wishes to exchange and remain, and as I prefer a good gallop after a pack of fox hounds to dragging along one leg after the other, I shall most certainly indulge him, except I get something to make it worth my while staying for. I begin to get a little reconciled to the heat and to feel as I used to do, though I was very unwell the first two days. I endeavour to accustom myself to the sun as much as possible, as I have a light brigade which is to land first and most likely shall have to move about from one part of the island to the other the whole time, however I think myself as capable of enduring fatigue as anyone. I have hired a negro to carry me a small portmanteau on his head, with a ham hock and boat cloak, this composes the whole of my *kit.* I have my old servant with me, but as he is a *Johnny Newcome*, I am obliged to be careful of him and keep him out of the sun as much as possible. Tom Thompson is here and is going with us, he is very well.

4 January 1809. Since writing the above Sir George Prevost with his army have arrived and we are now, instead of immediately getting under weigh for Martinique, all at a compleat [*sic*] stand still, owing as far as I can understand to some misunderstanding between the two commanders, each one fancying his instructions were to be as Commander in Chief, but this is all conjecture and I should hope that either would give up a great deal rather than the publick [*sic*] service should suffer, a few days will determine. Let me hear how you get on with your land suit. Remember me to Mrs U[nett] and all the young ones and believe me dear John, your affectionate brother G[eorge] W[ilkes] Unett.

Two months later George wrote of their successful capture of Martinique. He believed he would be mentioned in the official dispatch but was to be sorely disappointed.

Negro Point,[13] Martinique, 28 February 1809

My dear John,

After a short but successful campaign here, I am once more in my old quarters and as well as most of my brother officers after sleeping upon the ground and wet through almost every day for near a month. I landed with a light brigade on the windward side of the island but had very little to do except fagging very hard in getting my guns along, which from the quantity of rain lately fallen had made the roads almost impassable. I very soon got appointed to a mortar battery [on] *Morn Tartenson*.[14] I beg you will *remember the name*, consisting of four 13-inch mortars and four 8-inch howitzers and have been much complimented on the shells thrown from it. Fort Bourbon is literally one heap of ruins and scarcely one stone left upon another, all the magazines are blown up, except the principal one which contains 1,700 barells [*sic*] of powder and which is so shook by the number of shells falling upon it, that they expected every next one to send them all in the air together.

Villaret upon the whole has made but a bad defence, he neglected clearing the country in the neighbourhood of Fort Bourbon, and by these means enabled us to go on erecting our batteries unperceived; but his greatest fault was in giving up Fort Edward,[15] which we immediately took possession of and turned four 13-inch mortars against himself with great effect, in short he knows nothing on shore. We have not yet taken possession, except of the Boullic [Bouille] Redoubt and some outworks, but we understand they all embark as prisoners of war in three or four days.

You must not expect a long letter. I am appointed one of the commissioners for taking an account of the stores and have enough on my hands at present. I have been given to understand I should be appointed Captain of the Fort, but at present we are all confusion as you may suppose and I know nothing certain.

The magazine in the rear of my battery where I fix my fuzes and fill my shells, exploded and occasioned the most striking scene

13. Pointe des Negres lay just to the west of Fort Royal (modern-day Fort-de-France).

14. Mount or Morne Tartenson lies about three miles north of Pointe de Negres on a 1780 map of the island.

15. Fort Royal was renamed Fort Edward by the British and Fort Bourbon on the hills overlooking the capital as Fort George. When the French retook possession of the island in 1802 they renamed Fort George as Fort Desaix.

I ever beheld. It happened in the middle of the night, my post had been close to it for two days and nights and I had but just quitted it when it blew up. 9 poor fellows were blown to pieces and 9 severely wounded (including sailors who assisted me). Our greatest loss was on the heights of Suriere [Surirey].[16] I know not what account will be given of it, but it was badly ordered, to attack redoubts by the *bayonet* and we smarted for it severely, had our field pieces been brought forward, our loss would have been trifling. No troops ever showed more courage; I don't know whether positive orders were given to attack the redoubts or not, but they no sooner came in sight of it, than away they went the Devil take the hindmost, charging and cheering up a steep hill, to the very muzzles of the guns, where they remained near half an hour exposed to a most destructive fire of grape & musquetry, each endeavouring to get in from the ditch, but without effect. We lost a great number, but the official details will explain it to you better. I have spun out my letter longer than I expected my time would allow. Direct to me at this island. Love to all, your affectionate brother G[eorge] W[ilkes] U[nett].

George wrote to Richard the same day, addressing him at Woolwich, where he was now stationed.

28 February 1809, Negro Point, Martinique

Dear [Richard] Wilkes,
Here I am once more at Martinique after an active but short campaign of only 28 days. I intended to have written you the particulars, but find I have not time, having been appointed one of the commissioners to take an account of the stores, you may conceive therefore, I have enough upon my hands. I am just returned from Fort Bourbon [Desaix] on this duty and never witnessed such a scene of desolation, you would not know the place again, all the barracks have scarcely one stone left upon another, you are obliged to step over shell holes every yard, guns turned topsy turvy, every magazine but the principal one blown up and that so much shook, that they expected another shell would have sent them all in the air together and 1,700 barrells [*sic*] of powder. Villaret has not made so good a defence as we expected in many respects, he gave up Fort Edward [Royal] immediately, which we took possession of and turned 4 13-inch mortars, which he left there, against himself, thus he is universally blamed for, even by his own soldiers, and in many other respects he acted quite different to what a good general would have done.

16. These heights lay to the east of Fort Desaix.

I believe I remain here with the command (provided I do not make the exchange); Sir George Prevost sent me word yesterday by Phillott,[17] I was to have the fort. We are at present all bustle, the French are not yet out of the fort, but we have possession of the Boullic [Bouille] Redoubt, and some of the outworks. I had rather they were onboard a ship.

A most melancholy scene happened at my battery, by the blowing up of the magazine for filling shells, fixing fuzes &c. I had 9 killed and as many wounded including sailors, who assisted. My post had been close to it for two days and nights previously and I had not quitted for five minutes when it happened.

I had four 13-inch mortars and four 8-inch howitzers; by the bye, you must look in the dispatches for the battery at *Morn Tarteson*. I have been much complimented on the occasion of the good shells thrown & am told it is particularly mentioned. I have written a long letter to Fisher.[18] I am in very good health, after our fatigues. Love to all. Your affectionate brother G[eorge] W[ilkes] Unett.

Write to me here.

George wrote to his sister Fanny, explaining that they were embarking again in preparation for landing on the Saintes.

To Miss [Fanny] Unett, Mr Wards, Acton Hill near Stafford

Fort Royal, Martinique, 8 April 1809

My dear Fanny,
I am become quite anxious for letters from you all, not having received one from any of you yet. We had just compleated [*sic*] the dismantling of our batteries and were in hopes of getting ourselves and men into some little order and to collect their little comforts, for the poor fellows have been fagging incessantly and latterly without shoes, being disappointed in money that was to arrive from Barbados, when here we are again, all alive for another expedition. We have already embarked the principal part of our stores and expect to be off on Monday next. Three line of battle ships, with several frigates, who left France under the idea of preventing our taking this island and finding they are too late, have taken shelter at the Saintes, three small islands laying close to Guadeloupe, where they are so well protected by batteries, that the admiral finds he can do nothing with them and has therefore applied

17. Captain Henry Phillott Royal Artillery (Kane 755); he died at Bathford, Somerset in 1839.
18. Lieutenant Colonel George Bulteel Fisher Royal Artillery.

for troops,[19] 2,500 men are accordingly going, with [Brigadier] General Stehelin, myself, 4 subalterns and 120 gunners of the artillery. We have some heavy mortars and having *lately* given them a pretty good specimen against *this place, of our skill* in that way, I hope a very few days will settle their business and that you will have the pleasure of hearing of their safe arrival in some British port. We are already calculating very largely upon our Prize Money. From being second in command of the artillery, I had nearly missed going, as I expected General Beckwith would have kept me here on that account. I came the old soldier over the next captain who commands the expedition and got him to apply for me, which settled the matter at once. When this is done, there will be nothing left but Guadeloupe, which I have no doubt we shall soon have in our possession and that once over, I will get Mr Ward to *attack them again.* There will in a very few months be two troops vacant in the horse artillery and I think my claims will weigh against anyone's, for one campaign in this climate certainly ought to ballance [*sic*] two at once; and if necessary I can get letters from sufficient general officers under whom I have been, I almost feel as though I had one leg in the stirrup. This is a compleat [*sic*] military letter and will tell you very little and probably uninteresting, but I really can neither write or think upon anything but shot, shells &c and getting heavy guns and mortars into ships, we talk of nothing else the whole day through and I dream of them all night. I believe I have written to you all as often as I had an opportunity, if you see John, tell him I will send him word all about it. Tom Thompson is here and goes with us, he dines with me today. I hope the next packet will bring letters for me, they are the greatest pleasure of our life in this part of the world. I understand a ship sails today for Liverpool & have no more time to spare. I am in good health and spirits though my face is the colour of mahogany from being in the sun all day long. Remember me to Mr & Mrs W[ard] and friends and believe me dear Fanny, your affectionate brother G[eorge] W[ilkes] Unett.

George's next letter to John one month later brought news of their success and his return to Martinique.

Martinique, 5 May 1809

My dear John,
We have done our business handsomely, I wish Admiral Cochrane could have given as good an account of the ships. When he requested

19. Commodore Amable Troude was sent with a squadron of three ships of the line (the 74s *Courageux*, *Polonais* and *D'Hautpoul*) and two frigates *Felicite* and *Furieuse* both armed *en flute*, acting as storeships.

our assistance, he promised if we would drive them out from under the batteries, that he would be answerable for the remainder; this we soon did and took the place afterwards.

To their very great astonishment, I landed two 8-inch howitzer mortars, had them got up a very steep hill, with a supply of ammunition and fired two shells *within an hour* from the time the boat was alongside the ship. This put them into the greatest confusion and after blazing away at them for about an hour and a half and bursting shells over their heads in all directions, they cut their cables and stood out to sea, having previously landed 500 soldiers and a supply of provisions. We have just heard of the capture of one of them a 74, the two others escaped by superior sailing. The next morning we drove the two frigates out, pursued by the *Intrepid*,[20] who got so roughly handled by the batteries with hot shot from Guadeloupe, that she could not prevent them coming to an anchor there, where they now remain closely watched.

Having got away the ships, we changed our position and moved to another part, for the purpose of erecting a mortar battery against their forts. This was completed; two 13-inch and three 10-inch mortars were mounted, loaded and almost in the act of being fired, when the white flag made his [appearance]. They were crowded together in two small forts, without any bombproofs; that had our battalion opened, the destruction would have been dreadful; this they knew and therefore surrendered, though upon the whole they have defended themselves better than their countrymen did at this place. They fought every inch of ground, until they were beat into their forts and certainly threw their shot and shells exceedingly well. I do not recollect how many we have had killed, but we have 75 wounded and many of them badly. My old servant who has been with me so many years, had his cap taken off by a splinter, and I never had a shot come so near my nose before, it lodged in the bank opposite. We have destroyed all the guns, burnt their barracks & in short completely demolished the whole of their fortifications before we quitted. I had great expectations of Prize Money and we now think it will be better than the capture of this island, we brought away all the brass guns, powder, horses, which with the 74 gun ship,[21] will make altogether about £80,000 to be divided amongst us.

General Stehelin is returned to England leaving me commanding officer of artillery at this place, I have my hands full I assure you, but hope soon to have a little time to look after my own people, who from having been at work so long and not a parade these six months, are as ragged a sett [*sic*] as need be, but they are '*rough and ready*'

20. HMS *Intrepid* was a 64-gun ship of the line.
21. *D'Hautpoul* of 74 guns was captured by HMS *Pompee* also of 74 guns.

and your fine rosy cheeked gentry in England would stand but a poor chance with theirs if they were obliged to work, as they do all day in the sun, like horses, many of them without shoes and a *soft plank* to lay down upon at night.

I am quite anxious to hear from you all, it is now 6 months since I left England and not a line from anyone. You must all have supposed me returning immediately, but it is the most difficult thing in the world to get away from hence and I shall certainly not think of it if there is the least chance of our going against Guadeloupe. I am exceedingly well and I think fatter (notwithstanding the exercise I take) than ever I was in my life. I do not think I shall be able to write either to [Richard] Wilkes or Fanny, though I should like to send her a good long story of hairbreadth escape &c. *My Deputy Captain of the fort-ship* is answering well, I calculate it will bring me in about 150 or £200 a year. Let me hear how your lawsuit goes on. I dine with General Gledstane[22] tomorrow. Love to all, your affectionate brother, George W[ilkes] Unett.

His letter a day later to Fanny gave a few other details.

Martinique, 6 May 1809

My dear Fanny,

I told you in my last of my being on the point of sailing on another expedition to the Saints [Saintes], where three French line of battle ships and two frigates had taken shelter under the batteries. The admiral promised to give a good account of them, provided we would send them to sea. I wish he had succeeded and done his part as well as we did ours, our Prize Money would have been handsome. Since my return we have intelligence from him, he has taken one of the ships (the *D'Hautpoul*).

We sailed from hence about 2,300 men and 130 artillery under General Maitland and the next day I landed with two 8-inch howitzers, and after firing at the ships for about an hour and a half, and bursting some shells about their heads, they *cut their cables* and stood out to sea, pursued by our squadron, who by the bye, from not being in the situation they ought to have been (as far as us poor landsmen were able to judge) were considerably in their rear. The next morning, I blazed away at the two frigates who did not go out in the night, and they very soon *cut* and run. The *Intrepid* was on the lookout for them, but they were so close under the land at Guadeloupe and the *Intrepid* got so roughly handled by the batteries, who fired hot shot at her, that they both got safe to anchor, where they are now closely

22. Brigadier General Albert Gledstane.

watched. Previous to their sailing they landed 500 soldiers, which with those already there made near 1,000 men; these were in three small forts situated on the tops of hills of amazing height, exactly in [the] shape of sugarloafs and our next operation was to take these. We accordingly moved to a place nearer them and began throwing up a mortar battery, which we had compleated [*sic*] the third day. They were all loaded and on the point of being fired, when the white flag made its appearance.

Upon the whole, they defended this place better than their countrymen did Martinique, they fought every inch of ground and did not surrender until they were driven into their forts and knew that the instant our battery opened would be destruction to them, as they had no bomb proofs and were crowded so thick, that a single shell dropping in, must destroy numbers. They annoyed us considerably during the time we were erecting our battery, both night and day and threw their shot and shells exceedingly well. My old servant, who has been with me these ten years, had his cap taken off by a splinter and I myself never had a shot so near my nose before, it buried itself in the bank opposite my head.

I remained to the last and effectually destroyed all the guns and carriages, the barracks were burnt down and blockhouses blown into the air, as it was not meant for us to keep any garrison there. Thus has *successfully* terminated our little campaign, as far as the *army* was concerned. The brass guns, powder, flour, with a number of government negroes we brought away, which are to be sold for the benefit of the captors,[23] this with the ship of the line will make about £90,000 to be divided amongst us. We had not many killed, but had 75 wounded, many dangerously.

I am now here commanding the artillery for a short time, General Stehelin having gone to England and notwithstanding all the fatigues I have undergone for the last six months; often with my cloaths never off for a week together and generally speaking on the ground with nothing but a boat cloak; I think I never found myself so well in this country and certainly never was so fat. I am afraid I shall have to pay enormously for my horses, when I [torn- return, as I?] shall be such a dreadful weight.

I think I have given you a [torn – full account?] of this last business and shall now [torn – hope for some?] tough stories from all of you. I have not yet had a single line from anyone since my arrival. The bag is now making up at the Post Office and I have not

23. An interesting comment for the moralist. The slave trade had been abolished in 1806, but not the possession of slaves in the West Indies and therefore it seems they were viewed as valuables and the proceeds of their sale would be shared as Prize Money.

more time than to beg to be remembered to all at the Hill, and believe me dear Fanny, your affectionate brother, G[eorge] W[ilkes] Unett

George's next letter at the end of that year was to Fanny again.

Fort Desaix [Bourbon], Martinique, 15 December 1809

My dear Fanny,
I am not quite certain whether I have written to you since 28 July by the *Latona* frigate,[24] but shall be most exceedingly disappointed if that letter did not arrive safe,[25] as I therein enclosed you one from General Beckwith who commands the forces in this part of the world to Lord Chatham, *strengthening my claims* to a troop of horse artillery.[26] I have been anxious to hear of its arrival, and that Mr Ward had acted upon it, as *this* is a time that may never happen again, there being no less than *six troops* of horse artillery vacant by the promotion of the next twelve senior captains and by everything I can hear, it may take place in a few months, as we are given to understand there will be a considerable promotion in the regiment. General Stehelin promised me to speak to Chatham and I really think if Mr Ward will *once more* make a push, I stand every prospect of success; he cannot with any face again talk of claims on account of service, for I have been almost constantly on actual service ever since & are now making every preparation for our attack on Guadeloupe and from thence to the island of St Martins, (the only remaining island the French will have in these seas)[27] on which service I am *promised* the *command* of the artillery.

The admiral is arrived here from Halifax [Nova Scotia] and our exertions are now increasing, we have began the embarkation of our stores and the men of war are gone round to the different islands to collect the troops, the greatest part of the artillery are already brought here, so that about the beginning of next month we shall be hard at it and be able to give a much better account of them than they do with their expeditions at home.

At all events, I expect to return [home] afterwards, as I think I shall be able now to effect the exchange I mentioned on my first coming out, that officer is now appointed Captain of a fort and means to stay a few years longer in the country to endeavour to realize [*sic*] a little cash for his children. I told you he had lost his wife and I then thought

24. HMS *Latona* of 38 guns.
25. It is not extant, therefore we cannot be sure of its safe arrival.
26. Presumably this was forwarded to the proper people.
27. Sint Maarten was actually held by the Batavian Republic, but this was closely associated with the French.

he would no longer wish to exchange, but I find now that he will do it, but do not let Mr Ward wait my arrival, nor slacken on that account and I feel so confident that I have already *one foot in the stirrup.*

The packet which arrived yesterday, brought me a long letter from Mary Anne [Fraser], she writes in high spirits & says she is now as happy as the day is long. I find the two Miss Forrester's are at the same school and that they are great friends. I hope it will be the means [of?] improving her in her singing, for she had very little idea of it some time ago.

18 December. Since writing so far, the 2 November packet has arrived, but no letter, I trust you are waiting to give me some good information. I have been talking to Captain Cleeve[28] and think I shall be able to shake you all by the hand in a few months. Four French frigates full of troops have taken one of our frigates (the *Juno[n]*)[29] and chased a brig about 200 miles to windward of Guadeloupe, they are intended to reinforce that place, the admiral has gone with three sail of the line besides his own (the *Pompee*) and all ships &c &c to endeavour to intercept them, but I am afraid he will be too late; however since his sailing, two line of battle ships with troops (French) passed this place for the same destination and we are in hopes he will take them both; these reinforcements, so far from putting an end to our expedition, only raise General Beckwith's spirits and we are all alive and using every means to be in readiness to pay them a visit and I have no doubt of our giving a good account of them. We have collected a fine parcell [*sic*] of artillerymen from the different islands, old weather-beaten faces, but their hearts lay in the right place. The mail closes at four o'clock, so that I have not time to say any more than that you must remember me very kindly to all at the Hill and believe me my dear Fanny, yours most affectionately, G[eorge] W[ilkes] U[nett].

George's next, again to Fanny announced their success at Guadeloupe.

From Bellain [Belle-Eau?], Guadeloupe, 6 February 1810

My dear Fanny,

I take the earliest moment to tell you that this place is ours and that here I am exceedingly well after six days constant fatigue, I have had so much moving about and my quarters so often changed, that my servant has never been able to overtake me and I am now in the same

28. Captain William Cleeve Royal Artillery (Kane 935); he died at Dover in 1831.

29. HMS *Junon* had been recently captured (10 February) from the French, but was recaptured within months (13 December). *Junon* was deceived by four French frigates commanded by Commodore François Roquebert which were flying Spanish colours. When near she was overwhelmed by their far superior fire and burnt.

cloaths I disembarked in, without ever having washed or shaved, consequently as dirty a looking a *ragamuffin* as you ever set eyes upon.

I landed with General Harcourt,[30] who commanded the Second Division of the army,[31] in command of the artillery attached to him and as I have had all the fatigue &c shall feel very much disappointed if you do not see my name in his dispatches, as no guns were landed on the other side of the island and Colonel Burton[32] who commands the whole artillery never came ashore until two hours before the white flag was hoisted. This will give me another *lift towards the saddle.* I have no time now to tell you of all *my hairbreadth* escapes but trust soon to give them to you in person. I expected to have been off again in a day or two against the island of St Martins [Sint Maartens] but have just heard that place is included in the capitulation, so that now we have compleat [*sic*] possession of all the islands in these seas.

Continue to direct to me at Martinique as usual, as I know not whether I shall remain here or there, I should prefer this place, as it is a much finer island as far as I can judge, but then I shall lose the Fort at St Pierres, except General Beckwith will give me one of the two that are here, but a few days will determine it.

We have lost a good many men in killed and wounded, but I think only one officer killed, a Lieutenant Elliot of the Navy,[33] who was attached to me to bring forward my guns with a party of seamen and was killed by a 12-pounder shot in my battery by my side; he was a very fine fellow & I am sorry I have not time to fill my paper. Remember me very kindly to all at the Hill and believe me always dear Fanny, your affectionate brother G[eorge] W[ilkes] Unett.

George wrote three months later to John, indicating that his exchange had been effected with Captain William Cleeve.

Basseterre, Guadeloupe, May 1810

Dear John,
I have just received yours of 18 March, together with one from [Richard] Wilkes, the first I have had from him for many months.

30. Brigadier General George Harcourt was appointed Governor of St Croix and died there on 19 December 1812.
31. The dispatch states that General Harcourt commanded the Second Division, consisting of two brigades. First Brigade consisting of 500 light infantry, 300 of the 15th Foot, and 400 men of the 3rd West India Regiment. Second Brigade consisting of 300 grenadiers, 600 of the 25th Regiment and 350 of the 6th West India Regiment.
32. Colonel George Burton Royal Artillery (Kane 555); he died at East Cowes, Isle of Wight in 1830.
33. Lieutenant William Elliott Royal Navy.

I would not have you proceed any farther with the estate at Smithfield,[34] as from your description of the roads, I do not think I should like it, there can be no society in the neighbourhood and I have now been so accustomed to it for so many years, that I should get on but poorly without it; besides I have now accomplished the exchange of companies which I have so long had in view and should like to *see* any place previous to its being purchased. I sometime back received a letter from Captain Cleeve saying he had no objection to the exchange, provided I had sufficient weight with Sir General Beckwith, as to get him to remain at the island he is now at (he being Captain of the fort) without running any risque [*sic*] of being removed. I went instantly to the Commander of the Forces and got the thing done, and moreover permission to return to Europe on the arrival of the first captain from thence, of which I am daily looking out and have no doubt of very soon shaking you all by the hand.

I forget whether I wrote to you on the capture of this island, but rather think I did, since which I have been a good deal employed, in collecting all the ordnance and stores from various parts of the island. Removing heavy guns in this country is I assure you a very serious undertaking and I have been left the whole of the fag, both here and at Martinique, but I have a constitution of iron that bids defiance to all climates and never was better. I am now taking a particular survey of all the guns & ordnance stores in the island, in order to send to the Board of Ordnance that they may be enabled to fix the *quantum* of Prize Money to be allowed us for them. They are very particular in this return and require not only the nature, whether French or English, serviceable or unserviceable &c &c; but even the length, weight & the year made, of every piece of ordnance. There are batteries all around the island and I leave you to guess of the number of cool rides I must take before this can be ascertained.

This place is still continued as headquarters, though but for a short time longer, when Sir George [Beckwith] and Staff remove to Barbados. I hope ere then to have my face turned towards old England, or I should be very sorry for it, as he always has been exceedingly kind to me and I find him the pleasantest man in the world to do business with, I attend him every morning between nine and ten, either to report what has been done, or receive his orders and having been now constantly under him since I left England, we must each of us have had a pretty good trial of each other.

Did I tell you of my having an excellent house, with a good cook and a *sort of an establishment.* Tom Thompson is living with me and by giving dinners now & then, we get on very well together. He is not at present here, having been ordered round to different islands to

34. An area of Birmingham.

> collect the invalids who are going home in the next convoy; he is just promoted to Deputy Inspector General [of Hospitals], which doubles his pay and secures him 15 shillings a day, Half Pay, in case of a peace, so that he is a most fortunate fellow. Who is to be appointed new Master General [of the Ordnance]; as I find by the papers we are to have one? I hope Mr Ward will be able to get at him and to have another push for a troop; Parliamentary interest, nothing else does now. I think my claims ought to weigh as heavy as most, if not I must come to your part of the world, for there are no more laurels to be gained now, we are all a most peaceable sett [*sic*] here, having no enemy but the climate to contend with.
>
> With respect to the money that I owe you, on Tom's account, I must get you to let it lay by until my arrival, which I trust will be in time to knock down a few partridges at Marston, on the 1st of September. I have been at more expense here than I intended; my house rent being between £70 and £80 a year without furniture and I shall have occasion to draw for what I have in my bankers hands at Canterbury, as I calculate my passage with my servant who is a married man, will cost me little short of £100. Remember me kindly to all at home and to Mrs [Ann] Unett and Letty [Letitia] if they are at Southwick. I expect to see great improvements there and believe me dear John, your affectionate brother, G[eorge] W[ilkes] Unett.

George returned home that autumn and now commanded 7 Company 3rd Battalion, based at Colchester, where they remained until 1 May 1812 and therefore his correspondence draws to a close.

THE FRASER BOYS IN THE PENINSULA

James Fraser with the Fusiliers

Here we have to introduce the first of two new correspondents, Richard's nephew James Baillie Fraser, who was commissioned as a Lieutenant in the 7th Foot on 21 June 1810. We find him arrived in Portugal only ten weeks after he was commissioned as an officer.

Both battalions of the 7th Fusiliers were abroad in 1809; the 1st Battalion had served at the capture of Martinique and had then proceeded to Halifax, Nova Scotia, while the 2nd Battalion was initially at Clonmell in Ireland, but later were sent to Portugal; they landed at Lisbon on 7 April 1809. The 2nd Battalion arrived at Oporto just after the battle ended, but they were placed in the 4th Division and were fully engaged at the subsequent Battle of Talavera, losing one officer and six men killed, with a further three officers and fifty-four men wounded, many of whom were captured subsequently by the French, when Wellington was forced to hastily abandon Talavera. The battalion wintered at Olivenza. In June 1810 the 1st Battalion was ordered to Portugal, where they disembarked at Lisbon on 31 July, numbering 27 officers and 978 men. On 9 August the 1st Battalion marched to Ponte de Mucela, where it formed a brigade of the 1st Division with the 1/79th. The 2/7th was at Seia.

Richard had only been in Portugal a week but seems to have a remarkably good understanding for the place already.

> To [Lieutenant] Colonel [Richard] Unett, Woolwich, Kent, England
>
> Lisbon, 1 September 1810
>
> My dear Mary Anne [Fraser],
> As it is your turn to have a letter from me, I shall treat you with a very long one, beginning by letting you know that I arrived here on the 26 [August] after a pleasant passage of 9 days from Falmouth,[1] enjoying the most delightful weather the whole time and being in as good health as if I was on shore. This place is very dirty and disagreeable at first, but by degrees one gets accustomed to it. The streets are wide and regular, the squares beautiful and everything requisite to make it a very nice town if it was not for the inhabitant's excessive filth which presents anything of the sort. Fruit is cheap

1. He must have sailed on the mail packet; this would have cost him a pretty penny.

and plentiful but not so fine as I expected. I dined with Colonel [George Bulteel] Fisher the other day in a magnificent palace belonging to a Marquis in the French service, whose houses we take care of while he is fighting against his country.[2] I have just been billeted at the house of a Mrs Chaut, who is very civil to me. The first billet I was sent to, I was forced to get a police officer to go with me and at last it turned out there was no room. The waiter at the hotel speaks French very luckily for me. The rascals robbed my trunk of every sixpence I had the other day and as I cannot get all the pay due to me, my Uncle [Richard] must not be surprised if he receives an *Order* for some cash when received. If we march, it is absolutely necessary I should have a mule and I have hardly money enough to get my dinners. We go either tomorrow or the next day but are not sure whether we go by sea to Coimbra[3] within 2 day's march of headquarters or whether we march the whole way from here, a long and fatiguing [one] I assure you. News is just arrived of the fall of Almeida,[4] I do not know the particulars, it is kept secret as yet from the inhabitants. The [1/]79th & [2/]88th have arrived from Cadiz and other troops are expected daily.

The [1/]23rd are coming from Halifax and when they come up, Pakenham of our regiment is to have the Fusilier Brigade, consisting of our two battalions & the [1/]23rd and it is reported we are to relieve the Light Brigade, which have suffered so much. The First Battalion of the 7th landed here a month ago *1,000 strong* every man in health and one of the finest battalions that ever was on service. The people here were quite astonished at them. A very fine young man, a private in it, was murdered the first night by some of the inhabitants. Upwards of 200 deserters have been sworn in here this week, some of them very fine men. Before you receive this letter, I shall probably be at headquarters of the regiment. I expect very soon to be able to speak Portuguese as it is a very easy language.[5] I have been since to the opera, it is a fine building, several tiers of boxes to an immense height above one another and a pit are the place for spectators. If you go to a box, you pay for the whole of it 3 dollars. The performance is bad, but the music pretty good. I generally breakfast at some of the coffee houses, (which are much frequented by the English officers) &

2. This must refer to Major General Pedro de Almeida, 3rd Marquis of Alorna, who was assigned to the Staff of Marshal Massena.
3. Seagoing ships could not proceed up the Mondego River to Coimbra, but would discharge the men at Figueira de Foz on the coast and they would march to Coimbra (52km), but this was far more preferable than the 215km march from Lisbon.
4. Marshal Massena captured Almeida on 27 August after the explosion of the main arsenal killed a large number of the defenders.
5. The editor begs to differ!

dine with my brother officers at a hotel which is not very expensive as the wine though dear at present, is very cheap compared to England. 2s 6d for Colares[6] a wine the very same as Claret, 1s 6d for the best Carcavellos[7] & other wines cheaper. About the middle of the day it is quite necessary to go into a coffee room and drink lemonade; the weather is uncommonly fine but very hot and I am getting as brown as a berry. The Tagus is crowded with ships of war and transports, upwards of 300 sail of them to carry the army or best part of it, off where requisite, but there are no fears I assure you, [of] their army advancing and everyone is certain we shall succeed in driving the French from the position. The banks of the Tagus are not so beautiful as I expected. I went across the water to Almida [Almada] yesterday and 4 of us got horses or mules for a dollar as long as we chose to have them and 4 boys to drive them. We went to a vineyard and watched the wine making and eat [*sic*] grapes. The people call us *Signor, Signor Capitano* and take off their hats to us. It is a high treat to see these wretches in rags with cocked hats on. A little satisfies the Portuguese for their trouble, I gave 1 person for carrying my luggage from the boat to the hotel one vintem or 3 half pence. They will row you up and down the river for a pisseta [peseta] or a shilling. I have been forced to enclose this letter; I had written all the sides without perceiving it and the packet now making up for this evening and I should not have time to write it over again. My very best love to my Uncle Richard & Aunt [Ann] & Alex [Fraser] & all relations and believe me my dear Mary Anne, your affectionate brother, J[ames] B[aillie] Fraser.

His next letter was again from Lisbon, but this time having already seen his first action with the 1st Battalion at the Battle of Busacco, having been sent back with the wounded. Neither battalion were seriously engaged, the losses of the 1st Battalion amounting to one man dead and Lieutenant John Mair and twenty-two men wounded, the 2nd Battalion suffering no casualties at all.[8]

10 October 1810 [Lisbon]

My dear Uncle [Richard],
I have just arrived for the second time at Lisbon, having been detached from the regiment with the sick & wounded to take them to the General Hospital here. I have been appointed to the 1st Battalion and have been with them 3 weeks. I am in the grenadier

6. Colares wine is a traditional prestigious wine region on Portugal's central Atlantic coast.
7. Carcavelos is a very rare wine, being aged from 7 to 15 years, made in only one tiny enclave near the town.
8. An error in the *Record of the Royal Fusiliers* allocates the losses to the second rather than the first battalion.

company but have the pleasure of carrying the Colours, being junior in this battalion. I have never slept in a bed since I joined as we never by any chance go into villages but are always bivouacked in the open air, I joined them at Ponte di Murcella [Ponte de Mucela], from thence we marched to Coimbra, then a small village called Mealhada, where we halted some days, during which time I took the opportunity of calling on Brigadier General Campbell,[9] then marched to our line on the position at Busacco, We were on the top of an immense high hill, from whence we saw the surrounding country around, with the French troops & saw as plain as possible every manoeuvre they made. Our brigade,[10] the 79th and ourselves under Colonel Pakenham in Sir Brent Spencer's[11] Division arrived on the ground (after a very fatiguing march) towards evening at which time the piquets just under us were firing away as hard as they could, and from the top of the hill, saw everything as safe as if we were 10 miles off. The next day about daylight the firing began and at last came on to a general engagement, the men about the centre of the line in the very steepest part of the position, so that our division was not engaged the whole time and it was only our own brigade in the division that had anything to do. The body of the regiment was not engaged at the same time, but only the piquets which we changed every six hours and supported by 2 companies occasionally as they wanted it, so that we were all in the business, though not at the same time. Our regiment lost one officer and 30 [22] men & the 79th 1 officer & another taken prisoner.[12] The part of the regiment that was not engaged was drawn up in line in case our advanced posts were driven in, to be ready and receive them, but we were so well posted as to be able to keep them back the whole day, for the firing never ceased all that day & part of the next. The situation being on two hills over a valley, there was such an echo that I was quite deaf for a long time. The balls made such a whizzing about my ears that I kept bobbing my head every minute when they perhaps were not near me. When it first began, I felt myself very awkward and my teeth chattered & in spite of [all?] I tried, all I could do to look cheerful, for fear the men should observe me. In a short time, when I found they did not hit me, I began to look up and before I came off piquet did not care much about it. Some regiments suffered severely,

9. Brigadier General Alexander Campbell commanded the 1st Brigade of the 4th Division, consisting of 2/7th, 1/11th, 2/53rd and a company of the 5/60th.
10. He was now in the 1/7th, which was brigaded with 1/79th in the 4th Brigade of the 1st Division, commanded by Colonel the Honourable William Stewart.
11. Major General Sir Brent Spencer commanded the 1st Division.
12. The 1/79th lost seven men killed, one officer and forty-one men wounded and one officer and six men missing.

the Portuguese behaved enormously well. We took a General[13] and a stand of Colours and it is supposed they lost 6,000 men. They decamped shortly after and Lord Wellington having discovered their intention to come round him by the way of Oporto, gave orders for the retreat, to the position which he has had in view all the campaign only fifteen miles from Lisbon; but where it will be madness of them to attempt attacking us, there is nothing but immense hills, batteries, entrenchments, abattis and in fact every 30 yards is a new position.[14] We have had such bad weather that the army is not yet in the lines but can be in them at a moment's notice. I shall be back [with the regiment] tomorrow or next day. The cavalry skirmish every day, they took 40 officers the other day. The march for 6 days, sometimes night & day to this position, during which I never as much as took off my sword & belt to sleep.

The French are not far off and their communication being at present cut off with France, they must fight, as they have no provisions, they find no one in the towns & villages, the country is bare, the bullocks & sheep driven away for our use, the corn fields burnt & they being now so far advanced, if they are beat they are ruined. In less than a week will be the finale of all this, Lord Wellington says he will be in Oporto in a fortnight. I received Mary Anne's letter. The person I sent for some of those things was because I heard they were in the 2nd Battalion, but I having joined the First, they are of no use. I have been forced to draw for 50 pounds as we do not receive our pay regular here and I had an opportunity of getting it done without paying, but if I stay here for 3 years, I shall not have occasion for any more, unless in the event of sickness. There are several things such as a canteen, a patent cloke [*sic*] and other campaigning articles I [have] been much in need of, having been forced to eat with my fingers for a week together & sleep under a hedge without cloaths. But the only way of sending them is by officers coming out. I wished particularly to write to John Greene but I have not really time as I have several commissions for my brother officers to execute and I set off for the regiment tomorrow so that if Alex could write just a line telling him it is by my request and let him know how I am going on it would be as well. My best love to my dearest Aunt [Ann], Mary Anne, Alex, my Aunt Elizabeth & Mrs Godwin & all friends & send me out as many letters as you can. Believe me your very affectionate nephew J[ames] B[aillie] Fraser.

13. French General Edouard Simon was wounded and captured.
14. He describes the famous Lines of Torres Vedras, which the French found too strong to attack and eventually retreated.

Another month still found him in Lisbon.

Lisbon, 11 November 1810

My dear Uncle [Richard],
You will perhaps be astonished to see me direct from Lisbon again, but the reason is that I have had another attack of my old malady the ague. When I last wrote to you, I had come to this place with sick & wounded men. When I returned to the regiment I found them close to the French lines. They were in cantonments on account of the season, but a camp was pitched (on the hill which we are to occupy in case of an attack) ready for them to go to, and to this camp in the meantime our company was detached and there we staid [*sic*] about ten days in very bad weather which gave me the ague. When we came down to the village where the regiment are, I had a bed of straw which was rather better than the one I had at camp, but still I got worse & worse, as I stood out as long as I could and did not like to complain, but at last I was forced to send for the surgeon and the consequence was that notwithstanding my remonstrances they put me into a bullock waggon, in which I was 2 days coming here over the most horrid road in Portugal; and as these vehicles are enough to kill a man *in health*, you may imagine my agony. I was forced to submit, as I could not stand if I had got out, so that the whole way I was roaring out with pain, every jolt shook all my bones. I have taken physick here which has cured me of everything but an excessive weakness for which I am going to take bark,[15] so that in a short time I hope to be in a state to return to the regiment. General Campbell has behaved with great kindness to me, he offered me a room in his house and insisted upon sending me money. I told him I did not want any as I did not at that time, but since that, having found that I had not enough for my necessities, I have complied with his positive *orders* to let him know if such was the case and he is going to send me some.

An order is come out to wear epaulettes as usual, but of course before you get this letter, the box with my things will have been sent off.[16] I received a letter from Mary Anne [Fraser] dated the 4 October, best you should have sent me one of a later date and let me know what the people in England think of Busacco. By the same packet we

15. Cinchona tree bark from South America was used from the seventeenth century in Europe to fight malarial fevers, it contained quinine.

16. An Official Order of February 1810 stipulated that Subalterns were to wear one epaulette on the right shoulder, while captains also wore one of a more ornate design again on the right. Field officers were to wear two epaulets, with a crown and star for a Colonel, crown for Lieutenant Colonel and star for Major. Fusiliers and light infantry were also directed to wear wings in addition to the epaulet, but he seems to indicate that there was some delay in these changes.

got the Gazettes and some of the officers got letters about it. After our hard retreat & incessant marching from Busacco we expected as soon as we got to the lines to be attacked directly, instead of which they are directly opposite to us, staring at us without making the least signs of attack and it is thought they never will. We have skirmishes every day. A company & piquet of ours the other day charged nearly a thousand of them, to the utter astonishment of General Cole[17] who was looking on and who commands our division now, we having been changed from the 1st to the 4th Division of the army.[18] I believe I shall soon be sent to my proper battalion, the 2nd. They are within ½ a mile of the 1st though in different divisions [brigades].[19] The French are now within 2 days march of Lisbon, but they don't like the appearance of our position and it is even thought will decamp sooner than make an attack on it. The duty is very hard, we furnish 2 guards, 2 working parties and a piquet every day. The working parties are occupied in fortifying the hill that we are to defend. The *'turn out'* and *'stand to'* serves 3 hours every morning before daylight, to which I think I may owe a little of my ague. I should have no objection to make one of [*sic* – those at] the fireside I assure you this Christmas, this sickness has made me long for England more than ever possible or hunger or thirst (and I suffered them all in the retreat) made me do.

I have nothing more to say in the way of news and I dare say there will be none for some time. Give my best love to my Aunt [Ann], Mary Anne & Alex & all friends at Woolwich & Greenwich & believe me your very affectionate nephew, J[ames] B[aillie] Fraser

Nearly a full month later, James wrote again from Lisbon.

Lisbon, 30 November 1810

My dear Uncle [Richard],
I told you in one of my former letters, that I should be obliged to draw again in case of sickness and though I thought I should not have been obliged, in this instance I have unfortunately found the absolute necessity of it. General Campbell I told you was going to send me money. The army has made a movement, his division advanced suddenly and he has

17. Major General Sir Galbraith Lowry Cole commanding the 4th Division.
18. An Order of 6 October 1810 moved Pakenham's Brigade from the 1st Division to the 4th Division consisting of 1/7th, 1/61st and Brunswick Oels regiment. However, on 12 November, the Brunswickers were moved to the Light Division, with only single companies attached to the other divisions; their place being taken by the 1/23rd just arrived from Halifax, Nova Scotia. On 17 November the 1/61st were drafted out and the 2/7th were drafted in, forming the Fusilier Brigade of the 1/7th, 2/7th & 1/23rd.
19. They were now both in the 4th Division, but not yet in the same brigade.

of course been prevented from relieving me. That you may not think me extravagant, I must tell you that since I have been at Lisbon nearly a month, I have never been out except to several Medical Boards, to each of which I was forced to go in a carriage and it being some distance from my billet, it cost me sometimes 2, sometimes 4 dollars according as they delayed me at the hospital; and I paid no more than was just and what is paid by every inhabitant of Lisbon.

I have taken a great deal of porter[20] (on my getting better) which is very dear here, as you may imagine and several other things in the English style, which I longed for and which have contributed to increase my expenses. We have been disappointed in not receiving our bat and forage allowance, as they are waiting for money from Gibraltar. A months pay I got when I came to Lisbon sick, rations and Income Tax deducted; the utmost dollar of which has gone long ago and I am under orders for the regiment, have bills to pay & baggage mule to get, besides necessary articles to take with me, so that you see the necessity I am in of doing what cannot but be necessary to me, from an idea that you may imagine that I am not going on profusely. The method I have taken is the common one with officers and certainly the best. I draw on Greenwood & Cox[21] and write to them myself to say what I have done and I have taken precautions with my Uncle [Richard], saying who you are who will have the money paid into their hands, the sum is £40; owing to a want of the certificates, the surgeons have ordered me up before I am recovered, the least riding or walking knocks me up and I have every now and then returns of the ague and as there is little prospect of anything to do with the enemy it is useless sending me. The rainy weather has set in and not a day passes without heavy rain, so that the first night's piquet will certainly lay me up again.

However, he added a further note.

The 29 [November], I have arrived and with our 2 battalions, form a Fusileer Brigade under Colonel Pakenham. We are at Azambuja near the Tagus, rather advanced. I believe Massena having received his reinforcements, if the weather gets favourable for operations, we may expect something to do in a short time. The Portuguese have 12,000 sick and indeed the whole army is sickly. Pray remember me to Captain Campbell,[22] headquarters having been a long way from us for some time, I have not had an opportunity of waiting on Colonel Campbell lately. Give my best love to my Aunt [Ann], Mary

20. Porter was supposed to help build up bodily strength when poorly.
21. Greenwood, Cox & Hammersley Army Agents, of Craigs Court London.
22. Captain Alexander Campbell Royal Artillery (Kane 819); he died at Weedon on 7 May 1819.

> Anne & Alex, not forgetting Mrs Godwin, my Aunt Elizabeth and Mrs [Gascklin?]. Believe me my dear Uncle [Richard], your very affectionate nephew J[ames] B[aillie] Fraser.

Within a week he was in Lisbon yet again!

> Lisbon, 8 December 1810
>
> My dear Mary Anne [Fraser],
> I have just received your letter of the 4th after dated 15 November[23] and as you so anxiously wish to hear of me from me, I can easily let you have that pleasure as a packet sails every Tuesday for England and while I am here, I have plenty of leisure to write. I see letters you had not received when your letter came away. My Uncle [Richard] will find by one of them that I have been obliged to draw again, but I hope when I once get up again and [will] not come to Lisbon till I embark for England. I have slept out many a night in nothing but my coat and have woke up wet with the dew; we have suffered a good deal otherwise, but never had a moment's illness till I went to that unctuous camp. A party from each regiment in the brigade was ordered to be pushed forward to encamp on a high hill near the French lines; being the right company we are sent and staid [*sic*] a fortnight before we were relieved. There was a valley between us and the French picquets, the nearest of which was not quite a quarter of a mile distant. Junot with his division was 2½ miles from us only, so that we were generally turned out every night with a false alarm, besides the turning out in a morning before daylight and it is to these I think I owe my ague. When I got to Lisbon I was delirious, left my billet and had it not been for an officer of the 16th Dragoons (an old college friend) I do not know what would have become of me. I am now detained here to march up a party of convalescents when ready, my own leave being refused. The whole army lies on the banks of the Tagus. We are in a better village than the generality I understand. The officers of a regiment in our division, 30 of them, were all quartered in the same room, *a long stable*.
>
> At headquarters and other places, they are building chimnies [*sic*], which looks as if we were in our country quarters. The theatre here is now as fine as our Mary. The rain has cleared, but they say we shall have it again soon. I am learning Portuguese rapidly, I can ask for anything and carry on a conversation on some things. The Portuguese captains wear two fringe epaulets, so that with my two fringe wings, I pass with everyone for a senior captain. If you wish, you may go to as many parties &c in the English stile [*sic*] as you like. I am now in a part of the town called Buenos Ayres [Buenos Aires] the cleanest part

23. Started on the 4th and posted on the 15th.

owing to there being a great many English families resident [in] it. I live in the same street as the admiral[24] and have a delightful view of the Tagus and its banks. There is a nice family near me with some very nice senoritas, or young ladies in it who are very civil to me and speak French to me out of their balconies as I pass by.

I met an old acquaintance in the streets the other day, in the person of Wilson,[25] who did not recollect me at all. I called him and asked him if he knew me, he said not, when I told him who I was he cried out '*Good God, Sir, is it you*' and seemed very glad to see me and enquired after you all and says he wishes he had enquired after my uncles. He met with some accident when he came here and has in course scarce ever gone up the country and has got a very good employment as mess man to the officers in Lisbon & takes care of the wounded and is exempt from all duty. I asked him if I could do anything for him, if he wanted money &c but he said he was very comfortable & that Colonel [George Bulteel] Fisher[26] & the officers were very kind to him. I saw Mr Alder at Busaco, but not being quite sure, he not seeming to know me, I always speak.

You must give my love to Mrs Godwin and compliments to Mrs [Brown?] and remember me to Captain [Alexander] & Mrs Campbell and my Aunt [Ann]. My best love to my Uncle [Richard] & brother Alex, whose turn it is to send me a letter. Believe me my dear Mary Anne, your ever affectionate brother J[ames] B[aillie] Fraser.

I hope you will allow this to be a good letter; I say nothing of the army in the way of news, for everything is quiet and seems as if it would be so for some time yet. You do not mention my Uncle George & when he is expected.[27]

James was back with the regiment when he wrote two days before Christmas. He was transferring to his official battalion, the 2nd.

Azambuja, 23 December 1810

My dear Mary Anne,
I received your letter of the 28 November yesterday and am satisfied that you received a letter from me immediately after that period. I wrote 3 letters from Lisbon, which you will have received before now. I am now as well as ever I was and as we have the most delightful weather, I hope I shall remain so. Though within 2 days of Christmas, the trees

24. Admiral Sir George Berkeley commanded the Lisbon Station from 1810–12.
25. Richard Unett's servant back in 1795–6.
26. He was Officer Commanding the Royal Artillery at Lisbon until November 1812.
27. His uncle, George Unett, was due to arrive home from Martinique.

have their leaves and the weather is as hot as our June, but they say that after January we shall have months of rain. We are in a very good place and perfectly secure, having a division in front of us, and do no more duty than if we were in quarters at home. We have field days, races, Balls &c, quite gay; and the French officers have sent us (by a flag of truce) a message saying '*That with Lord Wellington's permission, they will be very happy to see any British officers at an opera they have at Santarem*'.[28] Being near Lisbon and on the Tagus, we have plenty of everything and have laid in stock for a Christmas dinner. We shall have roast beef and plum pudding. Four of us live in a clean little room just like the room of a cottage in England. We are busy perfecting the light manoeuvring and they still say that we shall relieve the Light Brigade. I hope I may soon expect my things, being in want of them. If they come safe, I hope my Uncle [Richard] will let me [have] some other things in the spring. I want a great coat and some books, which would be the greatest comfort to me imaginable. Our sentries at Santarem are on the same bridge within 20 yards of the French and apparently talking to each other, in fact the campaign at present is carried on in the most polite way. At headquarters the other day they took out of a well (which had been used by Lord W[ellington] and his Staff and the troops for nearly a fortnight) the bodies of 2 dead Frenchmen. The houses and the roadside when we first came here, had produced many shocking spectacles and so this minute in several places there are the carcasses of dead men & horses in the middle of the road. On Xmas day there will be performances at headquarters and in the evening every Englishman in the army intends to keep up the old customs here. If we stay here long enough, I intend to keep my birthday also on the 17 [January].[29] 2,000 bullocks were drove into Santarem the other day for the use of the French there.[30] It is confidently reported that we are to have another battalion, but our 2nd is so weak that I can hardly believe it.[31] Tomorrow, I go to my proper battalion the 2nd. It is not unlikely that we shall have to turn our men to the 1st and come home to recruit, if the thing takes place there is not a doubt of it. You must not expect a long letter now as there is nothing to tell you and I only wrote because I wished to tell you that I had arrived here quite well. If any officer is coming to this country, send me books on anything you think will amuse me, for in cantonments we have nothing to do. I expect a letter by every packet.

28. It is peculiar how the British and French treated each other so cordially apart from when in battle, while the French treatment of the Spanish and Portuguese was often savage, which provoked an equally savage response.
29. He would be 18 years old on 17 January 1811.
30. An interesting comment, confirming that the French were succeeding in gaining substantial supplies at times.
31. He was correct; the 7th only ever had two battalions.

Give my best love to my Uncle [Richard] and Aunt [Ann] and Alex, and believe me your affectionate brother J[ames] B[aillie] Fraser.

If you write to Mrs Hood pray remember me to their nephew Mr Colley & Mrs Colley.

James' next letter to his Aunt complains bitterly that he had not received any letters from home, but he forgot the change of year.

Avarez do Cima [Aveiras de Cima], 29 January 1810 [1811]

My dear Aunt,
Packet after packet, I do not know how many, and I receive no letters from any of you, which I cannot account for as I have not heard of any accident having happened to the mails lately. We left Azembuja [Azambuja] on the 24th and came to this place, which *is not* near so good a town and being farther from the Tagus, of course we lost our supplies, the country people being afraid to leave the river with their goods. Headquarters still remain in the same place and everything is perfectly quiet now, though we were alarmed the other day by the French coming on in a large body to the left of Cartaxa [Cartaxo]; however, it turned out to be one of their strong foraging parties, which after a sharp skirmish with the 95th and German Hussars retired again. In this affair Junot[32] was wounded severely and we have had a report these 3 or 4 days that he is dead and I believe it is true.[33] The *Spaniards* have all gone away again to their own country, to the great joy of the whole army, who plainly saw that they were nothing but a cowardly, indisciplined race. The Marquis of Romana they say is dead,[34] it is supposed he was poisoned. My things are not yet arrived; I thought perhaps you might have got Colonel Drummond[35] to bring them. I have not seen him since he arrived, but I shall take an early opportunity to go to headquarters and call upon him. We have bats and balls made and in those idle times, we amuse ourselves by playing cricket to the astonishment of the natives. We may call ourselves friends to the Portuguese, but I am certain they all hate us except their soldiers, who I believe are fond of the English. Whenever we come to a village, if there are inhabitants in it, they are immediately turned out to accommodate the soldiers and they can get no redress, for if [they] try, they are told to go and live with the men, which they know better than to do. On the other hand, they steal our horses and everything they can belonging to us. In

32. General Jean-Andoche Junot.

33. Junot was wounded by a ball striking his nose; he did not die.

34. General Pedro Caro y Sureda, 3rd Marquis of Romana died of dyspnoea (breathing difficulties) on 23 January 1811.

35. Lieutenant Colonel George Duncan Drummond 24th Foot arrived in the Peninsula in January 1811 on the Staff, commanding a brigade in the Light Division.

fact, they equally detest the English and French with this difference, only that sometimes the latter kill and burn, which makes them more afraid of them than they are of us.

We are living with the French in a most extraordinary manner. Our sentries are in the same fields, the same bridges now with theirs, and they are regularly relieved without taking the least notice of one another. If you could see us, you would never imagine that we were within a hundred miles of the enemy. Everything is going on [in] the different towns as if we were in garrison in England. We have our Balls, parties, races, reviews, cricket matches and are in fact as happy as possible. I have got accustomed to this manner of living. It makes no difference changing our quarters, one village is as good as another and I can sleep as well between my cloak and blanket, as I did in England between a pair of sheets in a warm room with a floor to it. We dine well with our ration beef and wine and only feel the want of beer and milk, which we never see up the country; but these are only luxuries, which we can easily do without. I have spun out a tolerable long letter out of nothing and I hope you will never forget to let me have one every packet. I do not care about news.

William Boyle[36] is here with the 27th, I have never spoken to him as he does not recollect me, nor do I wish he should. Give my best love to my Uncle [Richard], Mary Anne and Alex [Fraser] and believe me your very affectionate nephew J[ames] B[aillie] Fraser.

His next describes excessive marches and the regiment's part in driving the French out of Portugal.

Elvas, 2 April 1811

My dear Mary Anne [Fraser],
I arrived at this place yesterday after a month's continued marching and enduring as much hardships and privations the Army ever suffered in the country. Long ere this, the dispatches will have informed you of the retreat of Massena and the subsequent events, it is therefore unnecessary that I should enter into a long detail. Our division was present at the affair of Redinha,[37] but owing to the precipitate retreat of the enemy on *our* advance, we had merely a few shells which went over us. At Condeixa[38] again, we were once more inactive spectators of an engagement between the light troops, which lasted the whole day and in which by the particulars, you will perceive that the Light Brigade suffered considerably. The same

36. Ensign William Boyle 27th Foot.
37. Fought on 12 March 1811.
38. Usually referred to as the Action of Casal Novo fought on 14 March 1811.

night 2 divisions, our own (the 4th) and the 2nd commenced the march under Marshal Beresford to cross the Tagus and proceed to the relief of Badajoz. On our arrival at Thomar [Tomar] we heard of its fall[39] and lost no time in crossing the river in order to prevent the French penetrating [into] Portugal by the Alemtejo. When we got to Portalegre we found that they had besieged and taken Campo Mayor [Campo Maior], a frontier town, to which we immediately proceeded and they retired to Badajoz in a great hurry on our approach. The 13th [Light] Dragoons[40] and some Portuguese cavalry came up with them in a plain near the town and a most desperate skirmish took place which continued to the gates of Badajoz; they lost a great many killed but not many prisoners. The whole business was carried on by the sword; I walked over the ground about half an hour after and I never saw such horrid spectacles as it presented. The 13th suffered a good deal.[41] We marched here yesterday, this place [being] the strongest in Portugal is about 3 miles from Badajoz, but being situated on a hill and the country round a level plain, we can see them as plain as possible. It is supposed that tomorrow we proceed to the siege, but they will not be such fools as to stand the event of one. We are here, so far from Lord Wellington that we are perfectly ignorant of what he is about; but we understand that he has made a great many prisoners and that headquarters are at Almeida. We are very comfortable on this side of the water, as the French have never been here, but on the other we were miserably off. We never, by any chance get much cover, the French burning every city, town or village they passed through. The baggage and stores could not keep up with us and as there was no inhabitants we could buy nothing. I was two days without tasting anything but half a biscuit and sleeping out without any cloak or blanket. We marched constantly 20, sometimes 30 or 35 miles a day; the day we marched [to] Thomar [Tomar], I marched 32 miles with a hungry stomach, drenched with rain and for the last 5 miles with a fit of the

39. The Spanish-held fortress of Badajoz was captured by the French on 11 March 1811.

40. The 13th Light Dragoons lost twelve men killed, four officers and twenty-five men wounded and twenty men missing.

41. A French force of two infantry battalions, half a battery of horse artillery and eight squadrons of cavalry was removing a siege artillery train from Campo Maior to Badajoz when attacked by elements of the 13th Light Dragoons supported by part of the 1st and 7th Portuguese cavalry regiments (totalling about 700 cavalry) and two cannon. The French cavalry were broken and pursued rapidly all the way to Badajoz, leaving the cannon and escorting infantry to those following. Unfortunately, Marshal Beresford mistakenly believed that the 13th were captured in their entirety and called off the pursuit. The French infantry then safely escorted the siege guns into Badajoz. The French lost 200 men and one cannon, the 13th lost 10 killed, 27 wounded and 22 captured, the Portuguese losing 14 killed, 40 wounded and 55 captured.

ague, which however thank God, I felt no more of the next morning, as we got into houses and I changed all my things and got a good night's sleep. This is a most beautiful town and the country about is much prettier than any I have ever seen in the country. For miles and miles are nothing but plains of corn and groves of orange & olive trees; and at a distance are seen the Spanish mountains bounding the horizon. I see by the Gazettes that I have got 11 [lieutenants] under me and as we still have some vacancies, I hope to have good promotion. I am indeed truly happy to hear that my Uncle George has arrived at last and do not doubt that he will speedily recover. I am very glad to hear Alex is so comfortable [at] Dr Glennan's [school] and hope he will be continued so, I have got so completely brown that you would not know me, the features of my face are all turned into a perfect sheet of brown. Let me know how the people at home like Massena's retreat. What [does] Mr Cobett say of it?[42] My best love to you all and believe me my dear Mary Anne, your very affectionate brother J[ames] B[aillie] Fraser.

James' next letter tells of his harrowing experiences in the dreadful Battle of Albuera, in which the Fusilier Brigade played such a significant part, but at a tremendous cost.

Albuera, 20 May 1811

My dear Uncle [Richard],
Doubtless before you receive this letter the public prints will have informed you of the sanguinary action of the 16th between this corps of the Allied army under Marshal Beresford & that of the enemy under [Marshal] Soult. I shall not attempt to describe the movements that took place previous to the event but shall merely tell you that on the first news of Soult's coming to raise the siege of Badajoz, the whole army advanced to meet him; except our brigade, which was left till the stores and heavy cannon could be got off to Elvas. On the night of the 15 [May], we received an order to march immediately and after marching the whole night, about eight o'clock in the morning we arrived on the plains of Albuera, where we found the army's [*sic*] drawn up cannonading each other hotly. For the whole particulars of the action, I must refer you to the dispatches, as I can only speak of our part of the business.

Our brigade advanced to support an attack made by the Spaniards and 2 brigades of British, upon the principal force of the French, situated on a hill, lined with cannon. Whatever may be said at home of this; I must tell you (as a secret) that they were completely routed,

42. William Cobbett, the radical journalist and politician.

after having done all that men could do and absolutely forced to run in the utmost confusion through our line, pursued by the enemie's [*sic*] cavalry, who cut down and made prisoners an immense number. This was owing to the great superiority of the enemy in cavalry & likewise to our people being brought up in an injudicious manner. We gave them a volley, which made them sheer off & when the smoke cleared we perceived opposed to us on the hill a heavy column, and behind them a line [of infantry] flanked with cavalry, besides several guns which played round and grapeshot on us. The Marshal sent to General Cole to tell him we must advance, to which he replied '*We should be sacrificed if we did'*, the answer was *'The fate of the day depended on it'*. Sir William Myers[43] who commanded the brigade, rode up and said *'I will take the hill';* he put himself in front and cried *'Fusileers advance'*. We did so in the best order, the enemy firing on us tremendously without our returning a single shot. When we came within ten paces, we gave them a cheer and rushed on them; they turned immediately and for nearly half an hour, a complete slaughter took place. We took the heights and retook some cannon of ours, but found ourselves in danger of being outflanked by their cavalry & besides received the fire of another fresh line, upon which we received orders to retire behind the Portugueze [*sic*] who had had time to form and were advancing in the best order; we formed in the rear and the French retired, completely foiled in all points, not daring to try a fresh attack.[44]

Our loss has been immense; we were not engaged an hour and our battalion has 2 officers killed and 14 wounded, with about 360 men.[45] All the British regiments have suffered, but most of them in a different way from us. I am concerned to say that the 48th 2nd Battalion & 66th have lost their Colours; do not mention it unless it becomes public; it could not be avoided. Our cavalry was employed in watching the greatest part [of] theirs on the right, while they had others to charge our infantry. We were not supported on either flank in our advance. Our First Battalion has had 16 officers wounded,

43. Lieutenant Colonel Sir William Myers 7th Foot.
44. It is interesting that he gives such credit to the Portuguese, who shielded the Fusilier Brigade from a fresh counter-attack. This is supported by other eyewitnesses from this brigade.
45. The 2/7th went into the action with 435 men and left the action numbering about 80 men, having 47 men killed and 286 wounded. As regards officers, the losses of the 2nd Battalion were eventually worse than James' initial report at three dead and thirteen wounded. Captain Gaspar Erck, Lieutenants Holt Archer and Edward Irwin were killed; while Lieutenant Colonel Sir Edward Blakeney, Captains John Orr, Henry Tarleton and Henry Magennis wounded and Lieutenants John Healey, Thomas Wray, Charles Lorentz, George Seaton, James Fraser, John Holden, Martin Orr, Thomas Lester and Adjutant Timothy Meagher wounded.

2 of whom are since dead.[46] The 23rd have lost 3 officers killed & 13 wounded.[47]

Sir William Myers had his thigh broke, he died the next day of a mortification; he is a great loss, he behaved in the most gallant stile [*sic*]. General Cole & all [most of] his Staff are wounded; he went up with us. In the list of the wounded, you will I believe see my name; you must not be alarmed, it was a ball which struck my right thigh, but merely grazed [*sic*] it. It is already well. The wounds are in general very bad, several officers and men have lost legs and arms and some are not expected to live. It is expected that the 2nd Battalion will come home. The regiment have [*sic*] lost 32 officers and 700 men. The oldest soldiers in the army say they never saw such fighting; some regiments have lost more than us. Talavera and Barossa were a mere joke to it. If Marshal Beresford gives us credit, he will say we saved the day. The French retired on the 18th, pursued only by the cavalry; tomorrow we follow. Soult says he is retiring to meet a reinforcement of 10,000 men. We expect today Lord Wellington & 2 Divisions of the other army; he has again beat the French in the north.[48] The loss of the enemy according to a deserter's account is 8,000; we are supposed to have lost 4,000 English and 3,000 Spaniards & Portuguese. It has been a bloody day. Buonaparte is expected by the French army to take the command.

I received my box safe & wrote to let you know a long time ago. I beg to want shirts and stockings. I am sorry to say I was obliged to draw for £30 in favour of the Quarter Master of the 2nd Battalion.[49] On the 21st of next month I have been a year in the army and shall have overdrawn my [allowance of] £100 by £20, but which I hope to be able to save out of my next.

Massena's army is moving down this way and another desperate action is expected soon. Although I hope I shall always do my duty as a soldier, I must confess I should be sorry to see such another day as that of the 16th of May; a day that will be always memorable in the annals of British history. My best love to my Aunt [Ann] and sister [Mary Anne] & brother [Alexander] and everyone and believe me your very affectionate nephew. J[ames] B[aillie] Fraser.

---

46. In the 1st Battalion the losses were 65 men killed and 277 wounded; regarding officers five were killed and nine were wounded, Lieutenants Henry Prevost (died of wounds), Thomas Moultrie, Stephen Johnstone and Henry Jones (died of wounds) and Captains William Cholwich, James Singer and John Crowder with Lieutenants Charles Wemyss, Thomas Mullins, Thomas Moses, George Henry, Edward Morgan, Richard Johnson and Frederick Gibbons were wounded.
47. The 23rd suffered two officers and 74 men killed and 12 officers and 341 men wounded or missing.
48. Wellington had won the Battle of Fuentes d'Onoro fought between 3–5 May 1811.
49. Quartermaster John Hogan.

A note added to the letter states:
We are very happy that James is in a regiment which has distinguished itself so much & very thankful that he is safe.

The effective men of the 2nd Battalion were ordered to transfer to the 1st Battalion by a General Order dated 26 June 1811 and the officers, non-commissioned officers and Staff of the 2nd Battalion were ordered to march to Lisbon for homeward transportation. They sailed to England (including James) in the July and formed a depot at Maidstone, where large numbers from the Militia were drafted in, meaning that the battalion was soon deemed effective again and sailed to Jersey in November 1811, where it remained for the rest of the war.

Petworth, 17 August 1811

My dear Mary Anne
I am so far on my journey to Maidstone, where we shall arrive on the 22nd. The marching is so different from that in Portugal, that I quite like it. A good bed every night and something to amuse one on the road instead of marching all day over miserable roads with the pleasure of sleeping under a tree at night, by way of dinner a fight. Our appearance just now enforces respect and much as John Bull dislikes soldiers, we are everywhere paid attention. Our small number, old caps & coats, our Colours in rags with the poles of both shattered in halves are objects to which we owe a great deal.

I understand we are to have an order to state what place we wish to go to, Recruiting. It is not the kind of thing I should like by any means, but if I am obliged, I wish to know what spot I should choose. I shall trust to find a letter at Maidstone. I have not time to write a long letter now, all my news I reserve till I see you, which will be shortly. My best love to all and believe me your affectionate brother, James B[aillie] Fraser.

James was placed on the recruiting service, which he hated, but he was trying to get back to Spain as he now belonged to the 1st Battalion; he was happy however to hear that Alex had gained a commission in the 52nd Foot, a renowned regiment of light infantry.

Meanwhile George Unett's company moved to Weedon Barracks during May, remaining here until November 1813, although they were temporarily stationed at Sutton Camp from July till October 1812.

Leicester, 26 May 1812

My dear Mary Anne,
I am truly rejoiced to hear that Alex has obtained a commission in so good a regiment as the 52nd[50] and which is indeed another proof

50. Alexander was appointed to the 52nd Foot as an Ensign on 12 May 1812.

of Captain [Alexander] Campbell's kindness. They have been lately fighting with the Fusiliers at Badajoz and like them have suffered immensely. My promotion has been very great lately, I am effective in the 1st Battalion and have *written* to beg I may be allowed to take my tours of duty, from besides my detestation of the Recruiting Service, I am as anxious to go out to Portugal now as I was at first. We have had 7 officers killed[51] and all of them senior to me, but it is the last kind of way in which I should wish to obtain promotion. I know several officers of the 52nd, but there are most of them abroad. The 2nd Battalion [52nd] has just come home, so that there is no chance of Alex going out very soon; when he does, I dare say he will like the service much, for they are a dashing corps and are always present when anything is going on. I have got acquainted with very few of the gentlemen about here, for the *army* is not much liked in this part of the country. Sir R Lawley[52] told my Uncle John he would get me introduced to a Mr Pares, a banker, who is one of the first people in Leicester,[53] but I have not heard anything about it since. There is a Miss Linwood who is pretty well known in England from the exhibition in London belonging to her,[54] who gives the most dashing parties here and always asks me, when instead of playing cards all night, we dance, have music and spend the evening rationally. There is also a Mr Burnaby, who has been very civil to me from having known a son of his at [school?], which son is now at Woolwich.[55] The people here are very disaffected, but are afraid to show it openly, they insult us at night and where they think they can do it with impunity but have not proceeded to any great lengths as yet. Weedon Barrack is *not* very far from here and I think I could manage to see my Uncle George in a short time perhaps. I suppose he would *be some time* in *recognising me.* I think this is rather a long letter *about nothing* for I have not the subjects to write about now, that I had in posting a line. My best love to my Uncle [Richard], Ann & Alex & believe me your affectionate brother J[ames] B[aillie] Fraser

51. At Badajoz the 1st Battalion lost Major James Singer, Captains Robert Cuthbert and William Cholwich, Lieutenants Paul St Pol (died of wounds), William Pyke, Thomas Wray and Robert Fowler were killed.
52. Sir Robert Lawley had been MP for Newcastle until 1806; he became Baron Wenlock in 1834.
53. Mr Thomas Pares formed Pares & Co. Bank in Leicester in 1800. It eventually became part of the National Westminster Bank.
54. Miss Mary Linwood exhibited her needlework art in both Leicester and London, producing in her lifetime over 100 full-size copies of famous masterpieces in wool. Apparently the stitching was so fine that it resembled brushwork.
55. Gentleman Cadet Richard Beaumont Burnaby Royal Artillery (Kane 1565).

In his next letter, he admitted to his aunt that he had been foolish and was now heavily in debt, but that he desperately needed money to prepare for going abroad again.

Leicester, 10 June 1812

My dear Aunt [Ann],
I have this moment received your letter and answer it by saying that the scrape into which I have got took place 4 months ago and likewise most of my debts were incurred about that time. It is needless relating the story, I can only repeat that it was through another's fault that I got into it and that I must divide the expense with him. I have been obliged to pay a good deal of money on account of my Recruiting party through casuals, which have happened since I have had it. I own that my debts are great, but I also maintain that I am not deaf to advice, for my conduct for the last 2 months has been different from what it was before and the major part of my debts have been acquired a long time ago. As to being reserved as to my affairs, I did not think it necessary to hurt you by relating them when I had prospects of settling them and which I still should if I was to remain at Leicester any time. But now that I am ordered away and that my character with my regiment, my everything, depends upon it, I prefer laying my conduct before you; and all I can say is that you can never think so ill of me as I myself do. At any rate it would have cost me a great deal of money going to Portugal, as besides my things to be got in England, when I got there, there are things to be got which cannot be done without, mules &c. Therefore, I must once more declare however great the sum and however difficult to be obtained, I cannot go to Portugal without it and it will most probably be the least money I shall ever have. I cannot get more from Hillear and must take my chance whether they choose to supersede me or no. Notwithstanding whatever you may think, the loss of your esteem will ever be a source of misery to me and will render me careless of anything that may happen to me abroad. J[ames] B[aillie] Fraser

James wrote again from Portsmouth seeking more money.

Portsmouth, 21 June 1812

My dear Uncle [Richard],
I am put down to go onboard when the wind permits, which may be tomorrow, or in a day or two. I ought to [have] desired you to send me some money in my last letter, as I have not enough to buy my sea

stock. I have bought a canteen £4 15s,[56] a portmanteau £2 5s[57] and a boat cloak £4 4s,[58] so that you see I am in want of more. I would not wish to have much now but would rather draw when I get to Lisbon for some, to allow me to purchase a mule &c. I have received one month's pay and it will probably take £10 to get my place of mess on board this ship. In case we should be delayed by the wind at Plymouth or Falmouth, it will take much more, so that I ought to be provided for such events. I think the best way would be to draw here on Taylor & Lloyd[59] for £20, but the bankers I am afraid will not give me the money, so that if we sail directly I shall be in a pretty way. If not, you had better send me the money by return of post and I will leave directions for the letter to go back if I am gone, and if I go directly I must take my chance of the bankers accepting the bill if you will give Taylor directions to accept it. When I wrote to you last, I had not the least idea of going soon, but they have orders to be away without waiting for the Major.[60] Give my best love to my Aunt [Ann], Mary Anne & Alex & believe me your affectionate nephew J[ames] B[aillie] Fraser

56. About £250 today.
57. About £125 today.
58. About £225 today.
59. John Taylor & Sampson Lloyd of Birmingham began banking in 1765 and this was the forerunner of Lloyds Bank.
60. This must refer to Major Robert Burton 7th Foot, who arrived back in the Peninsula in September 1812.

Alexander and James in the Army

James' brother Alexander had joined the 52nd Foot as an Ensign on 12 May 1812 and his correspondence now begins to appear alongside his brother's.

Brabourne Lees Barracks, 29 June 1812

My dear Mary Anne,
I arrived here on the evening of the 23rd with all my clothes, books &c &c. There was an officer's wife & daughter on the outside of the coach, who were going to Ashford to join the 73rd Regiment of which the lady's husband was a captain. We had not proceeded far on our journey when it began a violent shower & Cargill[1] & myself gave up our inside places to them & went all the way on the outside; we escaped with two or three *duckings*, for which we were amply compensated by the beauty of the country through which we passed & the pleasure of having obliged the wife & daughter of a brother soldier. We passed by Lee[d]s Castle, which is a most beautiful old building, standing in the midst of a delightful park & surrounded by a moat. The country all the way was highly cultivated, every half mile was some gentleman's seat. What made it more entertaining, there was a gentleman on the coach who knew to whom every house belonged & the character of the owner. I was sorry when we came to our place of destination as with such a companion I could have travelled twice as far with pleasure. I found Matthews[2] waiting for me & had obtained leave from evening parade on purpose to [be] with me. Cargill has an uncle in the 52nd to whose room he went on his arrival & I to Matthews's [*sic*]. Matthews *knocked* me [up] a bed in his room till I could get a quarter & have my baggage & bed removed into it. I soon got acquainted with all the officers in the regiment who are the finest, most gentlemanlike young men I ever met with. They were all willing to assist me & would have gladly accommodated me with half their quarter but I prefered [*sic*] an

1. Ensign James Stewart Cargill 52nd Foot.
2. Almost certainly Ensign John Echlin Matthews 43rd Foot.

old friend's. They allmost [*sic*] all know James [Fraser] very well as they were in the same brigade with him & many are old Marlow friends.[3] Brabourne Lees is a most desolate place. I have not seen a single person except soldiers since my arrival, but we can do very well without & what time we have from drill we employ in cricket, *duck hunts*[4] & other boy's games. We have not got a field officer[5] in the garrison, the commanding officer is a young captain. I believe the oldest among us is not more than 25. I want some more buff pantaloons & blue web pantaloons as it is a fine of 5 shillings for every officer who does not dress for dinner in buff pantaloons & wear blue in the morning, no such thing as grey are ever worn, they are not regimental & you are not allowed to appear on parade with them. Cargill & myself have obtained leave to wear them till we get blue. I have written to Ashton [tailor] to beg he will take back one pair of grey. The short boots are not of any use to me except on a march, then the officers wear overalls. If Smith [bootmaker] could take back one pair & give me a pair of hessians[6] instead, or if he would both pair I should be much obliged to him.

I have no more room to write any more but answer this soon & you shall hear from me again. Give my love to my Uncle [Richard] & Aunt [Ann] & remember me [to] Mrs Scott & Captain [Alexander] Campbell to whom I shall for ever be grateful for having got me into the best regiment in the service. I remain your affectionate brother A[lexander] J[ohn] Fraser

Within two weeks, Alexander was writing to his sister again querying the non-arrival of his trunk.

Brabourne Lees Barracks, 10 July 1812

My dear Mary Anne,
Day after day have I been expecting to receive my trunk containing my drawings &c, but am now at a loss to conceive what can have become of it. I have enquired at all the inns at Ashford & at the house where the coaches & waggons stop here, but can hear nothing of it, they all assure me no such trunk has ever arrived. Pray inquire of the waggoner or whoever had the charge of it, what he has done with it, as I cannot do anything without I receive it. I am extremely obliged to Mrs Borthwick for her kind recommendation & beg you

3. Royal Military Academy at Marlow.
4. Also called Duck Stone. The object is to knock a stone off a rock by throwing stones at it.
5. A field officer included all officers of the rank of Major and above.
6. A mid-calf boot with a low heel and a tassel on the top.

will present to her my sincere thanks. I called at the gentleman's house but was told that he would not be at home before Saturday. I went over to Hythe the other day & visited the Martello Towers & the other batteries erected along the coast.

General Mackenzie[7] comes over to see us very often & as we are great favorites [*sic*] of his, he has applied to get us removed to Shoreham Cliff [Shorncliffe], where we shall be more immediately under his eye. We are delighted at the thought of going there as it is a delightful place, the sea coming almost close up to the barracks. The weather here is uncommonly fine, but excessively hot, which makes the drill before breakfast very fatiguing. All my drilling at Woolwich avails me nothing, as it is quite different from what is practiced here. The Marlow Cadets are more fagged than a person who has never seen a firelock, as they are obliged to break them of their bad habits & careless exercising, however I expect to be dismissed drill in about 6 months.[8]

I have just paid half a guinea subscription to a fencing club; fencing & rabbit hunting being our chief amusement in this *out of the way* place where there is not a town for five miles. I have bought a very fine terrier & a ferret. Every officer has his dog & his ferret, as *rats & rabbits* are the only game we are allowed to pursue. We have church every Sunday morning at the drum-head out on the common. The mornings & evenings are entirely taken up with drill, but in the middle of the day all the officers in the garrison play at cricket by which I can assure you I am pretty well knocked up this hot weather. My face is peeled by the sun & my lips so sore that I can hardly touch them, but this is only a little seasoning & which I like very well. I wish we had a few of the Artillery gentlemen down here who do nothing but march past every evening parade, a few months under the hands of one of our drill sergants [*sic*] would do them a great deal of good. I do not think they would like standing for 5 minutes upon one leg to give the body a proper position, till one is ready to faint, or skirmishing for two hours with a heavy gun, running at one time as hard as possible, then laying down on the belly & behind the hedge & all the other maneuvers [*sic*] which *light bobs* are obliged to practice & which all the officers here fag at every day. Recruits are coming in to us every day, we now muster near 500 strong, which is immense considering that on the return of [the] 2nd Battalion from

7. Major General Kenneth Mackenzie.
8. Newly commissioned officers were required to learn the manual of arms and drill of the soldier, as well as to perform the commands for company drill before they could be considered ready to go on active service.

Portugal, had not 50 men.[9] Write immediately & tell me something about my trunk, what can have become of it, as I am put to great inconvenience without it. Give my best love to my Uncle [Richard] & Aunt [Ann] & all friends & believe me every Your affectionate brother A[lexander] J[ohn] Fraser.

In July, we find James landed in Lisbon and requiring more money.

Lisbon, 23 July 1812

My dear Uncle [Richard],
I have been absolutely obliged to draw on this bill for £20 on Greenwood & Cox, as it was impossible for me to proceed up the country without money, and all I had was taken in buying mules & other things requisite for the journey. You will of course think I am going to be as extravagant as ever, but I assure you upon my honour, that you shall see no more bills from me for some time, in fact no more I hope this year. Tomorrow, I start for the army which is [in] full pursuit of the enemy. Of course, you will have the glorious news before this letter.[10] My best love to all & believe me your affectionate nephew, J[ames] B[aillie] Fraser.

Four days later he wrote a more fulsome letter.

Lisbon, 27 July 1812

My dear Uncle [Richard],
I departed in such a hurry from Portsmouth that I had no time to write to you. I was quite able to throw my things into a trunk and sent it off and had the wind been fairer, should have lost my passage. They ordered us onboard at 9 & at 10 the ship sailed. We had a pleasant passage and arrived on the 25 [June]. I got a letter from Thompson the day I sailed, to say my [old things?] would come the next night. I left directions with 3 different officers to bring them, and I am in daily expectation of receiving them as another fleet was to sail 2 days after us. We have 25 days continued marching before

9. Before the 2nd Battalion left Portugal in the spring of 1812, it transferred 504 other ranks into the 1st Battalion to bring up its numbers; a number of junior officers and sergeants were also transferred. They were exchanged for 100 sergeants and other ranks who were unfit for duty. They, as well as the remaining officers and sergeants went back to England, where they would spend the next two years rebuilding the 2nd Battalion before going on active service again to the Netherlands in December 1813.

10. Of the Battle of Salamanca.

us, before we can join the army and the weather is more noticeably hot than I ever before felt it.

I have been obliged to draw for £30 instead of 20 the discount being high and I fear I shall be obliged to draw more before I get settled, as the army is 5 months in arrears of pay and Lord Wellington has given an order for no detachments to be paid at Lisbon. I should have got one month's pay and bat and forage money had it not been for this. I have got a billet at Belem in order to live cheaper than I could do at Lisbon and as soon as I get a march I shall depart for the army, which I hope will be in two days; but mules are so dear it is impossible to get one to carry baggage under 150 dollars. I believe the Paymaster will advance me some money on my bat & forage allowance. There is a great deal of manoeuvring going on between the armies but not much fighting. Our men are in good health and spirits although they have had constant marching since [storming] Badajoz and sleep every night in the fields. The men and some of the officers got a great deal of money and plate &c at Badajoz; as Lord Wellington could not and they say would not, prevent plunder for 2 days. A private in our regiment got 700 dollars and gave *most of them to* anyone who would take the trouble of carrying them. There is a report just spread of General [obliterated] having had an affair with Drouot's Corps[11] and that Lord W[ellington] has retired a short distance before the enemy. Write to me as soon as you can. Give my best love to my Aunt [Ann], Mary Anne and all friends & believe me your affectionate nephew J[ames] B[aillie] Fraser.

Alexander wrote again, explaining where his money had gone.

Brabourne Lees Barracks, 13 August 1812

My dear Mary Anne,

You have no doubt been surprised at my long silence. I can assure you I have determined day after day to answer your last letter, but some drill or inspection has continually interrupted my intentions; however this night having been obliged to make out a long statement of the company I belong to, which has taken me above an hour, while my *hand was in* I formed a resolution to put it off no longer. I paid Mr Ball a visit & delivered Mrs Borthwick's letter & was invited to meet a very pleasant party of the neighbouring gentlemen the next day. Mr Ball himself is indeed a delightful old gentleman, full of all manner of fun & excessively fond of the soldiers & I hope my Uncle [Richard] will not think me extravagant when in this letter I request a

11. General Antoine Drouot was actually then involved in the Russian campaign and subsequent fighting in Germany.

small supply of money. You must remember I only took with me from Woolwich 14 pounds. I have been obliged to give my servant a livery, as every officer's servant must wait at the mess & those who come in regimentals are fined. Though the clothes I got for my servant were not at all of an expensive sort, they cost me upwards of 6 pounds.[12] As for what pay I have received, the Mess fees,[13] Commission fees,[14] Charity fund,[15] Band, Income tax[16] &c have made such a hole in it that there is very little indeed left to receive. Beside these, I have been obliged to buy breakfast things, blacking brushes, boot trees, a couple of pair of shoes & spats as my boots if constantly worn would soon be good for nothing & a number of articles which though singly trifling yet altogether come to a good deal. Add to this my messing & breakfasting.[17] I assure that except the two or three first days I joined, when it was absolutely necessary & yesterday, being the Prince's birthday,[18] I have never tasted a drop of wine that you might not consider me extravagant in that respect. I *am happy* to say I do not *owe anything*, but *sorry to say* I have *nothing left* in case anything might happen, when I should stand in need of it. I therefore *submit* it to *your consideration* whether or not I have been extravagant. It is impossible for a young officer to be in a better place than this for learning his duty. After drilling, before breakfast we go home tired out.

At twelve the junior officers are obliged to go round the barrack rooms, parade the company & see that the beds are properly folded up & everything clean in rooms. At one, ball firing till four. At four go home & dress for dinner. A ½ past four we dine. After dinner [is] evening parade & a long drill of an hour & ½. At 9 visit your company's rooms again & finish the evening by making out a statement of every man in the company, which takes me every night about an hour or more. What time we have is from 9 o'clock till twelve which we

---

12. In addition to providing appropriate dress the officer would have to pay his servant around 6 pence a day.
13. This would include his dinner and any wine he consumed in the mess. One officer in the 50th Foot said his mess fees were 3 shillings a day. The 52nd Foot's fees, because it was a fashionable regiment, were probably higher.
14. He would have paid £4 11s 10d commission fee in addition to £400 for the price of the commission.
15. An officer was expected to donate a day's wage per year to the Chelsea Hospital.
16. An ensign's daily pay was 5 shillings 3 pence. His annual pay was £95 16s 3d. His income tax was 10 per cent of his pay or £4 1s 9½
17. All these bills added up. One officer claimed that after paying his expenses he had only 5 pence a day left. For more information on this see Robert Burnham and Ron McGuigan, *The British Army against Napoleon: Facts, Lists, and Trivia 1805-1815*, Barnsley: Frontline, 2010, pp. 140–50.
18. The Prince Regent's birthday was on 12 August.

employ in cricket, quoits &c. I must [torn – now?] leave off as it is one o'clock in the morning [torn – I do not?] know how I shall be able to awake tomorrow morning for drill if I do not go to bed immediately. Give my love to my Uncle [Richard] & Aunt [Ann] & Aunt Elizabeth & remember me to Mrs Scott & the Campbells. Believe me ever my dear Mary Anne, your affectionate brother A[lexander] J[ohn] Fraser

Brabourne Lees Barracks, 19 August 1812

My dear Mary Anne,
I take the earliest opportunity of acknowledging the receipt of your letter enclosing the half notes. I have likewise this day received a letter from Mr Garstin who is on the Company's establishment at Croydon,[19] in which he expresses how much he wishes to renew our old acquaintance & encloses a letter to Mrs Loftie at Canterbury his grandmother, which if I deliver any time I may happen to go over there, she will be happy to pay me every attention in her power.

(21 August) I had just begun my letter when I was disturbed by the bugles sounding for the skirmishing parties to go out, I was therefore obliged to take my musket & accoutrements & join them[20] nor have I been able till now to address you [again]. This day being the anniversary of the glorious Battle of Vimeria[21] in which the Light Division so highly distinguished itself, our regiment & the 43rd have boughs of laurel in their caps. In this *out of the way* place it is impossible for me to have anything to say that could entertain you. All our society is among ourselves. I must therefore conclude this short letter by begging you to give my love to my Uncle [Richard] & Aunt [Ann] & Aunt Elizabeth & believe me ever your affectionate brother A[lexander] J[ohn] Fraser.

Alexander continued his pleas of lack of time and lack of money.

Brabourne Lees Barracks, 20 September 1812

My dear Mary Anne,
I can assure that I have been intending to write to you day after day for some time past, but my time has been so employed that I have been

19. Cadet Edward Garstin attended the Addiscombe Military Seminary, which from 1809 prepared young men for service in the forces of the East India Company.
20. Newly commissioned officers were required to learn how to skirmish as a soldier before they were taught their duties as an officer controlling a group of skirmishers.
21. The Battle of Vimeiro was fought on 21 August 1809. The 2nd Battalions of the 52nd and 43rd Foot were brigaded together under the command or General Anstruther, but they were not in the Light Division, which was not formed until 22 February 1810.

always prevented. We have three drills a day besides two garrison parades, which together with visiting the rooms twice a day, inspecting the company &c &c prevents a subaltern from having an hour in the day to himself & by 9 o'clock when all our duty is over it is as much as I can do to make out a long parade state which we are obliged to do every night. However I am happy to day that I was yesterday dismissed drill, having got over it sooner than almost any officer in the regiment was known to do, for which I may thank Captain [Alexander] Campbell for getting me so well drilled at Woolwich.[22] Matthews who joined two months before me has not yet got over it & Cargill who joined with me the same day has not yet taken a musquet. I can assure you that I am very sorry I shall be obliged to draw for £15 as the expences [*sic*] that I have unavoidably incurred renders it absolutely necessary. I shall therefor prove to you how it is impossible for anyone to have acted with more economy than I have done.

To begin therefore, every officer on being dismissed drill he is obliged to pay one guinea, on mounting his first guard which I did two or three days ago one guinea more.[23] I have been obliged to buy a white belt & silver breast plate which I bought from an officer going abroad & though the regular price is £3 I got it for 25 s[hillings] & wear them on all field days, reviews &c. General Mackenzie has ordered us to wear grey trowsers & gaters [*sic*] for which I paid 2 guineas. I have likewise been obliged to buy a new pair of wings[24] as I only got one pair from Ashton. Ashton[25] wings are very bad indeed & he charges 6 guineas, whereas the ones that I have bought, of which the bullion is much larger I have only paid 5s 6d. All these expences [*sic*] were absolutely necessary & are alone more than the £10 which you sent me. I should therefore be obliged to you to write & inform me in what manner to draw on Taylor & Loyd [*sic*]. I think it is shameful in Thompson [tailor] requiring £4 10s[hillings] to exchange the bed,[26] as you can get the best common camp bed for £12. I really now must conclude by assuring you that now I have done with the *laborious part* of drill I shall become a more regular correspondent. Give my love to my Aunt [Ann] & Uncle [Richard] & Aunt Elizabeth & remember me kindly to the Campbells & Mrs Scott. Alexander Fraser.

---

22. At the Royal Military College.
23. In some regiments the tradition was that a newly commissioned officer would give the first soldier to salute him a guinea. In others the tradition was when the officer served as the officer of the guard for the first time, he would give the sergeant of the guard a guinea to buy drinks for the guard once it was dismissed.
24. Wings were worn on the shoulders and designated the individual was a light infantryman.
25. I could find no reference of a military tailor with that name.
26. Although an officer's room was furnished with basic furniture such as a table and chair, he had to provide his own bed.

It was three months before Alexander wrote again, when he wrote to let them know that he might have leave from Christmas Day.

Shoreham Cliff [Shorncliffe], 6 December 1812

My dear Mary Anne,
I am afraid you must by this time have thought me very negligent in not having written for so long a time, my reason for having delayed it, was my not being able before to know when & for how long I should be able to obtain leave.

Having so lately joined & a great number of wounded officers wishing for leave, it will be impossible for me to obtain a month's leave of absence, however (provided we have enough officers to do the duty of the garrison), I am promised leave from the 25th of this month till the 10th of the next being the interval between the Returns & which General Mackenzie will be able to grant me without an application to the Commander in Chief. You have no idea of the difficulty a young officer has to obtain any leave & my being the very junior officer with the regiment, everyone has prior claims. It is unfortunate that I cannot be with you on Xmas day but that will be impossible. I received my bed two or three days ago, it seems an excellent bed itself, but he only sent one blanket. I shall therefore keep the pair I had with the other bed, (as they fit very well) & send him the old one with the bed.

I received the other day a very kind invitation from Garstin (as he has now left Addiscombe) to dine with him & go to the Ball at Canterbury in the evening. It was not in my power to accept his invitation, [for] not knowing that we had left Brabourne Lees he had directed the letter to that place & it did not reach me till the morning after the Ball. Notwithstanding the coldness of the weather (which here is intense) we have as much drill as ever, about a fortnight ago we were reviewed by the Earl of Rosslyn.[27] General Mackenzie made us perform a variety of light manoeuvres, the rapidity of which completely astonished him. In a very handsome speech, he expressed how much he was pleased with our appearance & state of discipline. I see Harris[28] almost every day, he seems very comfortable & keeps a very good horse. Every day while we are skirmishing & running through mud & leaping hedges &c, the *gentlemen* of the Staff Corps are quietly seated on their horses viewing us; they seem indeed a different race from us, they are always riding about, giving Balls &c and living in the greatest luxury, yet I assure you I do not envy them; although their pay[29] & allowances are fully twice as

27. James St Clair-Erskine, 2nd Earl of Rosslyn.
28. Ensign Thomas Harris Royal Staff Corps.
29. An infantry ensign's pay was 5 shillings 3 pence per day. A Royal Staff Corps ensign's pay was 8 shillings a day.

good as ours, yet there is not one of us that would exchange places with them. The only thing that I envy them is their being allowed forage for horses which is certainly the greatest luxury.[30]

8 December. I was interrupted while writing by the bugle sounding for parade & yesterday it was not in my power to proceed with my letter as we marched a good way into the country & did not return till long after the post had left. I had just sat down to finish today when I received your letter. As to Thomson's bill it is all very correct, except (as I have mentioned in a former part of the letter) there is one blanket wanting. I have been reading Lord Byron's *Childe Harold*,[31] which has delighted me very much. I now beg leave to submit to your consideration the state of my *finances* which you must be aware from the length of time that has elapsed since they were replenished, must [torn – be?] inadequate to the various expenses I must [torn – incur?] in my journey up to you. You must not [torn – ever?] think me extravagant if I request supply for that purpose. At the same time, I beg you will rest assured that I have not deviated from my plan of economy. When you consider the smallness of an Ensign's pay (exclusive of all the different deductions) & that in the 52nd Regiment he is obliged to make just as must figure as a captain, my present demand cannot appear to you extravagant. I am sorry to hear you have all [been] suffering from rheumatism & colds though not surprized at my Uncle [Richard] being unwell as the weather is cold enough to hurt any person. I am afraid you will not be able to make out this scrawl. Remember me to the Campbells & Huddlestones, Scotts &c &c & give my love to my Aunts [Ann & Elizabeth] & Uncle [Richard] & believe me ever my dear Mary Anne your affectionate brother Alexander Fraser.

The next long letter from James in Spain was copied to Uncle John and Aunt Fanny. He had endured the retreat from Madrid to Salamanca and the even worse retreat further back to the Portuguese border; but he had also suffered from severe fever.

To Miss [Fanny] Unett, Stafford

11 February 1813

Dear Sister,

By desire of Mary Anne, I send you a copy of James Fraser's last letter [not last ever]. The poor fellow has suffered dreadfully. We

30. An infantry ensign was not authorized a horse and thus he received no money for buying it forage. A Royal Staff Corps officer was authorized a horse and would receive money to feed his horse. In Portugal he was authorized 6 pence per day.

31. Lord Byron's long narrative poem was produced in four separate Cantos between 1812 to 1818. Canto I issued in 1812 describes the journey of a youthful man, reckless of life, who experiences the savagery of the French invasion of Spain and Portugal.

are all very well. Mrs [Elizabeth] Unett joins me in kind love. Yours sincerely J[ohn] W[ilkes] Unett.

St Juan de Piscalos [San Joao da Pesqueira], 6 December 1812

My dear Mary Anne,
I had the pleasure of receiving your letter on the 23rd of last month, but as we were then on our march to this place, where we only arrived 2 days ago, I have never before had an opportunity of answering it. I have been at so many different places since I left Lisbon, that it would be utterly impossible for me to describe them; you must therefore be content with a short account of my adventures &c, some of which I cannot think of without shuddering, for never since I have been in the Army have I suffered so much from sickness, severe marching, the inclemency of the weather [&] a want of provisions as I have for the last 3 months. I left Lisbon on 30 July and after 31 days march, passing through Abrantes, Castello Branco [Castelo Branco], Ciudad Rodrigo & Salamanca, I arrived in safety at the Escurial,[32] where the regiment was quartered. I found nothing to admire in Salamanca but the cathedral & the public square, which excel everything of the sort I ever saw, but for description of which I refer you to history, until I have the pleasure of giving you a verbal one. The Escurial is built in the shape of a gridiron, and one part of it projects for the handle. There is a small town round the palace, which is built under the Guadarama mountains, 18 miles from Madrid. On the 1 September, when out with a foraging party on the summit of the mountains, I was seized by a faintness, fell of[f] my mule and was carried home senseless. This attack was followed by a severe one of the ague, which never left me till the 28 October, during which time we moved to the other side of Madrid as far as Aranjuez on the Toledo road. Madrid is a most beautiful capital & the streets &c are cleaner than any other I ever was in; and I regretted much that I was not in a state to see the lions.[33] At Aranjuez, a very nice town, I saw a palace built by Charles the 4th, every floor and staircase of which are built of the different marbles of Spain and the walls lined by the most beautiful tapestry, which employed hundreds of people several years to make, in short foreigners allow it to excel everything of the kind in Europe.[34]

From this place we commenced our retreat after making a slight defence of a large bridge over the Guadarama; we passed through Madrid & retraced our steps, closely pursued by the enemy to Alba de Tormes, where we crossed the river and took a position on the other side near to Salamanca. Necessity forced me to rise from my

32. The battalion was quartered in the Escurial from 19 August to 6 October.
33. The 'lions' were the main attractions.
34. He refers to the Casa del Labrador built by King Charles IV.

bed and march, had I remained I should at this moment have been a prisoner, or perhaps have died from bad treatment. We marched [from Aranjuez] on 28 October, it rained all day and night. I got upon a gun carriage wrapped up in a cloak & when we halted next day at 11 o'clock at Madrid[35] where we took a position, I felt quite well. All the rest of this march, which only ended 2 days ago I have walked, been wet through 9 days out of 10, waded through rivers above my knees and slept every night in my wet things; our baggage being ordered from us, not to impede the line of march. To add to all this, we took it in turn to be the rear-guard and having to show a front to the enemy kept us from 3 hours before sunrise till after dark every night on the march, after which came piquets &c to amuse us. The officers and men were 5 days together without bread, which is the greatest want I ever experienced. At one time we had unground corn served out to us, and when that failed, we picked acorns, which in this country are as good as chestnuts.

At Alba de Tormes, we halted in the open air [for] 3 days. On the 4 [November] at night, the French crossed the river and next day after a good deal of skirmishing (in which having command of the light company, I had my share; the dragoons fired at us all day, but [we] being behind walls they did no mischief). We set off for Ciudad Rodrigo and crossed the Agueda where the French halted and left us to pursue our route to quiet winter quarters, where we hope to have a long rest. We were joined at Salamanca by Lord Wellington from Burgos with 4 divisions & some cavalry.

On the 17 [November] a smart affair took place, but the Light Division took the rear guard that day and suffered some loss; we were formed close behind them but lost no men, though 2 or 3 shells fell near us. Officers who were on the retreat to Corunna say it never was at the worst, so bad as ours and the one from Busaco which I was at myself, although bad enough, was never either for length of duration or want of food and comfort, half so bad as the one from Madrid; and I have reason to think, that the one from Burgos was much the same.

From Ciudad Rodrigo to this place, we have taken our time & had our baggage with us, so that we have had no great loss on the Agueda; but *entre vous* [between us], I imagine 5,000 men is not the least exaggeration; in one night our own division left behind 1,000, upwards 300 of whom were taken or died of cold, the others got round by the mountains. I never saw men keep up their spirits on [the] march so well in the midst of difficulties as the regiment did, and yet we are told in England that the British soldier sinks under the smallest [trial]. It is quite impossible that any letter of mine can give you an idea of what I felt when dragging my shoes through mud above my knees, wet

35. The Regimental records show that the battalion arrived in Madrid on 31 October.

to the skin, a hungry stomach, knowing that if I stopped at any hovel I should be a prisoner. I have felt a slight attack of the ague here, the first since the march began, but having changed to a warmer house, I feel already better. We are in hopes of being very comfortable here if we remain the winter, as it is only 16 leagues from Oporto, from whence we can get English goods, some of which I want, all my shirts having already suffered in the war. Mr Thompson's (the tailors) things I have got all safe, but they do not fit me as the other things he sent me [did], and I have been obliged to alter them.

16 December. Since writing the above I have been confined to my bed with a delirious fever. I am still in bed, but the fever has left me. As soon as I can move, I am going to Oporto, for which purpose I shall want money and have therefore drawn on Greenwood & Cox at 8 days sight for £30. I could not have done without money at any rate, for we have had none these 6 months. I almost despair of having my health again in this country, for the moment I came to quarters I was taken ill directly. I hope the length of this letter will make up for my silence before. Give my best love to my Uncle [Richard] and Aunt [Ann] & Alex [Fraser] if with you and believe me your affectionate brother, J[ames] B[aillie] Fraser.

Alexander wrote again just days before Christmas, giving bad news.

Shoreham Cliff [Shorncliffe], 22 December 1812

My dear Mary Anne,
I am extremely sorry to communicate to you the tidings that I must yet defer the pleasure of seeing you for some days. You must recollect that although I was very sanguine in my hopes that I should be able to obtain leave, yet it was with the proviso that there would remain a sufficient number of officers to do duty with the regiment, which I am sorry to say (owing to a number getting leave & others on leave getting theirs prolonged) is not the case. It is a double mortification to me, my being thus disappointed, (as independent of the pleasure of meeting you all at the present season) my friend Matthews & I had formed a scheme for paying a visit to Dr Glennie & family during the vacation, which will now be expired before I can get leave. I have been for these last three days on duty & have this morning come off guard.

The Commanding Officer cannot therefore in justice grant leave to one subaltern while the duty is so hard upon the others. You may rest assured however that no applications on my part shall be wanting to obtain leave on the 10 January, the next interval between the Returns & I make no doubt but I shall be able to accomplish it at that time. It is unfortunate that I wished to obtain leave at a season which everyone as well as myself wishes to spend with their family & which is the reason we are so weak in officers. If it had been at any other time, I should not have had any difficulty in procuring leave for so short a period.

I now beg leave to inquire whether my quarterly allowance is not due the 28th of this month, as far [as] I recollect it is, but however I will not be certain. I only request that if it is, my Uncle [Richard] will either send it or give me directions to draw for it on Taylor, Lloyd &c, money being always acceptable but more particularly so at present, as we have received an order to provide ourselves with buff breeches & long black gaiters. Give my love to my Uncle [Richard] & Aunts [Ann & Elizabeth] & remember me most kindly to Mrs Scott & the Campbells & Believe me ever my dear Mary Anne, your affectionate brother Alexander Fraser.

George wrote to Richard Unett from Weedon Barracks, enclosing a letter which was meant for Richard from an old acquaintance. He wished to buy or rent some land in Scotland that Richard managed for his nephews.

Weedon, 7 February 1813

Dear [Richard] Wilkes,
This letter was intended for you, I have written to Mr Patterson to say you will answer it. Love to Mrs [Ann] U[nett], Mary Anne [Fraser] & Elizabeth. Your affectionate brother G[eorge] W[ilkes] U[nett].

Inverness, 1 February 1813

Dear Sir,
I dare say you will hardly recollect the signature to this letter as it's so long since I had the pleasure of seeing you at St Pierre, Martinique, where I think we both spent many a pleasant day during three or four years stay in that island. I have been almost all the time hence in Demerara, a very unhealthy climate which I left only last July. My reason in troubling you at this time is at the request of a friend. My wife's aunt has lived long in the neighbourhood of a place belonging to your nephews Belladrum[36] who are under your charge. This place I am told brings in a rent of £50 per annum, pray would you be inclined to dispose of it, or is it to be let [?] In either case if agreeable to you, I should like to have the refusal. If the first, how much might be expected [?] If the last, how long a lease would be granted and would a tenant be allowed [?] the valuation of his friends at the end of his lease for improvements & buildings, the place at this moment looks poor enough, hardly a house upon it & such. If the place

36. Belladrum had passed through the Frasers for centuries. It lies 8km west of Inverness.

is sold, I could procure as much for it as any other person, most likely thirty years purchase of the present rate. I would not wish to offend any of your friends or agents here, nor could I wish the contents of this letter to go farther than yourself; I shall be happy to hear from you on receipt & please say in either case what you would expect. Do you ever meet my old garrison friend Colonel [John] Sheldrake & where is he quartered [?]

The present high price of cotton will add much to his comforts, should you ever see or meet our worthy friend Colonel [James] Forster, please remember me kindly to him. Maclean[37] has like myself taken to himself a wife and lives about forty miles from this, he has now one or two *white* children, you know what a flock of a different breed he left in the West Indies. I dare say you know my father-in-law, the old cock served twenty years in the Ordnance Department (John Haywood) he the greater part of the time lived at St Kitts (Brimstonehill).[38]

If you get a short leave of absence during the summer months, I am sure you would meet with many of your old acquaintances in this quarter & believe me none would be more happy in seeing you than dear Sir, yours very truly G Patterson[39]

PS I frequently meet Miss Bell Fraser, she is well and in very good health.

James wrote again to explain his dire need for funds.

Ervedaya [Ervedosa do Douro], 17 February 1813

My dear Uncle [Richard],
I have been obliged to draw another bill for £25 dated 10th of this month, [payable] 31 days after sight. I was driven to it to obtain the common necessaries of life and if we march tomorrow, I shall commence the campaign without several things that I ought to have for want of money. I have had a horse and a mule die from the fatigues of the retreat and I positively cannot walk any longer. Every officer has two animals and is allowed forage for them and I must provide [for] myself or drop on the road. It is now 6 months since I joined my regiment and I pledge my honour that during that time I have received but 30 dollars pay & I have due to me more than 200. I have the ague every third day and am so pulled down with continued illness, that the commanding officer has desired me to attend a Medical Board to

37. Lieutenant F Maclean 11th Foot (in 1795).
38. Brimstone Hill Fortress on St Kitts is now a UNESCO World Heritage Site.
39. Ensign George Paterson 11th Foot (in 1795).

obtain leave for England, but which I certainly shall not do, as I expect to get well when we march in the spring.

When the campaign opens is quite uncertain, but the common idea is that we march for Spain the beginning of next month, when I suppose it will be the old thing, fighting all summer and running away all winter. What kind of a constitution I have, I cannot find out, at the Escurial and the villages round Madrid and now at this place, where comparatively speaking we live in comfort, I have never had one day's health. On the retreat (when we had a mostly continued march and where half the time I was to the middle in water and never had an opportunity of changing my clothes) I enjoyed perfect health, had a famous appetite and was as strong as any man. I had better be killed at once than live the life I do now. Every third day I am in bed all day and the others almost poisoned with bark & draught.

The country we are in is enough to make one hang oneself; it is 10,000 times worse than the worst part of the highlands of Scotland that I passed through and which were bad enough certainly. We moved to this town, which is close on the Douro about a month since. We are all delighted at the success of the Russians, as the opinion here is that it gives a chance of peace and we should have no objection to go home by that means. I am sorry to say the army is very unhealthy, the men are dying very fast. My Uncle John blamed me for not writing to him before and I discern the same concern now, but I am going to write to him soon. Give my best love to my Aunt [Ann] & Mary Anne & all friends & believe me my dearest Uncle, your affectionate nephew J[ames] B[aillie] Fraser.

A Disastrous Campaign

Alexander wrote his first letter home after landing in Portugal with a detachment of the regiment and commencing his march to join the army.

Abrantes, 5 April 1813

My dear Mary Anne,
After a prosperous voyage of 9 days we landed at Lisbon, a place which at first sight seems a beautiful city, but which on a closer inspection is one of the most filthy places in the universe. On my arrival I inquired if Sir J Bateman[1] was there but found he was still in Ireland. I should have written to you before I left it but was for three days employed in getting a billet which I at last did. I had then to purchase animals which are immensely dear, nothing to be had under 150 dollars.[2] It was my intention to have procured two of them one for my baggage & one to ride, but owing to the enormous prices, my finances would only allow of one for my baggage. The city still bears marks of the earthquake, in many parts there are heaps of ruins & grass growing.[3] I had not time to visit Cintra [Sintra] or any of the adjacent villages, for after giving us a few days to get horses we received orders to march for the army. We entered this town yesterday & halt here today to give the men a little rest.[4] We march every day 20 miles, beginning before daylight & get it over by 11 o'clock. The heat is excessive much hotter than in the middle of summer in England.

I confess I felt rather tired when the march is nearly over, but we have had no hardships as yet. Our only provisions are salt ration pork & biscuit. The old officers who have been out before, call it living in *clover* to what we shall when the army is in motion. The marching

1. This would appear to refer to Sir John Bateman (1782–1858) who bought Knypersley Hall in Staffordshire in 1809. He was a famous horticulturist. Why Alexander thought he might have been in Ireland or Portugal is not known.
2. One dollar was equal to 4.5 shillings; 150 dollars was equivalent to £33 15 shillings.
3. The Great Lisbon Earthquake occurred on 1 November 1755.
4. Abrantes is about 150km from Lisbon.

here is much more fatiguing than in England owing to roads which are either up to your knees in sand, or over stones & lumps of rock. This day we marched from Santarem, it poured in torrents of rain from before daylight till six o'clock in the evening, we had to wade up to our middle in water almost the whole way & as the baggage could not proceed we had to stay in our wet clothes for several hours. It has had no bad effect on me, in fact except ten minutes sea sickness in the Bay of Biscay, I have never had a moment's illness since I saw you.[5] Our march has been along the Tagus the whole way through the most romantick [*sic*] country that can be imagined. We passed yesterday by the walls of Tancos which you may perhaps have heard of. This city is immensely strong indeed the hills you have to ascend to it are almost equal to a day's march. The French were never here. When they retreated from Santarem burning every village they came to, they left Abrantes to their right. The inhabitants are very uncivil to the English, everywhere else the Portuguese take off their hats to us. Our division being much in advance we have 140 miles[6] father to march, the 52nd are now at Fuente Guinaldo [Fuenteguinaldo]. From all accounts the 7th Regiment are near Opporto [*sic*], if this is the case I shall not see James before the army commences operations when the 7th are generally nearer the Light Division than any other division of the army. On my joining the 1st battalion I shall have to pay the Mess subscription of 7 guineas,[7] & on my being gazetted lieutenant my Commission fees [are] about 6 guineas, the army are now 5 months in arrears, so that I shall not have any pay for a long time. I must therefore draw a bit some time or another for 20 or 30 [torn – pounds, but?] you may depend upon my being as economical as possible but staying so long at Portsmouth & horses being so dear have completely made me a ruined man. I have not time now to write to my Uncle John or anyone else. I shall write to them all when we join the army, if we have another halting day, I will write again to you. You must give my best love to my Uncle [Richard] & Aunt [Ann] & Aunt Elizabeth & Mrs Godwin who, I hope are all well & remember me most kindly to Captain & Mrs Campbell. Tell Captain [Alexander] Campbell that his friend Mr Dornford[8] is marching up with us. I mentioned to you that a gentleman amateur was with us, he has already had a *sickening of campaigning* & has given *it up as a bad job*.[9] I must now bid you

5. Presumably he had gained leave in the second half of January.
6. 224km.
7. A guinea was worth 21 shillings or £1 1 shilling.
8. Volunteer Joseph Dornford 95th Foot.
9. Individuals who could not afford to purchase a commission could volunteer to serve with a regiment in hope of being commissioned without having to pay for it. They would mess with the officers but would serve in the ranks in combat.

goodbye as the rest of the officers are now waiting for me & have a bath in the Tagus. Adieu my dear Mary Anne & believe me ever your affectionate brother. A[lexander] Fraser

Alex's next confirmed that he had reached the regiment on the Portuguese border.

25 April 1813, Fuenteguinaldo

My dear Mary Anne,
We have at last finished our march for the present & are now comfortably settled here. This is a very good town & is occupied by our regiment alone so that we have plenty of room. I have been lucky in getting into a good company (Captain Patrick Campbell's) he is very much liked by everyone & is remarkably kind to his subalterns. One of the towns we passed through on our march was Niza [Nisa] the Commandant of which place is an officer of the 7th Fusiliers & having found out that [the] brother of James was with the detachment of the 52nd immediately called upon me, invited me to dinner & behaved with the greatest attention to me. He told me that everyone was truly concerned at the bad health that James has lately had & that General Cole offered to procure him leave to go to England for the recovery of it, but that he preferred trying this campaign. I wrote to James that night & he got the letter conveyed to him & on my arrival here I found an answer from James. He says that he is much better & writes in good spirits & I hope will be quite strong again by the time the Army is in motion. The 7th now are at St Juan de Pisquara [San Joao da Pesqueira] about 11 leagues from us. I should have liked to have gone over to see him but cannot obtain leave as operations are expected to commence immediately. I never was so much struck as with the appearance of our regiment, we are on parade every morning 900 strong. The men are hardy, sun-burnt ruddy fellows, that have been in the country & in every action for the last 5 years. Everyone allows them to be the finest set of men in the Army, no one can help being proud of commanding them. We are now commanded by Colonel Hunt[10] a most gallant officer & a friend of Colonel Colin Campbell's.[11] We expect Colonel Colbourne out soon to join us, who will then take the command.[12] Colonel Campbell had spoken to Colonel Hunt about me so that he treated me with great attention & has already

10. Brevet Lieutenant Colonel John Philip Hunt 52nd Foot.
11. Brevet Lieutenant Colonel Colin Campbell was an Assistant Quartermaster General.
12. John Colbourne was seriously wounded in the shoulder and leg during the assault on Ciudad Rodrigo on 16 January 1812. He returned to England in June 1812 and did not rejoin the regiment in Spain until late July 1813.

invited me twice to dine with him. We give balls here very often & the Spanish ladies are to have a superb one tonight. We expect to move the 2nd of May. The French have taken a position along the Douro; we shall begin by turning their flank & then march direct to Burgos, into which place they have collected their plunder & have fortified very strongly.[13] We only wait for an immense battering train, which they are bringing from Badajoz & from Lisbon. We see parties of guerillas every day, who are collecting under their chiefs Don Carlos,[14] Don Julian[15] &c &c. They are very fine men & have a most ferocious appearance, clad entirely in the uniforms of the French that they have set upon & butchered, with long cloaks thrown over their shoulders, such men properly organized might at once clear the country of their invaders, but notwithstanding their great bodily strength & martial appearance they never shall attack the French, unless 3 or 4 of them fall upon some unfortunate straggler whom they butcher without mercy. The city of Ciudad Rodrigo is about 4 leagues from us, which I intend going to see, not wishing to leave this part of the country without visiting so memorable a place. I mentioned in my letter from Abrantes, that I should be obliged to draw for a small sum soon. I have not done so as yet, but I shall soon be obliged as I must buy another animal & I shall not receive pay for these 6 months. I must therefore beg my Uncle [Richard] to tell Taylor & Lloyd to accept a bill that I shall draw upon them. Write to me soon & direct to 52nd Regiment, Light Division, Spain. Be sure & put Light Division as it is very seldom we now are with the rest of the army.

I will write again very soon. I dare say the next letter you will have from me will be from Burgos. Give my love to my Uncle [Richard] & Aunt [Ann] & Aunt Elizabeth & Mrs [Andrews?] such I hope have all have been well lately. Remember me to Captain [Alexander] Campbell him & all friends & believe me ever my dear Mary Anne, your affectionate brother Alex Fraser.

Alexander wrote another long letter on the eve of the Battle of Vitoria and relating having met his brother James on the march.

To Colonel [Richard] Unett, Royal Artillery, Woolwich, Fleet, England – redirected to Mr John Wilkes, Square, Birmingham

From our bivouack [*sic*] 3 leagues from Vitoria, 20 June 1813

13. He shows a clear understanding of Wellington's strategy for the campaign.
14. General Carlos de Espana.
15. Don Julian Sanchez Garcia, nicknamed *El Charro*, 'the Salamanca Peasant', was a guerilla commander.

My [blank – Dear Uncle]
So many events have taken place since my last letter that I hardly know where to begin my relation of them. I shall however begin by informing you that we left our comfortable cantonments at [Fuente] Guinaldo on the 20th of May & moved forward upon Salamanca. The whole army was divided into 3 separate columns and took 3 roads. The 2nd Division, 30,000 strong under General Hill moved by the right; the 1st, 3rd, 4th, 5th, 6th & 7th advanced under General Graham by the left & the Light Division under the superintendence of Lord Wellington took the centre. We advanced rapidly without seeing a Frenchman till we arrived at Salamanca! They did get out of the city [in] time enough for our cavalry & horse artillery who had a skirmish with them on a plain close to the town, 200 of them were taken prisoner & about 60 killed. The loss on our side was nothing except 2 horses killed. We halted one day at Salamanca which afforded me an opportunity of seeing so noted a place. The cathedral is beautiful, *Te Deum* was sung there that day, Lord Wellington with all the British officers were present. Ours was the only division that went by Salamanca. The reason of General Graham going so far to the left was to turn the position the enemy had taken up on the other side of the Douro & thus oblige them to retreat. Owing to an immense march of 30 miles which we accomplished in 10 hours we came upon the French before they could get clear out of Toro but could not get at them owing to the bridge across the Douro being blown up. The cavalry however forded the river & coming up charged their rear guard, took 200 prisoners. The blowing up of the bridge did not delay us, for notwithstanding our forced march the day before, we crossed the Douro at daylight the next morning, some by flying bridges[16] & some by boughs of trees & ladders placed over the ruins. Here we joined the 4th Division who had been under General Graham & here I fell in with James. Without giving us a day's rest we were pushed to Palencia, which city we entered amidst the acclamations of thousands of the inhabitants. The balconies of the city's houses were festooned with ladies who threw roses and flowers down on us. King Joseph himself & his army had just left the city an hour before us. We moved to the camps outside the town which they had just occupied, we discovered their fires yet burning & huts constructed ready for us. Palencia is a beautiful city it is surrounded on all sides with walks & cooled with rows of trees. There are a great number of nunneries in the town, the nuns here are notably civil to us & gave us sweetmeats and flowers. I should have liked much to have stayed a day to have seen something of the city, but we were off

16. Flying bridges were formed by a single guiding rope being laid across the river, by which boats of troops were hauled across.

the next morning before daylight as usual. We continued our march towards Burgos. When we came within 3 leagues of the place, the 4th Division were allowed to halt & rest for a day or two while the poor Light Division were pushed [on to engage?] the enemy who were drawn out in the plain in front of Burgos. When we came to a hill about 4 miles from the city it was our first glimpse of the place which had resisted the attacks of our engineers last year so successfully.

The castle stands very high above the town & appears an immense pile of building. The only hill it is possible to breach it from, the French had raised immense fortifications on it and connected with the castle. In the meantime, our artillery began to play upon their columns from a hill, which causing some confusion a squadron of our cavalry dashed out & killed or made prisoners 40 or 50 of them. Our division was drawn up in line expecting to be engaged every moment, but we being not above 4,000 strong, Lord Wellington let them retire behind the town having accomplished his object viz finding out their force. The whole of this day it rained incessantly without respite from 4 o'clock in the morning till 8 o'clock at night, not having tasted a thing since the night before. We retired that night to a hill a few leagues from the town where up to our knees in mud, we lay down for the night & notwithstanding the rain, fell fast asleep. About 3 o'clock that morning, we were awoke by an immense explosion, which was succeeded by two others. We could not then imagine what it could be. About an hour afterwards we began our march towards Burgos, when what was our surprize, when on arriving at the hill from whence we saw it yesterday we discovered that the castle was blown up and the French [were] off. We then changed our direction towards the sea-coast & crossed the Ebro on the 16 [June]. We knew that the enemy had a corps of observation watching our movements among the mountains. We had seen none of the rest of the army for two days. It seems however that Lord Wellington's information was better than theirs, advancing [we] made a march of 25 miles over the highest mountains on the 17th, nearly cut off their corps of observation from the rest of the army. We lay concealed in the heart of an immense range all night and started before light on the 18th, after having marched for about 3 hours, we observed some French looking at us on the tops of the heights where we kept moving parallel with them for some time. They then perceived they were cut off & having halted, waiting for us on some heights above a small village. Having formed, they sent out their skirmishers at us but they were immediately driven [off] by 3 of our companies & 2 companies of the 95th. We then received orders to advance & take the heights, we advanced in line scrambling on our hands & legs; we arrived on the top of the hill without any resistance except a few shots which passed over our heads. We gave a shout & charged forward. They immediately took to their heels for we struck and pursued them without firing a shot down the other side of the hill, till they came to a narrow pass where one *by one* in about 5 minutes about 60 of them were laid dead & about the same number desperately wounded of whom many must die, upwards of 300 laid down their arms & were immediately sent off to the rear. It was no longer an action, we had nothing to do but hunt them down. They all took to the woods & mountains pursued in all directions by our men. One of our officers, a sergeant & 7 privates took 40 of them. I likewise saw another of our fellows bring in 6 others. The general commanding the 5th Division attempted to escape on his horse but was killed by one of our men, his aide de camp has likewise died of his wounds.[17] General Montfort's[18] Secretary, his wife & all his baggage are taken. What have escaped will fall into the hands of the guerrillas who are now hunting them down. Thus has a division of observation consisting of near 5,000 been defeated by 2,000 of the Light Division, only one brigade of us being engaged. Our total loss is one officer killed and 24 privates wounded. The loss has happened chiefly among the 95th. Our regiment has only 2 men wounded. This [is] now a month since we marched from [Fuente] Guinaldo, since which time we have never been inside a house, nor have I undressed more than taking off my jacket. We have been often for days together without a bit of bread & continual rains for a week together. We expect an action tomorrow morning, the French have a position on some heights close to us & as General Hill has come up today, they must either retreat or we attack them tomorrow. I have not seen James for some time. The 4th Division were engaged yesterday on our left, but we are in ignorance as to the particulars. I am sorry to say he suffers dreadfully from the ague, indeed so does almost everyone. A number of our officers are at this moment lying wrapped up in their boat cloaks almost dead with it. This is the first day we have halted since Salamanca. We were 16 hours yesterday under arms & marching the whole time, raining incessantly. It is now the 4th day since we have tasted bread. We have our rations of meat, cut hot off a bullock which we are obliged to roast or rather to smoke over a fire & eat without either bread or vegetables & then lay down at night with hungry bellies & rise in the morning with wet skins to match. I am afraid you will not be able to read a word of this account. I have no room to say any more, the first opportunity I will send again. Render my love to everyone & believe me ever your affectionate nephew Alexander Fraser

Mary Anne begs you will take care of the letters for her, as she wishes to keep all her brother's letters.[19]

17. No French general is recorded as being killed in Spain on 18 June 1813.
18. General of Brigade Jacques de Montfort commanded a brigade in the 5th Division of the Army of Portugal.
19. This note was attached when the letter was being forwarded on to John Wilkes.

The next letter was from James, recounting his part in the campaign and also mentioning that he regularly saw Alexander.

> Under the walls of Pampaluna [Pamplona]
>
> 9 July 1813,
>
> My dear Aunt [Ann],
> I little thought when I wrote to you last at the commencement of the campaign, that the British Army ever would have arrived at this town, or indeed that we should have passed the Ebro. Long before you receive this letter, you will have learnt [of] the different events that have taken place. We first met the enemy on the 18th of June, on that day and on the 19th we had some skirmishes with them and on the 21st attacked their position before Vitoria and by the bold and masterly manoeuvring of Lord Wellington, drove them from this and [a] succession of others, in which they attempted to check us. So rapid was our advance and so determinedly kept up over nearly 6 leagues (18 miles) of ground without a halt, that whenever they brought guns to bear on us, they were taken before they could put their horses to. 158 pieces of cannon, an immensity of baggage &c fell into our hands, and it was night alone that prevented us from making half their army prisoners. Our regiment, though continually opposed to their lines, escaped with hardly any loss,[20] owing to their losing all their cannon and being determined not to let us come in contact with them. Some of our men got bags of dou[b]loons and if I had not been occupied in keeping the soldiers in their ranks in passing the plunder, I could have made my fortune. I actually more than once saw soldiers breaking open boxes which were filled with dollars. It was in fact the plunder of Spain which they were carrying off; and [they] had not the least idea of our being able to force their chain of positions and deprive them of their ill-gotten booty. As a secret, there is a strong report in the army, that if the 18th Hussars had attended as much to fighting as to plundering, we should have made 6,000 prisoners.[21] I know Lord W[ellington] is taking steps to expose their conduct; but not a word of this unless you hear of it elsewhere, which I do not doubt you will soon.
>
> Since the action, the 3rd Division and some [other] divisions have been at Saragossa [Zaragoza] driving Clausel,[22] who was trying to join [King] Joseph; he has now joined [Marshal] Suchet and report

20. At Vitoria the 7th only suffered two men killed and two wounded.
21. The Duke of Wellington severely reprimanded the 18th for allowing their men to plunder.
22. General Bertrand Clauzel.

says they are coming to raise the blockade of this town, w[h]ere we are with the 3rd & 6th Divisions, waiting the arrival of a Spanish corps, when we go to join Lord Wellington, who is in the Pyrenees with the rest of the army, expecting an attack from Joseph and all the French army. This advance is 4 leagues in[to] France.

I first met Alexander [Fraser] at Toro and since then we have been almost constantly together; he has very good health and seems to like this kind of work very much; no doubt you will have a dispatch of the Battle of Vitoria from him. Mrs Godwin's death[23] was certainly a release from pain and an event more to be wished for than otherwise. I first saw the account in the papers. As to the house, I think it had much better be disposed of. I hope my Aunt Elizabeth will soon recover her health again. I was sorry to hear of your being troubled with the rheumatism last winter, but I suppose you mean to drive it away by a trip to the seaside. I still have the ague at times but am much better than I have been before these eight months. I hope my Uncle [Richard] continues stout. Give my love to Louise, Mary Anne and believe me your affectionate nephew J[ames] B[aillie] Fraser.

Alexander wrote in August from the foot of the Pyrenees at Bera. He reported that James had been wounded but saw no reason for concern.

Camp at Beara [Bera] 5 leagues from Bayonne, 3 August 1813

My dear Mary Anne,
So seldom has it been lately that we have a moments rest that I have not been able to put pen to paper for a long time. The last letter I wrote you was dated the 20th of June, the very night before the battle of Vitoria, but I had not an opportunity of sending it for some after afterwards, or have I till this day been able to write another. I that letter (which by the bye I am afraid no one will be able to make out) I mentioned that an action was expected the next day, but I little imagined [th]at the result would have been so glorious.

It is impossible that I can pretend to give you an account of this action, I refer you to Lord Wellington's dispatch. I can only say that after being engaged from 9 in the morning till 8 at night the French were beaten at every point & obliged to retreat in the greatest confusion, abandoning upwards of 200 pieces of cannon & 2,000 waggons, 5 millions of dollars & immense plunder of every description. The road to Bayonne for 6 miles was impassable owing to carriages they were obliged to leave. We pursued them long after dark till being as well as themselves in the most knocked up state possible (having been marching from 3 in the morning) we were glad enough to lay down

23. Mary Godwin was buried at St Nicholas, Plumstead on 20 April 1813 aged 87.

for a few hours. The next morning at daylight we continued our march after them. For three days after the battle our division kept sight of them & almost continually skirmishing with them. It was terrible weather, never ceasing raining till they arrived at Pamplona. What they must have suffered it is impossible to form an idea of, having lost all their stores they were half famished. The ditches on each side of the road were filled with wounded calling out on us as we went by. Our artillery kept close on them firing into their rear. Men with their arms & limbs knocked to atoms[24] lay at every step. Had the city of Pampelona [Pamplona] been 6 days march from Vitoria instead of 3, few of them would have escaped. Leaving Pampelona [Pamplona] to be invested by Spaniards we pursued Suchet[25] towards Saragossa [Zaragoza] undergoing every hardship. Never was a British army so harassed. We suffered nothing before the battle of Vitoria. Returning from Saragossa [Zaragoza] we have traversed the Pyrenees backwards & forwards marching day & night, our poor fellows dying on the mountains with fatigue. Soult[26] arrived in the greatest hurry from the north & took the command of the French Army. Having collected all the National Guard & every man capable of bearing arms, he brought such an immense force that Lord Wellington threw back his right. The 4th & 6th Divisions were ordered to cover Pampelona [Pamplona]. So certain were the garrison of being relieved that they illuminated [the town]. Soult attacked the 4th & 6th Divisions with immense force, yet in two attacks he was repulsed with great loss. The Fusileers [*sic*] behaved in the most gallant stile [*sic*] though the French were in the proportion of 5 to one & posted behind a wall, yet the 7th rushed forwards, leaped the wall & charged them with great loss.[27] The French have lost in their different attacks & in their subsequent retreat 20,000 men, a greater loss than they sustained in either of the battles of Salamanca or Vitoria. They are now posted strongly on a ridge of mountains, their right touching the sea. They are the last mountains in the Pyrenees & the only position they can take

24. The English chemist John Dalton had published the theory that everything was composed of atoms in 1801.
25. He means General Clausel: Marshal Suchet was still on the east coast of Spain.
26. Marshal Jean Soult.
27. The 7th suffered severely at the First Battle of Sorauren on 28 July 1813, with one officer (Captain Fernie) and 43 men killed and nine officers (Majors William Despard & John Crowder, Captains John Orr, Charles Wemyss & William Hammerton, Lieutenants George Loggan, James Fraser, John Nunn & Robert Garrett) and 159 men wounded. Captain Henry Tarleton was a prisoner of war. Lieutenant George King is also stated to have been slightly wounded, but he does not appear as such in any of the records. Three wounded officers subsequently died of their wounds, including Despard and Wemyss, the other one of which was James Baillie Fraser.

up for many leagues. Do not be alarmed when you see poor James' name in the list of wounded. I was not able to learn what casualties had happened in the 7th till this day. I received a note from the Staff Surgeon of the 4th Division stating that he had been wounded near Pampelona [Pamplona] & remains near there. What makes it doubly affecting is that it is impossible for me to go to him, as we are close to the French, our advance sentries within 50 paces [page is torn – ready?] to attack their positions every moment. [page is torn – We have?] a skirmish with them every day. Yesterday our division took a hill from them. So situated, no one can leave his regiment a moment & we are upwards of 40 miles from Pampelona [Pamplona]. I have written to him & told him that the first time I can with propriety ask leave I will go to him, but as we are now he himself could not wish me to do it. I think I am by this time perfectly hardened. I can sleep out without a cloak in [the] rain just as well as in a bed, we have marched 22 hours out the 24, but thank God I have never known an hour's illness since the campaign has begun. The scenery in the Pyrenees is grand indeed, I cannot attempt to describe it or to give you an account of anything, something happens every day that would take up a letter to write about.

Had I room I would give you an account of the siege of St [San] Sebastian, the forcing of the passes of Maya & Roncesvalles, the storming of some mountains by the 7th Division &c &c. Events which have displayed the gallantry of the British troops & ought to be remembered by the people of England. I have only received one letter from you since I left England whilst this is the 4th I have written to you. I hope soon to give you a favorable [*sic*] account of James, he is in a good town & will have every medical assistance. I hope you are quite well at home, write & tell me what the people of England think of the French being across the Pyrenees. Give my love to my Uncle [Richard] & Aunt [Ann] & Aunt Elizabeth & all friends. I would write to Birmingham, but having so much outpost duty when we by chance halt a day that I am glad enough to lay down for an hour. Adieu my dear Mary Anne & believe me as ever your affectionate brother, Alexander Fraser.

The next letter is the only one we have going the other way, from Mary Anne Fraser to Alexander, consoling him on the sad news on the death of their brother James, who despite all hopes had succumbed to his wounds on 4 August 1813.[28]

28. James was seriously wounded by a musket ball that struck his abdomen and went right through his body on 27 July at the Battle of Sorauren. He died from his wounds on 4 August. Sergeant Cooper of the 7th was ordered to take care of Charles Wemyss and James Fraser who were both clearly dying and soon succumbed; they were both buried in coffins made of old furniture in the garden.

From Mary Anne [Fraser] to Ensign Alexander Fraser, 52nd Regiment, Lord Wellington's Army. Spain

Woolwich, 27 August 1813

I will not my dearest Alex distress your affectionate heart by the various emotions which your letter of the 8th of August gave rise to. Colonel [Colin] Campbell's few lines dated the 4th had communicated the fatal intelligence to his brother[29] & my Uncle [Richard] & Aunt [Ann] were immediately informed of it by General Douglas,[30] who took the painful task on himself in the absence of Captain C[ampbell]. Colonel Campbell's account (which I shall copy for you) was however erroneous, which we attribute to the confusion & haste in which he must have written, but the generous tribute which he pays to the memory of my dear James will never be forgotten by us. He says as follows '*Your young friend Fraser of the Fusiliers, poor fellow! has fallen. A more spirited nor a finer fellow never was in his regiment & all the officers regret him very much, he was shot in the belly & immediately expired. Pray be so good as [to] break the sad business to his worthy uncle & tell him that he died as he lived, respected and beloved by all who knew him.*'

Your letter (which I received a few days since) with another dated the 3rd undeceived us, by relating the affecting particulars of his death which are instead *marvellous to me* & amidst the pangs which this cruel loss has inflicted, sometimes occasions feelings which soothe, at the same time that they increase our sorrow for his loss. I cannot yet help feeling frequently as if it was merely a dream, for the idea that I have been deprived of a brother & that I have now but one in existence is altogether so new & so dreadful to me that it almost suppresses my imagination. I hardly can hope for your return, for I have so often anticipated with raptures the resuming of our once happy family & so many winter card evenings so often furnished the [torn-hopes?] before [torn-and?] of my wishes, that I confess I am sensible enough to check the pleasure as I otherwise feel in the idea of [torn-seeing you?]. You will however believe [torn-sincerely?] it is the ardent desire which [torn-both?] Uncle [Richard] & Aunt [Ann] feel that *perhaps [if] you can with honour* you will obtain leave to spend the winter months in England; for when this campaign is over & the army is in cantonments, you will have little or nothing to do and may sincerely after what you have gone through, be allowed to taste some of the comforts of a warm fireside & to embrace once more those friends whose affections will ease by the hardships and

29. Captain Alexander Campbell Royal Artillery.

30. Major General Robert Douglas Royal Artillery.

privations you so cheerfully bear. Pray write me word about you, think of this plan & whether it will be possible for you to get leave. Not many days since and [close] to the first accounts of our news, we having received the same morning, letters from James & you, his was dated 9 July and yours 20 June. I had just also written a long letter to you reprehending you for your silence on describing the Battle of Vitoria, no doubt you have received it long ere this.

You had better always mention the date of thc letters you receive from me, that I may know whether you miss any of them, I have had 5 from you which I may truly say have been the source of pleasure to us. In one of them you desire I will tell you what is thought by the villagers of our army in Spain & to the best of my ability will answer you. Many there are my dear Alex, who like ourselves are mourning over some beloved relation whom this wretched contest has torn for ever from them & it cannot be wondered at if they forget the public cause of rejoicing, in their own private way wish, but the country in general is full of triumph & exultation & Lord Wellington is I really believe thought almost a demi God, by everyone but the poor artillery officers of whom he does not appear very partial. How little did I think the last words you said to me would have come to pass so immediately or that *when the French were driven over the Pyrenees* we should have deplored the loss of a brother in the cause. My aunt begs you will endeavour to obtain possession of poor James' watch as it has been so many years in the family & if his servant has it, perhaps you might get it by giving him something instead of it. I fear much of your being able to procure for me any trifle which belonged to him. He wore a broad gold ring on one of his fingers which I would give almost anything to possess, but I cannot hope for it. At any rate if *you will* my dear Alex, so oblige me in this particular. If you can see the humane surgeon who attended James in his dying moments, will you tell him that it is the particular request of my uncle & aunt that should he ever be near Springfield he will favour them by calling on this [torn-house, as it would be a?] satisfaction to us all to hear from [torn-him the full?] melancholy account of my brother's *death*. Where is Lieutenant Lorentz?[31] I pray accounts on how he received his friend's death & what character he beheld. My Uncle [Richard] has just received a note from your excellent friend Mrs Borthwick, in which she expresses herself most particularly interested in your welfare & safe return & desires to be particularly remembered to you. I wondered my dearest Alex if the affection & regard of friends could dull a day's [torn-heartache?] for many months & I need not tell how much the severe affliction will increase my bodily infirmities; he is now better than he was &

31. Lieutenant Charles Lorentz 7th Foot.

we hope will continue so. Now adieu my dear & *only* brother & in the hope brings '*a guardian angel down*' you would then be safe, for you have many, many friends. Write to me as constantly as you can for the receipt of your letters will be the only pleasure my mind is capable of receiving for a long time. My Aunt [Ann] has never known of our soon meeting, I am with increased desire and soon, your most affectionate sister Mary Ann Fraser.

NB My Uncle [Richard] & Aunt [Ann] desire most affectionate love.

Alexander wrote again a few days later as he tried to ensure that James' debts were all cleared.

Camp near Beara [Bera], 15 September 1813

My dear Mary Anne,
I yesterday received your letter dated 27 August & as we have now nothing but picquets & working parties to take up our time, I cannot employ myself better than in proving to you that whenever an opportunity of writing to you does occur, it should not be lost upon me. For a few days before I received your affectionate letter, I had been employed in the melancholy task of settling the accounts of our lamented brother. I am happy to say that I believe every sixpence due by him to anyone in this country is now paid. One of his last wishes were that his debts might be punctually discharged. I have been able to settle them all with the arrears of pay due to him with the exception of £15 due to a Commissary who enclosed me in a letter a note of hand of my brothers for that sum. I shall therefore give him an order upon Taylor & Lloyd for it. There is at the same time near 3 month's pay yet due him in the hands of Cox & Greenwood which would have paid everything, but I could only receive the arrears due to him up to May. There is not a single officer in the Fusiliers that does not regret his loss. He was well known to General Sir Lowry Cole who has since mentioned to Colonel [Colin] Campbell how much he regretted him & what a loss the 4th Division has suffered in him. I am sorry to say that I have not been able to obtain either his watch or the ring. I made immediate enquiries respecting his watch but was assured by Lieutenant [Charles] Lorentz who messed with him & was in the same company, that he never brought it from England the last time. I can well imagine what a shock you must have felt on the fatal news being communicated to you. You have I suppose by this time received the account of another glorious event, but which like all the others has plunged many families into affliction. I mean the storming of St [San] Sebastian & the attack of Soult the same day. I can only say that St [San] Sebastian was carried in the most gallant manner after as desperate fighting as ever was known. Our regiment has to lament the

loss of the gallant Lieutenant Harvest who was killed in the breach,[32] he being the senior subaltern was allowed to volunteer his services to storm. The same day Soult attacked the place where our division was with the intent of relieving the town. The whole of the French army crossed the river within 500 yards of our division who were posted on a hill. They then filed off on the road to St [San] Sebastian but were met by the 7th Division & the Spaniards & beat back with immense loss & after marching all night got back to their old position again.[33] It is vain for Soult ever to think of succeeding as we have now the 1st & 5th Divisions that were employed at St [San] Sebastian in the position. The wish of the whole army is to advance, it has never been more healthy or in better spirits. We are encamped on the face of a mountain, the French position on the other side of the valley. Our piquets are very fatiguing, once in 3 days & we have to stand to our arms an hour before daylight every morning. The scenery is wonderful. I very often climb to the top of the mountain on which we lay, from which I can see the sea & 50 miles into France, If I turn my eyes to the rear, nothing but immense mountains piled one upon another. In fact, it is impossible for me to attempt to describe it, I can only say that for the first time in my life I am most melancholy & perfectly tired of remaining so long stationary. As to my returning to England this winter it is impossible, indeed it is the opinion of everyone that we shall not go into winter quarters this campaign; at any rate it is difficult to obtain leave & was I once to go home I shall not be allowed to come out again till effective as a lieutenant in the 1st Battalion which will not be for 2 years yet.[34] In short I will on no account leave the country till the army itself does. Thank God I keep my health very well notwithstanding [torn – the?] incessant rains which have fallen for the last [torn – month?] I have not received any pay since I left England which with several extra expenses I have unavoidably been put to, has obliged me to draw two bills, one for £40 on Taylor & Lloyd, the other for £25 on Greenwood & Cox but you must remember that the pay due me is £40. Give my love to my Uncle [Richard] & Aunts [Ann & Elizabeth] & all my friends. This will be a dull, uninteresting letter to you. Were I to write as my spirits would prompt me it would be in a most melancholy stream, but we must bear with fortitude what we are all liable to. Adieu my dear Mary Anne & believe that though one brother is early cut off from you, that you have yet one left who will do everything to make you happy. I remain your affectionate brother, Alexander Fraser.

32. Lieutenant Augustus Harvest 52nd Foot was killed in the assault on 31 August 1813.
33. This refers to the Battle of San Marcial.
34. Fraser was the second senior Ensign in the regiment. Upon promotion he would be assigned to the 2nd Battalion which was stationed in England.

Four weeks later, a short note from Alexander simply informed them that he had been wounded in the action on 7 October to capture the heights above Bera but was now fine. Given what had happened to James, this news must have struck fear into the hearts of his family at home.

> Beara [Bera], 11 October 1813
>
> My dear Mary Anne,
> The Dispatch by Lord Wellington will inform you that the Light Division attacked & carried by storm the French position above the town of Beara [Bera] on the 8th of October. You will see my name in the list of wounded but to ease you of inquietude, I make this effort to write a few lines to let you know that there is no occasion to be alarmed. The ball passed through my thigh close under the groin, it has merely grazed the bone & has been cut out on the other side. I am now in this town but expect to be removed to Passages [Pasaia]. Adieu my dear Mary Anne. I will soon write you a more explicit letter. Give my love to my Uncle [Richard] & Aunt [Ann] & all friends & believe ever your affectionate brother A[lexander] Fraser.

The following letter written by Ann Unett to John Wilkes Unett was enclosed with the above letter.

> Dear Brother [John], you have no doubt been very much alarmed at seeing Alex's name among the severely wounded. We fortunately received his letter before the Gazette came out. I fancy Colonel [Colin] Campbell enclosed it with the dispatches. Colonel Campbell has also very kindly written very particularly about him to his brother,[35] he had seen the Surgeon who attended him & he said that the ball had not injured the bone nor any of the arteries & that there was no fear but he will do well. Colonel Campbell says he is a fine fellow & his colonel speaks very highly of him. Poor fellow he must have suffered a great deal in the operation of extracting the ball. I hope you will persuade Miss Quinnel to accompany you when you come to Town, it will be so good an opportunity & we shall be very happy to see her. I hope she did not think me uncivil in not writing the invitation to her myself; Mary Anne wished particularly to write to Mrs [Elizabeth] Unett & I was extremely unwell at the time, I am rather better now, though I still suffer a great deal of pain & walk quite lame.
>
> We received two very nice hares from you last night for which many thanks. I hope you will be able to come at the time you have

35. Captain Alexander Campbell Royal Artillery.

fixed, as I believe some of the legatees are upon the look out. Mr Thompson[36] has got some good appointment & is gone to Spain, he has given his mother a power of attorney to attend [to] all his affairs & she has impowered [*sic*] General Rimmington[37] to receive their legacies & settle with Mrs Godwin's Executors, Mrs Rimmington wrote about a fortnight since to inform your brother [George] of it. I wish you would send a copy of Alex's letter by post to George & Fanny as they will certainly be anxious to known how he is. Love to Mrs [Elizabeth] Unett &c &c believe me your affectionately A[nn] Unett.

John Wilkes Unett wrote to Captain George Unett Royal Artillery, Weedon Barracks, Northamptonshire, informing him.

21 October 1813, Birmingham

Dear George,
You would be equally alarmed with myself at seeing poor Alex's name among the list of severely wounded, but I have the pleasure to be able to dissipate your fears and to inform you that he is doing very well. Mary Anne received a letter from him before the Gazette appeared, and which I received from her yesterday, with a request that I would forward a copy of it to you and Fanny. I therefore send you a copy on the other side. Poor fellow, he has had a narrow escape. Colonel Campbell in a letter to his brother said that he had seen the Surgeon who attended him, and he assured him that the ball had not injured the bone nor any of the arteries, and that there was no fear but he would do well. Colonel Campbell says '*he is a fine fellow and his Colonel speaks very highly of him.*'

As I have some other business in London besides Mrs Godwin's I have postponed my journey until the second week in November. If you will ride my mare a hunting occasionally and you can conveniently take care of her, I think I shall ride her to Weedon and leave her with you until my return. I shall of course, expect to pay for her keep & grooming.

Colonel Cook,[38] Holden[39] & a party of gentlemen dine with me today. I have received my books safe. Mr Ward has met with a serious accident by falling through an unfinished floor. He has had his thigh

36. Thomas Thomson was now Deputy Inspector of Hospitals to the 7th Division.
37. Major General Samuel Rimmington (Kane 477); he died at Woolwich in 1826.
38. Most likely Lieutenant Colonel John Wilbar Cook retired.
39. Quite possibly Lieutenant John Holden 7th Foot, who was severely wounded at Albuera and retired on 9 April 1812.

> cut open since and it is supposed he will do well but will have a long confinement. Yours sincerely J[ohn] W[ilkes] Unett

The very same day their cousin Thomas Thomson wrote to Mary Anne with an update; it was not to be good news.

> From Staff Surgeon Thomas Thomson to Miss [Mary Anne] Fraser, John Ward's Esquire, Stafford.
>
> Echalar [Etxalar] 21 October 1813
>
> My dear Cousin,
> When I reflect that this will probably bring to you the first intelligence of the melancholy event it has become my duty to communicate, I feel quite at a loss in what terms to address you; if anything could add to the sorrow I feel for the loss of so fine a youth as your lamented brother, it is that I had not the opportunity afforded me of soothing his last moments & conveying to you his last wishes. How near I was having this melancholy satisfaction, you will learn when the first effects of so great a misfortune have subsided & reason & recognition to the will of providence shall have enabled you to peruse the following particulars. I had the pleasure of observing how much interest his fate excited in all who knew him & it will afford you some consolation to learn that his sufferings were not aggravated by the want of those comforts which have caused the loss of so many fine fellows, but that calmly resigned he expired in the arms of his most intimate friend Lieutenant Royds[40] of the same regiment who during his illness had attended him with the affection & care of a brother & whose attention merited the thanks of all his family. His friend Colonel [Colin] Campbell was in the same town & the first professional assistance was also afforded him, Dr McGregor [McGrigor] the Inspector General,[41] Staff Surgeon Hume[42] & Malling [Maling] had attended him with the most friendly care & when human aid was useless they kindly accompanied me to convince me that everything that art could do had been done. I arrived at Beara [Bera] the headquarters of the army the day before yesterday & dining at Dr McGregor [McGrigor's] the conversation naturally turned to the state of several wounded officers then in the town, but most unfortunately the name of poor Alexander was never

40. Lieutenant William Royds 52nd Foot.
41. Inspector of Hospitals James McGrigor was Principal Medical Officer in Wellington's Army from 1812.
42. Staff Surgeon John Robert Hume was assigned to the Army HQ.

mentioned, though his case and the operation it had that day been necessary to perform [on him] were spoken of. As I had not heard of his being wounded & knew that his regiment was at a distance, it was not till the next morning that I knew I had passed the night in the same village with the only relation I had in this country, which was doomed be the last [night]. I was no sooner acquainted with the loss we had sustained than I went to his lodgings accompanied by the gentlemen above mentioned to pay the tribute of a tear to the gallant boy & now my affliction was still to be increased by finding my duty would not allow me to remain at Beara [Bera] to attend his rending to the grave. The expectation of the right wing of the Army being ingaged [*sic*] the next day rendered it necessary I should join without loss of time. I was therefore obliged to leave Beara [Bera], but not till I had seen Colonel Campbell & communicated the fatal news to him

I also saw Lieutenant Royds to whom I gave my address & begged he would write to me, I was in hopes of finding some paper which might have contained his last wishes as he was aware of his danger for some days, or effects which you might wish to possess. The only papers were a letter from yourself with the statement of poor James' accounts there & a prayer book. The gentlemen with me thought I should take the letter, being the only thing among his effects I thought necessary to preserve & they shall be sent you by the first opportunity which offers, his servant who seemed a man of good character, told me his watch was left with the Adjutant of the regiment who wore it, he had a horse & mule. The former [his horse] the servant said had been stolen, the latter [hid mule] shot on account of an accident that had rendered it useless; It appears to me possible that any memorandum he may have left are in possession of some of his brother officers, to ascertain which I should write to the officer commanding, whose answer I will forward to you with the watch if it can be recovered, if possible I will visit Beara [Bera] & see Colonel Campbell & Lieutenant Royds again, but such is our state that we know not one hour where we are to be the next. I am obliged to close this to secure the post as now my dear cousin, having performed the painful duty assigned me, it only remains for me to assure you how sincerely I sympathize in your grief & in that of all his relations. Could you see the situation in which I write this you would excuse the imperfect manner in which I have expressed my feelings on this mournful event, need I say I shall be happy in executing any wishes you may have connected with it. Your Uncle [Richard] & Aunt [Ann] will feel severely on this occasion; remember me to them & particularly to your Uncle George. Adieu and believe to be your affectionate cousin Thomas Thomson.

The following letter was subsequently copied to Fanny by her sister Elizabeth.

To Colonel [Richard] Unett from Staff Surgeon Thomas Thomson[43]

Echalar [Etxalar], 21 October 1813

My dear Sir,
When I wrote the enclosed [to Mary Anne] I did not think time would have allowed me to address you, I am happy it has been afforded me by the detention of the orderly, as you will feel anxious to know more particularly the cause of poor Alex's death than I could with propriety state in a letter to his sister. I conclude you know the circumstance of his being wounded. The ball entered the thigh a little below the groin & was cut out behind, without wounding any of the great arteries so that for some days every hope was entertained of his doing well; about the 12th it was found that some small branch of an artery deeply seated had been wounded from repeated hemorrage [*sic*] taking place, by which he was much exhausted & on the 19th had increased to such a degree as to render it necessary at all risks to cut down upon & secure it. This is the operation alluded to in my letter to his sister & was performed the day of my arrival at Beara [Bera]. On viewing the limb on the 20th I saw that the vessel had been properly secured, for no further bleeding had taken place, but the previous exhaustion had been too great, much greater I apprehend than his medical attendants had an idea of, for they thought if the vessel could be secured he had every chance of recovering. The ball with which he was wounded was a rifle [ball][44] & was given me by his servant. In its passage it had wounded a small branch of the artery called (Profunda Femoris[45]). I feel the above is but an imperfect account, but it is all time permits me to say in addition to the particulars contained in the inclosed which I am glad to enclose to you as you can use your discretion in delivering it, for which account I leave it open. Adieu my dear Sir, believe me to remain with due regard your obedient servant Thomas Thomson

A new letter begins here to Fanny on the same sheet of paper, written by Ann Unett.

Dear Fanny,
Elizabeth has been so good as to copy Mr Thomson's letters as I wished very much for Mr Ward to see them. It is a great aggravation of our sorrow to think that our dear boy's life has been lost from the

43. Although he refrains from using the title, Thomas Thomson was made a Deputy Inspector of Hospitals in January 1813.
44. It is more likely to have been a musket ball; the French did not use rifles.
45. Also known as the deep femoral artery.

want of skill or attention of the medical people about him & I cannot be persuaded but that if the operation had been performed as soon as they discovered that the artery was injured & before he had lost so much blood he might have been saved.

I was very much obliged to you for the receipt for the saline draughts, but before I received it Mr Paton had ordered me some. I told him Mr Ward's opinion & he said the draughts he gave me were for the same purpose & in fact they succeeded in removing in a great measure the fever & my appetite is much better, but I still suffer very much from weakness & pains in my limbs & from some other unpleasant complaints, which I cannot very well commit to paper. I have been so very unwell lately again that I have at last been persuaded to send for a physician whom I expect today or tomorrow, but I very much fear no one can do me any good, my constitution seems so completely altered & weakened. [Richard] Wilkes is tolerably well & poor Mary Anne is recovering a little from the dreadful shock of her brother's death. It was so unexpected a blow, we were rejoicing so much at the thought of his coming home; he was the most amiable creature that ever lived & never gave us a moments uneasiness in his life, his death has occasioned a blank which nothing can ever fill up. With best compliments to Mr & Mrs Ward & love to Maria believe me yours affectionately A[nn] Unett. (Tom[46] has promised to get this franked)

Extract of Lieutenant Colonel [Colin] Campbell's Letter dated Vera [Bera] 25 October 1813

I believe I wrote to you that Fraser of the 52nd was wounded. I went to see him a few days after & he appeared to me to be doing uncommonly well & was poor fellow in high spirits & expected to be able to go about in a few days. On leaving him I called on Mr. Maling[47] the Staff Surgeon who attended him, who informed me that the wound did not appear to be a bad one, but he fears that it had touched the artery in his thigh & if that should be the case that he feared that nothing could save him. It turned out so, as the evening after I saw him, a hemorage [*sic*] took place. The surgeons there determined to perform an operation on him to endeavour to save him, by getting at the artery & tying it up, but he had lost so much blood before the operation was performed & during the operation, that he died a few hours after it took place. Thus have both the brothers lost their lives in the service of their country & two finer lads I never knew. Alex was an uncommon fine lad, it will distress their worthy Uncle [Richard]

46. Presumably Thomas Unett was visiting.
47. Staff Surgeon John Maling was assigned to the Light Division.

& Aunt [Ann] much. I feel most keenly for Miss [Mary Anne] Fraser who has thus been deprived of her two brothers. C[olin] Campbell

From William Royds to Miss [Mary Anne] Fraser, Spring Field, Woolwich

Chatham, 11 September 1814

Madam,
I feel beyond expression honoured by the attention of the sister & relations of my much-lamented friend but believe me your great kindness induces you to overrate my poor efforts to alleviate his sufferings. It was a melancholy satisfaction to me to be with your brother during his Illness which I could not deny myself & I conceive it would have been impossible for any person acquainted with his amiable qualities to have felt otherwise. Your very handsome present shall be held sacred to his memory[48] & your kind attention will ever be gratefully remembered by your highly honoured & obedient humble servant William Royds.

In the space of only ten weeks, a family which had until now been spared the pain of the loss of a loved one in these interminable wars, suddenly lost two young men. It undoubtedly ripped the heart out of the family and it may not be at all unconnected that their Aunt Ann was dead within six months aged 50 and was buried at St Nicholas, Plumstead, on 23 May 1814. Uncle Richard died at Woolwich 18 months later on 21 October 1815 aged 49 and was buried alongside Ann on 28 October 1815. Their sister Mary Anne Fraser died in December 1816 and was buried in the family vault at St Nicholas, Plumstead, on 24 December 1816 aged 22; it is possible she died of a broken heart.

48. Perhaps his watch or sword?

THE WATERLOO CAMPAIGN 1815

George Unett, now a Brevet Major in the Royal Artillery,[1] commanded a company (7 Company 3rd Battalion Royal Artillery) during the campaign in Belgium and France; with Thomas Browne as his Second Captain (Kane 1093) and Douglas Lawson (Kane 1399) and Willoughby Montagu (Kane 1450) his 1st Lieutenants. His company embarked at Tilbury Fort on 4 April and landed at Ostend on 6 April where they remained until late May. On 1 June the company was at Destelbergen, now a suburb of Ghent. His brigade of guns was formally attached to the 6th Division on 21 May,[2] commanded by Major General John Lambert, whose infantry served at Waterloo. George had been hoping to be allocated 9-pounders[3] but it would appear that they had been armed with 6-pounders. Being at Ghent the brigade could have reached the battlefield on the 18th, but it seems that they were either delayed in getting there or retained in reserve. His unit did go to Cambrai and was put into position to fire on the fortress and helped persuade the French garrison to surrender.[4] Unfortunately, no correspondence has been found from George or any of his officers during this campaign. George and his entire company all received the Waterloo Medal

Journal of John Wilkes Unett in France in 1815

It is clear that John Wilkes Unett travelled to France in early August 1815, both to see his brother George, but also to see Paris.

> Saturday 5 August 1815
> Here we are (at 7 o'clock in the evening) at Calais, eating a deficit of greengages and peaches (after a good dinner) and drinking Barsac & champagne. I can hardly believe myself in France. We set sail from Dover at 3 o'clock with a fair wind and landed at Calais at 6. A motley group of Frenchmen & boys were waiting by the waterside to carry us on shore and some of them ran up to their middle in the water. The passage cost 10 shillings 6 pence;[5] about 4s[hillings] more to be rowed with our luggage to shore and a shilling for being

1. He was promoted Brevet Major on 4 June 1814.
2. Reference General Order dated 21 May 1815. Reference the editor's *Waterloo Archive Volume XII* p. 103.
3. Captain Cortenay Ilbert wrote on 19 April 1815, that 'Another brigade of nine pounders is arrived, but it seems that they are intended for the King's German Legion, much to the annoyance and disappointment of Unett who expected to get them'. Reference the editor's *Waterloo Archive Volume III*, p. 152.
4. Lieutenant General Sir Charles Colville wrote to Wellington from Govy on 25 June to announce the surrender of Cambrai. He mentions 'The three brigades of artillery of Lieutenant Colonel Webber Smith and Majors Unett and Brome, under the direction of Lieutenant Colonel Hawker, made particularly good practise and immediately silenced the fire of the enemy's artillery . . .'. Reference *The Duke of Wellington's Dispatches 1799-1815, Volume* XII by Gurwood, p. 504.
5. About £40 today.

carried on[to] dry ground. We immediately proceeded to the inn called the *Silver Lion*, kept by an Englishman and ordered a good dinner.[6] [William] Holden and many passengers were sick on board, but I luckily escaped that unpleasant feeling & operation.

Sunday [6 August]
Awoke with a headache, hot and feverish (NB not to drink so much French wine again; all owing to drinking the health's of our friends in England). There has already been a good deal of travelling between this place and Paris and I understand that the road is perfectly open and safe. After breakfast walked through the streets of the town, which is a strong fortified place and went into the church during service. All the shops are open though it is Sunday. The landlord informed us that Mrs Webber Smith (whose husband I knew to be an officer of artillery)[7] was waiting in the house and wished to be conducted to Paris. I instantly sent to say that we were going there and should be happy to escort her to her husband. This produced an interview, which ended in our setting off together in her barouche. She travels with her man servant and a little child about 3 months old. She is very anxious to see her husband [Lieutenant] Colonel Webber Smith of the horse artillery; he was in the Battle of Waterloo. We could not conveniently set off from Calais until near 12 o'clock and have not been able to proceed farther than this place (Boulogne [-sur-Mer]) about 22 miles as there are no post houses to proceed. The house and harness at all the stages are the most miserable and ludicrous that can be conceived to an Englishman. From Calais to Boulogne we had only one driver to the 4 hours and he sat upon the near wheel horse and had reins to the leaders. He flogged them on, handled his whip and drove us with great care & dexterity. We arrived at this place (Boulogne [-sur-Mer]) about 5 o'clock and after dinner we went to look at the pier, the basin, the ramparts & fortifications &c and saw the place where all the flat-bottomed boats were moored, ready for an order to invade Old England. They are all decayed and are now seized for other purposes. This town is divided in politics, the lower class are in favour of Buonaparte and the middle & upper orders are all for the Bourbons. There was a play performed tonight called '*The Return of the King to Paris*'. The firing at the Battle of Waterloo was distinctly heard here at the time. The distance is not less than 80 miles. Sunday in France is the day for every amusement. We went this evening to a dance of

6. The Lion d'Argent is mentioned in 1814 as standing on the Rue Neuve in Calais and that it had an English owner.
7. Lieutenant Colonel James Webber Smith Royal Horse Artillery (Kane 877) commanded a troop at Waterloo and Cambrai. He was married to Eleanora Simeon, daughter of Sir John Simeon, in December 1807.

the middling class and I was highly delighted to see 50 or 60 couples waltzing round the room; some of them danced very gracefully; all cheerfulness and gaiety, pleasure in all their countenances and not a single person disgraced by liquor; 10 o'clock going to bed as we are to start tomorrow morning at 5.

Monday [7 August]
Started this morning at 5 o'clock and after travelling through Samer, Cormont, Montreuil (which is a strong fortified town) Nampion [Nampont], Nouvion, Abbeville and Arran [Airaines], we arrived at a miserable village called Paix at 9 o'clock in the evening. Mrs Smith's child being ill with the hooping cough & travelling, we would proceed no further. We supped in a room with 3 beds in it and our accommodations were uncomfortable in the extreme. With all our exertions and without stopping to dinner we have travelled only 70 miles today. The roads during this day's journey were better than any in England. The country is well cultivated, but there are no inclosures [*sic*]. Straight roads, hill and dale and (at present) very uninteresting. On a calculation we are travelling with horses at less than 2 s[hillings] a mile, including every expense except eating and drinking. Mrs Smith pays half.

Tuesday [8 August]
Started about 8 and breakfasted at Grandvillers [Grandvilliers] when Colonel Smith met his wife. Holden and myself entered Colonel Smith's cabriolet and passing through Bauvais [Beauvais] (where we went to see the cathedral), we arrived at 10 o'clock at night at Beaumont [-sur-Oise]. A robbery on this road is seldom if ever heard of, and it is safer to travel here than in England. A military police (called the Gens d'Armes) are constantly on the road. On arriving at Beaumont two British officers informed us they had just heard that the French National Guard had risen upon the Prussians, killed many and taken 7 pieces of cannon and that Paris (from which we were distant only 20 miles) was in great commotion. I did not believe it.[8]

Wednesday [9 August]
On rising I inquired [*sic*] from several people whether there was any disturbance at Paris, and the answer was that everything was perfectly tranquil. After travelling through Mouille & St Denis, we arrived at Paris about 1 o'clock, just in time to see much of the Russian army, which passed in Review today. The horses which drew the artillery (the cavalry and infantry having passed before our arrival) are the most beautiful Arabians I ever saw. The horses to every gun match; 6 greys,

8. It was false.

6 whites, 6 blacks, 6 cream colour &c. It was the most animating sight that ever was seen. The street was crowded with foot people, horsemen and carriages, and the windows & balconies of the houses (which are very high) were filled with females from top to bottom. After dressing at Colonel Smith's lodgings we walked in the Italian boulevards and met several officers whom I knew. We afterwards went to the Tuileries to see the king get in his carriage and the guard observing we were English, made way for us and I saw the good king with a most cheerful countenance and in high health and spirits come hobbling along and get into his carriage. I was within 3 or 4 yards of him. I soon found George who is very well. In Lord Wellington's dispatch respecting the capture of Cambray [Cambrai], the artillery commanded by Major *Knott*, is complimented. This Major *Knott* was Major *Unett*, it was a mistake of the printers. We dined (H[olden], George and myself) at Very's, a celebrated restauranteur in the Palais Royal. The room was filled with British, Russian, Prussian & Austrian officers. Two Russian officers who met (perhaps for the first time after leaving Russia) shook hands and kissed each other. The gardens are filled with thousands of well-dressed men & women drinking coffee, lemonade &c, and the different costumes of the officers give a novel and pleasing effect to the scene. Two months ago, the people were all desponding and apprehensive; now Paris is gay beyond conception, emperors, kings, princes &c, in short all the world is here; and though I have not been in Paris 10 hours (and have seen nothing to what I shall see). I am amply repaid for my journey.

Paris, Thursday 10 August 1815

My dear Bessy,[9]
I had written this far without considering that I am putting down rather more than a concise journal. We have taken lodgings for a fortnight in the courtyard of Galignam's Library and rooms,[10] where several officers, English newspapers and all the French journals are taken in. You will probably not receive this letter in less than a week, so if you or the boys write to me (and I shall be truly glad to hear from you if there is time) you must write immediately, directing for me at Major [George] Unett's, Royal Artillery, 6th Division of the British Army near Paris, taking care to pay the Inland postage. I have heard many interesting anecdotes respecting the late battle. Poor Major Lloyd[11] who was quartered at Stafford with [John] Fraser, had all his men either killed or wounded; still he refused to quit his guns,

9. His wife Elizabeth.
10. Galignam's Library was on the Rue de Rivoli in Paris.
11. They were in Stafford together in 1801.

he stood near them alone and a Frenchman came withing a few yards of him, took a deliberate aim and shot him. He died about 3 days since. This is devotion to the service! When you have read this letter, send it or a copy of it to my sister Fanny, it may amuse her. With love to the dear children and all at Southwick. I remain my dear Bessy, your affectionate husband J[ohn] W[ilkes] Unett.

Journal continued . . .

Thursday 10 [August]
Breakfasted at the English Hostel in the Palais Royal and afterwards went to see the Louvre, which contains an immense & most valuable collection of pictures and statues. One picture, supposed to be the best in the gallery (the descent from the cross by Rubens[12]) is valued at £25,000.[13] The statues are the finest in the world. The 3 most celebrated are the Venus de Medici,[14] the Apollo [Belvedere],[15] and the Laocoon.[16] The former has been broken in 13 or 14 places, quite through and pieced again. I afterwards walked in the garden of the Tuileries and went to dine at George's mess. He is quartered in Neuilly Park about three miles from Paris. The soldiers in his division (the 6th) are encamped all over the park, just as they were at Hill Common near Sutton. The house and grounds lately belonged to the Princess Borghese[17] and the latter appear to have been laid out with great taste. The soldiers have sent several of the trees & shrubs for fuel and have made their huts with the branches of others and in a short time the plan will be completely spoiled and will not have an original feature left. In the evening we went to Tivoli, which are gardens brilliantly illuminated like Vauxhall. The fireworks were very beautiful and whilst they were playing, two of the performers (a man and woman) walked up two ropes near together, in the midst of the fire and smoke to a platform on the top of a high tree. In descending, the woman tumbled down and caught by her hands. There was instantly a dreadful outcry by the spectators. She held by her hands as long as she could and then dropped; and I understand she was not much hurt. In tumbling, her pole struck the other rope, which vibrated and threw the man off, but he caught by his hands and feet and came down like a monkey.

12. It was returned to its original home at the Cathedral of Our Lady, Antwerp.
13. Around £1.3 million today.
14. Taken from Florence.
15. Taken from the Vatican.
16. Taken from the Vatican.
17. Pauline Bonaparte.

Friday [11 August]
The woman who tumbled off the rope appears to have been in the family way. She has been prematurely delivered this morning and her life is considered in danger. The report of the day is, that Marshal Ney that arch traitor, has been taken as well as Jerome Buonaparte.[18] The general opinion is that the king has not firmness enough to punish them. In my journal yesterday, I forgot to say that in walking through the picture gallery at the Louvre, I observed 10 or 12 large frames without pictures, the pictures it is said, have been removed by order of [Marshal] Blucher, being those which were taken from Berlin. This is as it should be. As I was leaving the Louvre, I observed some people taking away about 20 more. We this day dined with Sir Hew Ross[19] and his officers at their mess. They are quartered at a village on the banks of the Seine, a most beautiful spot, about half a mile from Neuilly. We drank light wine and champagne at dinner and claret afterwards. I begin to like the French wines so much that I am afraid I shall never relish English beer or port wine again.

Saturday 12 [August]
Went to see the palace of the Luxembourg where the conservative senate, similar to our House of Lords, hold their meetings. This room where these meetings are held & also the Council Chambers are beautifully fitted up. The pictures in one gallery by Rubens, representing the exploits of Henry the 4th are inimitably good. There is a large basin or sheet of water in the gardens, in which 50 or 60 Prussians (men & women) were washing their linen, and a little farther on there are wooden huts erected for their accommodation. This seems as if Paris would not soon be relinquished by the allies. I afterwards went again to the gallery of the Louvre, where I met [Dr] Tom Thompson whom I have not seen for 10 or 12 years. He is in good health and spirits and not much altered.

Sunday [13 August]
Took a cabriolet as far as Neuilly, where George lent us horses and Mr Montagu,[20] one of his subalterns, who speaks French like a native, rode with us to St Cloud, one of the palaces of the kings of France and the favourite residence of Buonaparte. The palace commands a view of Paris at the distance of 5 or 6 miles. The State Rooms and Bed Chambers are magnificent beyond conception. The beautiful paintings in every room, the profusion of gilding on

18. Jérôme Bonaparte was not captured, and went to live in Italy.
19. Lieutenant Colonel Sir Hew Dalrymple Ross commanded a troop of horse artillery at Waterloo.
20. 1st Lieutenant Willoughby Montagu Royal Artillery.

the ceilings, the walls, the pannels [*sic*] of the doors and windows and the tables and chairs and the taste displayed in hanging the drapery are inconceivably beautiful. We saw Buonaparte's bed and also Marie Louise's; adjoining the latter is her bath surrounded by mirrors and in another room near is a sumptuous bed upon which she reclined or dozed after bathing. From St Cloud we went to Versailles, another royal palace about 4 miles farther. It is a most immense pile of buildings. The gardens are extensive but laid out in the old formal way like Hampton Court gardens, with straight lines of trees, walks & fountains. Buonaparte never resided here. Being confined to time we did not view the inside of the house. There are no pictures and only a few rooms are furnished. I had the pleasure of seeing Colonel Tidy of the 14th[21] this morning; he is [in] good health & spirits and led his men on, after the Battle of Waterloo, in which they behaved very well, to the storming of Cambray [Cambrai]. He said he got through the ditch & scrambled up the breach as well as he could, when on looking up he saw some women who held out their hands to him and pulled him up. The town was surrendering or capitulating at the time, so the conflict was soon at an end to his great joy and surprise. We returned back to dinner at 6 o'clock and dined at the mess.

Monday [14 August]
Went to see the Catacombs but were not able to gain admittance in consequence of a recent regulation, that they were not to be shown to less than 8 people at a time; so being near the Observatory we ascended it and had a very commanding view of Paris.

Tuesday [15 August]
Went with Mr Montagu to see the Jardin des Plantes and was highly gratified. There is a Managerie [*sic*] of wild beasts; several of them have separate inclosures of half an acre or an acre to range about in, such as the elephant, the camel, the bear, the stags &c; but the live animals were nothing to be compared to the dead ones, which are preserved in glass cases in 4 large apartments. The collection is immense and consists of beasts, birds, fishes and insects; besides which there is a vast collection of minerals, petrifactions, earths & stones, the whole classed & arranged in the most admirable order. This being a holiday (a Saint's day[22]), the garden & the apartments were thronged with people. Everything is open to the public (except the theatres) free of expense.

21. Lieutenant Colonel Francis Skelly Tidy commanded the 14th Foot.
22. The Assumption of the Blessed Virgin Mary.

To Mrs [Elizabeth] Unett, Square, Birmingham, England

10 August [1815]

My dear Bessy
I dare say you are anxious to hear from me again. Everything here is new to me and I only wish you were with me for a fortnight; you would be highly gratified. I again dined yesterday with George at the mess and we are going this morning to see the Mint & the Cabinet of Medals. I propose setting off from this place on the 23rd instant with a Mr Richardson. Mr Holden proposes staying for some weeks longer. I shall hope to be at Dover on the 26th, from whence I intend going to Broadstairs to Mary Anne Fraser who is waiting for my return. I shall hope to arrive at Birmingham by the last day of the month, but should anything prevent my arriving quite so early, don't let John & Tom[23] set off to Rugby on the 2 September; if they have been good boys (which I have no doubt they have been) they may wait until I return. I shall endeavour to persuade Mary Anne [Fraser] to accompany me into Warwickshire. Everything is tranquil here & were it not for the presence of so many British and Foreign officers in the streets, you would not suppose that anything had happened. The inhabitants like the English best, the Austrians next, then the Russians and the Prussians least of all. The whole army, but particularly the Prussians are much vexed, that they had not the plundering of Paris. Dreadful would have been the scene if it had been permitted. Lord Wellington prevented it. From what I am able to see of the French people, I am convinced that unless Louis [XVIII] keeps a large army of the allies in France for several years, he cannot reign. With love to all J[ohn] W[ilkes] U[nett].
16 August
Desire Mr Walford to call upon Mr Steer (Mr Holden's partner) and tell him that Mr Holden expects to be in England on Monday next, when he will write to him. With love to the dear children and all at Smethwick. I remain my dear Bessy, your most affectionately J[ohn] W[ilkes] Unett.

Journal continued . . .

Thursday 16 August
Went to the Monnaie de Medailles at the back of the Mint and saw a fine collection of medals, chiefly struck in the time of Buonaparte to commemorate his victories and other remarkable events. They are admirably executed. I bought 8 or 10. I afterwards went to dine at the

23. John and Thomas were their two eldest surviving children.

mess at Neuilly where I met Colonel Tidy and several other officers. It is said there will be a Review of the British infantry by Lord Wellington, but I cannot learn when it will take place and am afraid it will not be until after my departure. In going to Neuilly I met Mr Edwin Pemberton[24] & Mr Crocket[25] in Rue Vivienne; they were just arrived.

Friday [17 August]
Having slept at Neuilly last night, I alighted this morning from my cabriolet opposite the residence of the Emperor of Russia, determining to see him if possible. I contrived to make one of his French footmen understand that I merely wanted to gratify my curiosity by seeing the Emperor. He was a very civil good-humoured fellow and placed me where I saw the Emperor go to and return from Mass. I also saw old Platoff, the Commander of the Cossacks,[26] the Emperor's two brothers, the Grand Marshal & many other generals; they were all dressed in full uniform. A company of Russian soldiers were drawn up in the courtyard. In returning home through the Place Vendome I met Mr Edmund Peel[27] & Mr Arthur Hinchley, who arrived at Paris on Sunday last. Holden & myself afterwards went with the former to a place called La Morgue, which is a receptacle for all the dead bodies which are found in the streets during the night. I had heard of this place in England but could scarce credit it. When we arrived there we were shocked to see the bodies of three men quite naked. We could not learn whether they had been murdered or killed by accident. One of them had been just taken out of the Seine; he appeared to be above 30 and had the countenance of an Englishman, he was beat about the head very much. The bodies lie 3 days to be owned [claimed] by their friends, and no inquest is held or any inquiry made by the police of the circumstances of their death. What a train of reflections did this shocking spectacle create in my mind. Oh happy England! Thy criminal laws are the protection of thy inhabitants and the admiration of the whole world. How seldom does it happen in England that murders are committed and how rarely do the murderers escape. In France (at least in Paris) anyone may gratify his malice, his hatred or revenge by killing his victim with impunity. Mr Crocket, Mr E[dwin] Pemberton, Holden and myself after dining at Very's,[28] walked in the gardens of the Thuilleries [Tuileries] and then strolled as far as the Duke of Wellington's residence in the

24. Mr Edwin Pemberton (1785–1851) was from a Quaker family living in Birmingham.
25. This appears to be a Mr James Crocket, a beer retailer of Birmingham.
26. Count Matvei Platov commanded the Don Cossacks.
27. Mr Edmund Peel, son of Sir Robert Peel, had married Amelia Swiffen in Weeford in Staffordshire in 1812.
28. Very's restaurant in Paris opened in 1765 and was renowned as the very best.

Champs Elisce [Elysees]. He gave a Grand Ball this evening and the front of his house illuminated.[29]

Saturday [18 August]
In walking through the picture gallery at the Louvre this morning, I met with Miss Williamson[30] and Mr & Mrs Charles Kemble;[31] they arrived last night only. Many more pictures have been removed [from the Louvre] since my last visit and many more will be removed. It is said that the Pope has put in a claim for 200, which were taken from Italy. There is some intention, it is said, of sending the celebrated statue of the Apollo Belvedere[32] to England. In the evening we went to the *Theatre Francais*, where we saw the famous Talma[33] (equal to Garrick[34]) and Madam George[35] in the play of *Britannicus*.[36] The playhouse is small and dirty in the extreme.

Sunday [19 August]
Unwell all day with a headache and disordered stomach, owing to my having partaken too freely of the French made dishes and wines. I yesterday engaged to set off with an Englishman on Wednesday, expecting to be able to reach Boulogne or Calais on Thursday evening or Friday at farthest, but I this day sent him word that I was afraid I should be too poorly to undertake the journey. Holden says he will return with me the latter end of this week. We this day heard that General Labedoyere,[37] who has been on his trial ever since our arrival in Paris, for taking up arms in favour of Buonaparte, was shot last evening at 6 o'clock according to his sentence. This and a few more salutary examples will tend to establish the king firmly on the throne. Ney will be tried immediately.[38] Stayed at my lodgings all day and took an emetick [*sic*] and went to bed early.

---

29. The Duke of Wellington bought the Hotel de Charost from Pauline Borghese on behalf of the British government and it remains to this day the official residence of the British Ambassador to France.
30. Almost certainly the Miss Sophia Williamson (daughter of Sir Hedworth Williamson 6th Bart) who married Thomas Dundas, 2nd Earl of Zetland in 1823.
31. Charles Kemble the actor was married to Marie Therese de Camp in 1806.
32. It was returned to the Vatican City.
33. François-Joseph Talma was Napoleon's favourite actor.
34. The English actor David Garrick (1717–79).
35. Marguerite Georges was a renowned French actress and lover of Napoleon.
36. A five-act tragic play by Jean Racine first performed in 1669.
37. Charles Huchet, Comte de la Bedoyere led his regiment, the 7th Line, over to Napoleon during his march on Paris in 1815. He was tried and executed after Waterloo.
38. Marshal Michel Ney was tried and executed by firing squad for going over to Napoleon in his march to Paris in 1815.

Monday [20 August]
Still unwell. Stayed at my lodgings all day and took a mixture of rhubarb, senna & magnesia, by direction of Tom Thomson. Most of the English have been ill from the same cause.

Tuesday [21 August]
Much better, but weak. Am going to view the French monuments and the fountain of the elephants[39] this morning.

Paris 22 August 1815

My dear Bessy,
We propose setting off from this place on Friday next and I hope to be with Mary Anne Fraser at Broadstairs on the Monday following. After sleeping one night there we shall proceed to Woolwich, from whence I shall be very anxious to set off towards home without a moment's delay. I received your letter by Edwin Pemberton, but have not heard from you since. I begin to have a home fever on me and long to see you and the dear children. I am afraid Mr Barker has been very much harried in the office, but I hope I shall arrive time enough to enable him to recruit himself by a little shooting in Cheshire. George has had pretty good shooting in the neighbourhood of Neuilly; two of his officers the other day killed 7 brace of partridges, 6 brace of quails & a hare.

[The journal ends here.]

George and his brigade were to remain in France with the Army of Occupation. They were at Paris on 14 July but moved to Neuilly-sur-Seine later that month, remaining there until late October when they moved to Saint-Germain-en-Laye. In January 1816 they were stationed at La Chapelle-en-Serval, at Sailly-Saillisel in February and then settled at Bapaume for the rest of the year and on till June 1817. They then moved to Fontaine-Notre-Dame in late June and remained there until October 1818, moving to Cambrai and then proceeded on to Calais where they embarked for England, being at Chatham in the December. They moved to Woolwich in February 1819 and on to Weedon in September of that year. George's company was then at Woolwich again from January 1820 until July 1825 when he was finally promoted full Major and he promptly resigned but died that December.

39. The Elephant of the Bastille was intended to be a huge bronze sculpture, but never went beyond a plaster full-scale model standing 24m high which Napoleon ordered to be built in 1811. It was removed in 1846.

Bibliography

Anonymous, *Army List*, Various.

Askwith, W.H., *List of Officers of the Royal Artillery (Revised Kane's List to 1899)*, London 1900.

Cooper, J.S., *Rough Notes of Seven Campaigns*, London 1869.

Dalton, C., *The Waterloo Roll Call*, London 1904.

Griffith, R., *Riflemen, The History of the 5th Battalion 60th Regiment 1797-1818*, Warwick 2019.

Hall, J.A., *A History of the Peninsular War Vol VIII, British Officers Killed & Wounded 1808-1814*, London 1998.

Homfray, Irving L., *Officers of the British Forces in Canada during the war of 1812-15*, Quebec 1908.

Johnston, W., *Commissioned Officers in the Medical Services of the British Army 1727 to 1898*, London 1968.

Kane, Lt John, *List of Officers of the Royal Regiment of Artillery*, Greenwich 1815.

Laws, Lt Col M., *Battery Records of the Royal Artillery 1716-1859*, London 1952.

Moorsom, M.S., *History of the 52nd Regiment 1755-1816*, London 1860.

NWK, *North West Kent Family History Society – Plumstead St Nicholas Transcript of Burials 1788-1859*, Kent 2019.

Oman, Sir C., *Wellington's Army 1809-14*, London 1913.

Vibart, Colonel H., *Addiscombe, Its Heroes and Men of Note*, London 1894.

Wheater, W., *Historical Record of the Seventh or Royal Regiment of Fusiliers*, Leeds 1875.